EXEGETICAL
GUIDE TO THE
GREEK
NEW
TESTAMENT

1 PETER

The Exegetical Guide to the Greek New Testament

Volumes Available

Colossians, Philemon	Murray J. Harris
James	Chris A. Vlachos
1 Peter	Greg W. Forbes

Forthcoming Volumes

Matthew	Charles L. Quarles
Mark	Joel F. Williams
Luke	Alan J. Thompson
John	Murray J. Harris
Acts	L. Scott Kellum
Romans	John D. Harvey
1 Corinthians	Jay E. Smith
2 Corinthians	Don B. Garlington
Galatians	William J. Larkin
Ephesians	Benjamin L. Merkle
Philippians	Joseph H. Hellerman
1–2 Thessalonians	David W. Chapman
1–2 Timothy, Titus	Ray Van Neste
Hebrews	Dana M. Harris
2 Peter, Jude	Terry L. Wilder
1–3 John	Robert L. Plummer
Revelation	Bruce N. Fisk

Greg W. Forbes

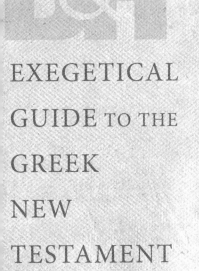

EXEGETICAL
GUIDE TO THE   1 PETER
GREEK
NEW
TESTAMENT

Andreas J. Köstenberger
Robert W. Yarbrough
GENERAL EDITORS

ACADEMIC

Nashville, Tennessee

Exegetical Guide to the Greek New Testament: 1 Peter
Copyright © 2014 Greg W. Forbes
B&H Publishing Group
Nashville, Tennessee
All rights reserved
ISBN: 978-1-4336-7602-4

Dewey Decimal Classification: 227.92
Subject Heading: BIBLE. N.T. 1 Peter—STUDY \ BIBLE—CRITICISM

The Greek text of 1 Peter is from *The Greek New Testament*, Fourth Revised Edition, edited by Barbara Aland, Kurt Aland, Johannes Karavidopoulos, Carlo M. Martini, and Bruce M. Metzger in cooperation with the Institute for New Testament Textual Research, Münster/Westphalia, © 1993 Deutsche Bibelgesellschaft, Stuttgart. Used by permission.

Printed in the United States of America

1 2 3 4 5 6 7 8 9 10 • 18 17 16 15 14

VP

*To my past and present Greek students
at
Melbourne School of Theology*

Contents

1 PETER

Publisher's Preface

It is with great excitement that we publish this volume of the Exegetical Guide to the Greek New Testament series. When the founding editor, Dr. Murray J. Harris, came to us seeking a new publishing partner, we gratefully accepted the offer. With the help of the co-editor, Andreas J. Köstenberger, we spent several years working together to acquire all of the authors we needed to complete the series. By God's grace we succeeded and contracted the last author in 2011. Originally working with another publishing house, Murray's efforts spanned more than twenty years. As God would have it, shortly after the final author was contracted, Murray decided God wanted him to withdraw as co-editor of the series. God made it clear to him that he must devote his full attention to taking care of his wife, Jennifer, who faces the daily challenges caused by multiple sclerosis.

Over the course of many years God has used Murray to teach his students how to properly exegete the Scriptures. He is an exceptional scholar and professor. But even more important, Murray is a man dedicated to serving Christ. His greatest joy is to respond in faithful obedience when his master calls. "There can be no higher and more ennobling privilege than to have the Lord of the universe as one's Owner and Master and to be his accredited representative on earth."[1] Murray has once again heeded the call of his master.

It is our privilege to dedicate the Exegetical Guide to the Greek New Testament series to Dr. Murray J. Harris. We pray that our readers will continue the work that he started.

B&H Academic

---

1. Murray J. Harris, *Slave of Christ: A New Testament Metaphor for Total Devotion to Christ* (Downers Grove: InterVarsity, 1999), 155.

General Introduction to the EGGNT Series

Studying the New Testament in the original Greek has become easier in recent years. Beginning students will work their way through an introductory grammar or other text, but then what? Grappling with difficult verb forms, rare vocabulary, and grammatical irregularities remains a formidable task for those who would advance beyond the initial stages of learning Greek to master the interpretive process. Intermediate grammars and grammatical analyses can help, but such tools, for all their value, still often operate at a distance from the Greek text itself, and analyses are often too brief to be genuinely helpful.

The Exegetical Guide to the Greek New Testament (EGGNT) aims to close the gap between the Greek text and the available tools. Each EGGNT volume aims to provide all the necessary information for understanding of the Greek text and, in addition, includes homiletical helps and suggestions for further study. The EGGNT is not a full-scale commentary. But these guides will make interpreting a given New Testament book easier, in particular for those who are hard-pressed for time and yet want to preach or teach with accuracy and authority.

In terms of layout, each volume begins with a brief introduction to the particular book (including such matters as authorship, date, etc.), a basic outline, and a list of recommended commentaries. At the end of each volume, you will find a comprehensive exegetical outline of the book. The body of each volume is devoted to paragraph-by-paragraph exegesis of the text. The treatment of each paragraph includes:

1. The Greek text of the passage, phrase-by-phrase, from the fourth edition of the United Bible Societies' *Greek New Testament* (UBS[4]). In the present volume on 1 Peter, nine textual changes (1:6,16 [2x]; 2:5,25; 4:16; 5:1,9,10) included in the Nestle-Aland *Novum Testamentum Graece*, twenty-eighth revised edition, © 2012 Deutsche Bibelgesellschaft Stuttgart (NA[28]) are noted that will also be adopted in the fifth revised edition of the UBS text (forthcoming, 2014).
2. A structural analysis of the passage.
3. A discussion of each phrase of the passage with discussion of relevant vocabulary, significant textual variants, and detailed grammatical analysis, including parsing. When more than one solution is given for a particular exegetical

issue, the author's own preference, reflected in the translation and expanded paraphrase, is indicated by an asterisk (*). When no preference is expressed, the options are judged to be evenly balanced, or it is assumed that the text is intentionally ambiguous. When a particular verb form may be parsed in more than one way, only the parsing appropriate in the specific context is supplied; but where there is difference of opinion among grammarians or commentators, both possibilities are given and the matter is discussed.

4. Various translations of significant words or phrases.
5. A list of suggested topics for further study with bibliography for each topic. An asterisk (*) in one of the "For Further Study" bibliographies draws attention to a discussion of the particular topic that is recommended as a useful introduction to the issues involved.
6. Homiletical suggestions designed to help the preacher or teacher move from the Greek text to a sermon outline that reflects careful exegesis. The first suggestion for a particular paragraph of the text is always more exegetical than homiletical and consists of an outline of the entire paragraph. These detailed outlines of each paragraph build on the general outline proposed for the whole book and, if placed side by side, form a comprehensive exegetical outline of the book. All outlines are intended to serve as a basis for sermon preparation and should be adapted to the needs of a particular audience.[2]

The EGGNT volumes will serve a variety of readers. Those reading the Greek text for the first time may be content with the assistance with vocabulary, parsing, and translation. Readers with some experience in Greek may want to skip or skim these sections and focus attention on the discussions of grammar. More advanced students may choose to pursue the topics and references to technical works under "For Further Study," while pastors may be more interested in the movement from grammatical analysis to sermon outline. Teachers may appreciate having a resource that frees them to focus on exegetical details and theological matters.

The editors are pleased to present you with the individual installments of the EGGNT. We are grateful for each of the contributors who has labored long and hard over each phrase in the Greek New Testament. Together we share the conviction that "all Scripture is inspired by God and is profitable for teaching, for rebuking, for correcting, for training in righteousness" (2 Tim 3:16 HCSB) and echo Paul's words to Timothy: "Be diligent to present yourself approved to God, a worker who doesn't need to be ashamed, correctly teaching the word of truth" (2 Tim 2:15 HCSB).

---

2. As a Bible publisher, B&H Publishing follows the "Colorado Springs Guidelines for Translation of Gender-Related Language in Scripture." As an academic book publisher, B&H Academic asks that authors conform their manuscripts (including EGGNT exegetical outlines in English) to the B&H Academic style guide, which affirms the use of singular "he/his/him" as generic examples encompassing both genders. However, in their discussion of the Greek text, EGGNT authors have the freedom to analyze the text and reach their own conclusions regarding whether specific Greek words are gender-specific or gender-inclusive.

Abbreviations

For abbreviations used in discussion of text critical matters, the reader should refer to the abbreviations listed in the Introduction to the United Bible Societies' *Greek New Testament.*

*	indicates the reading of the original hand of a manuscript as opposed to subsequent correctors of the manuscript, *or*
	indicates the writer's own preference when more than one solution is given for a particular exegetical problem, *or*
	in the "For Further Study" bibliographies, indicates a discussion of the particular topic that is recommended as a useful introduction to the issues involved
§, §§	section, sections

Books of the Old Testament

Gen	Genesis	Song	Song of Songs	(Canticles)
Exod	Exodus	Isa	Isaiah	
Lev	Leviticus	Jer	Jeremiah	
Num	Numbers	Lam	Lamentations	
Deut	Deuteronomy	Ezek	Ezekiel	
Josh	Joshua	Dan	Daniel	
Judg	Judges	Hos	Hosea	
Ruth	Ruth	Joel	Joel	
1–2 Sam	1–2 Samuel	Amos	Amos	
1–2 Kgs	1–2 Kings	Obad	Obadiah	
1–2 Chr	1–2 Chronicles	Jonah	Jonah	
Ezra	Ezra	Mic	Micah	
Neh	Nehemiah	Nah	Nahum	
Esth	Esther	Hab	Habakkuk	
Job	Job	Zeph	Zephaniah	
Ps(s)	Psalm(s)	Hag	Haggai	
Prov	Proverbs	Zech	Zechariah	
Eccl	Ecclesiastes	Mal	Malachi	

Books of the New Testament

Matt	Matthew	1–2 Thess	1–2 Thessalonians
Mark	Mark	1–2 Tim	1–2 Timothy
Luke	Luke	Titus	Titus
John	John	Phlm	Philemon
Acts	Acts	Heb	Hebrews
Rom	Romans	Jas	James
1–2 Cor	1–2 Corinthians	1–2 Pet	1–2 Peter
Gal	Galatians	1–3 John	1–3 John
Eph	Ephesians	Jude	Jude
Phil	Philippians	Rev	Revelation
Col	Colossians		

Dead Sea Scrolls

1QH	*Thanksgiving Hymn*
1QM	*War Scroll*
1QS	*Rule of the Community*
CD	*Damascus Document*

General Abbreviations

ABD	The Anchor Bible Dictionary, 6 vols., ed. D. N. Freedman (New York: Doubleday, 1992)
Achtemeier	P. J. Achtemeier, *1 Peter* (Minneapolis: Fortress, 1996)
abs.	absolute(ly)
ABRL	Anchor Bible Reference Library
acc.	accusative
act.	active (voice)
adj.	adjective, adjectival(ly)
adv.	adverbial(ly)
anar.	anarthrous
aor.	Aorist
apod.	apodosis
appos.	apposition, appositive, appositional
Aram.	Aramaic, Aramaism
art.	(definite) article, articular
attrib.	attributive
ANRW	Aufstieg und Niedergang der römisch Welt: Geschichte und Kultur Roms im Spiegel der neueren Forschung, ed. H. Temporini and W. Haase (Berlin and New York: de Gruyter, 1972–)
AThR	Anglican Theological Review
aug.	augment
AUSS	Andrews University Seminary Studies

Barclay	William Barclay, *New Testament Words* (Philadelphia: Westminster, 1974).
BBR	*Bulletin for Biblical Research*
BDAG	*A Greek-English Lexicon of the New Testament and Other Early Christian Literature*, rev. and ed. F. W. Danker (Chicago/London: University of Chicago, 2000), based on W. Bauer's *Griechisch-deutsches Wörterbuch* (6th ed.) and on previous English ed. W. F. Arndt, F. W. Gingrich, and F. W. Danker References to BDAG are by page number and quadrant on the page, *a* indicating the upper half and *b* the lower half of the left-hand column, and *c* and *d* the upper and lower halves of the right-hand column.
BDF	F. Blass and A. Debrunner, *A Greek Grammar of the New Testament and Other Early Christian Literature*, ET and rev. by R. W. Funk (Chicago: University of Chicago, 1961)
Beare	F. W. Beare, *The First Epistle of Peter*, 3rd ed. (Oxford: Blackwell, 1970)
Best	E. Best, *1 Peter* (London: Oliphants, 1971)
BGk.	Biblical Greek (i.e., LXX and NT Greek)
Bib	*Biblica*
Bigg	C. A. Bigg, *A Critical and Exegetical Commentary on the Epistles of St. Peter and St. Jude* (Edinburgh: T. & T. Clark, 1901)
BSac	*Bibliotheca Sacra*
BT	*The Bible Translator*
BTB	Biblical Theology Bulletin
Burton	E. D. Burton, *Syntax of the Moods and Tenses in New Testament Greek*, 3rd ed. (Edinburgh: Clark, 1898)
c.	*circa* (Lat.), about
Campbell, *Indicative Mood*	C. R. Campbell, *Verbal Aspect, the Indicative Mood, and Narrative: Soundings in the Greek of the New Testament* (New York: Peter Lang, 2007)
Campbell, *Non-Indicative Verbs*	C. R. Campbell, *Verbal Aspect in the Greek of the New Testament: Non-Indicative Verbs in Narrative* (New York: Peter Lang, 2008)
CBQ	*Catholic Biblical Quarterly*
Cassirer	H.W. Cassirer, *God's New Covenant: A New Testament Translation* (Grand Rapids: Eerdmans, 1989)
CEV	Contemporary English Version (1995)
cf.	*confer* (Lat.), compare
CGk.	Classical Greek
Colloq	*Colloquium*
comp.	comparative, comparison
cond.	condition(al)

conj.	conjunctive, conjunction
consec.	consecutive
cstr.	construction, construe(d)
CTR	*Criswell Theological Review*
Dalton	W. J. Dalton, *Christ's Proclamation to the Spirits: A Study of 1 Peter 3:18–4:6*, 2nd ed. (Rome: Pontifical Biblical Institute, 1989)
dat.	dative
Davids	P. H. Davids, *The First Epistle of Peter* (Grand Rapids: Eerdmans, 1990)
DBI	*Dictionary of Biblical Imagery*, ed. Leland Ryken, James Wilhoit, and Tremper Longman III (Downers Grove: InterVarsity, 1998)
decl.	declension, decline
Deissmann	G. A. Deissmann, *Bible Studies*, trans. A. Grieve (Edinburgh: Clark, 1901; reprint, Peabody, MA: Hendrickson, 1988)
def.	definite
dep.	deponent
DLNT	*Dictionary of the Later New Testament and Its Developments*, ed. R. P. Martin and P. H. Davids (Leicester / Downers Grove: InterVarsity, 1997)
DNTB	*Dictionary of New Testament Background*, ed. C. A. Evans and S. E. Porter (Leicester / Downers Grove: InterVarsity, 2000)
DOTWPW	*Dictionary of the Old Testament: Wisdom, Poetry, and Writings*, ed. T. Longman III and P. Enns (Downers Grove: InterVarsity, 2008)
DTIB	*Dictionary for Theological Interpretation of the Bible*, ed. Kevin J. Vanhoozer, et al. (Grand Rapids, Baker, 2005)
dir.	direct
DSS	Dead Sea Scrolls
Dubis	M. Dubis, *1 Peter: A Handbook on the Greek Text* (Waco, TX: Baylor University Press, 2010)
ed(s).	edited by, edition(s), editor(s)
EDT	*Evangelical Dictionary of Theology*, ed. W. A. Elwell (Grand Rapids: Baker, 1984)
e.g.	*exempli gratia* (Lat.), for example
EGT	*The Expositor's Greek Testament*, 5 vols., ed. W. R. Nicholl (Grand Rapids: Eerdmans, 1970 reprint of 1897–1910 ed.)
Elliott	J. H. Elliott, *1 Peter* (New York: Doubleday, 2000)
Eng.	English
epex.	epexegetic
esp.	especially
ESV	English Standard Version (2001)
ET	English translation

et al.	*et alii* (Lat.), and others
etym.	etymology, etymologically
EvQ	*Evangelical Quarterly*
EVV	English versions of the Bible
Exp	*Expositor*
ExpTim	*Expository Times*
f(f).	and the following (verse[s] or page[s])
Fanning	Buist Fanning, *Verbal Aspect in New Testament Greek* (Oxford: Oxford University Press, 1991)
Feinberg	J. S. Feinberg, "1 Peter 3:18-20, Ancient Mythology, and the Intermediate State," *WTJ* 48 (1986): 303–36
Feldmeier	R. Feldmeier, *The First Letter of Peter: A Commentary on the Greek Text* (Waco, TX: Baylor University Press, 2008)
fem.	feminine
fig.	figurative(ly)
fut.	future
gen.	genitive
Gk.	Greek
GNB	Good News Bible (1976)
Goppelt	L. Goppelt, *A Commentary on 1 Peter* (Grand Rapids: Eerdmans, 1993)
Green	J. B. Green, *1 Peter* (Grand Rapids / Cambridge: Eerdmans, 2007)
Grudem	W. Grudem, *1 Peter* (Leicester: InterVarsity, 1988)
GTJ	*Grace Theological Journal*
Harris	M. J. Harris, "Prepositions and Theology in the Greek New Testament," *NIDNTT* 3.1171–1215.
HBT	*Horizons in Biblical Theology*
HCSB	Holman Christian Standard Bible (2009)
HE	*Historia Ecclesiastica* (History of the Church)
Heb.	Hebrew, Hebraism
HGk.	Hellenistic Greek
HTR	*Harvard Theological Review*
HTS	*Harvard Theological Studies*
ibid.	*ibidem* (Lat.), in the same place
IBS	*Irish Biblical Studies*
IDB	*Interpreters Dictionary of the Bible*, ed. G. A. Buttrick, 4 vols. plus supp. (Nashville / New York: Abingdon, 1962–76)
i.e.	*id est* (Lat.), that is
impers.	impersonal
impf.	imperfect (tense)
impv.	imperative (mood), imperatival(ly)
incl.	including, inclusive

indecl.	indeclinable
indef.	indefinite
indic.	indicative (mood)
indir.	indirect
inf.	infinitive
instr.	instrument, instrumental(ly)
Int	*Interpretation*
interr.	interrogative
intrans.	intransitive
iter.	iterative
JB	Jerusalem Bible (1976)
JBL	*Journal of Biblical Literature*
JETS	*Journal of the Evangelical Theological Society*
Jobes	K. H. Jobes, *1 Peter* (Grand Rapids: Baker, 2005)
JOTT	*Journal of Translation and Textlinguistics*
JR	*Journal of Religion*
JSNT	*Journal for the Study of the New Testament*
JSOT	*Journal for the Study of the Old Testament*
JTS	*Journal of Theological Studies*
JTSA	*Journal of Theology for Southern Africa*
Kelly	J. N. D. Kelly, *The Epistles of Peter and Jude* (London: A & C Black, 1969)
KJV	King James Version (= "Authorized Version") (1611)
LB	*Linguistica Biblica*
lit.	literal(ly)
LN	J. P. Louw and E. A. Nida, eds., *Greek-English Lexicon of the New Testament Based on Semantic Domains, Vol. I: Introduction and Domains* (New York: United Bible Societies, 1988).
locat.	locative, locatival(ly)
LS	*Louvain Studies*
LSJ	H. G. Liddell and R. Scott, *A Greek-English Lexicon*, rev. and augmented H. S. Jones et al., 9th ed. (Oxford: Clarendon, 1940); *Supplement*, ed. E. A. Barber et al. (1968)
LTJ	*Lutheran Theological Journal*
LXX	Septuagint (= Greek Old Testament)
Macc	Maccabees
masc.	masculine
McKay	K. L. McKay, *A New Syntax of the Verb in New Testament Greek: An Aspectual Approach* (New York: Peter Lang, 1994)

Metzger	B. M. Metzger, *A Textual Commentary on the Greek New Testament* (Stuttgart: Deutsche Bibelgesellschaft / New York: United Bible Societies, 1994; original ed. of 1971 based on UBS³)
mg.	margin
MH	J. H. Moulton and W. F. Howard, *Accidence and Word-Formation*, vol. 2 of *A Grammar of New Testament Greek*, ed. J. H. Moulton (Edinburgh: T&T Clark, 1939)
Michaels	J. R. Michaels, *1 Peter* (Dallas: Word, 1988)
mid.	middle
MM	J. H. Moulton and G. Milligan, *The Vocabulary of the Greek Testament Illustrated from the Papyri and Other Non-Literary Sources* (Grand Rapids: Eerdmans, 1972; repr. of 1930 ed.)
Moule	C. F. D. Moule, *An Idiom Book of New Testament Greek*, 2nd ed. (Cambridge: Cambridge University Press, 1960)
Moulton	J. H. Moulton, *A Grammar of New Testament Greek, Vol. I: Prolegomena*, 3rd ed. (Edinburgh: Clark, 1908)
mng.	meaning
ms(s).	manuscript(s)
MT	Masoretic Text
n.	note
NABRE	New American Bible Revised Edition (2011)
NASB	New American Standard Bible (1995)
NCV	New Century Version
NDBT	*New Dictionary of Biblical Theology*, ed. T. D. Alexander and B. S. Rosner (Downers Grove: InterVarsity, 2000)
NEB	New English Bible (1970)
neg.	negative, negation
Neot	*Neotestamentica*
NET	New English Translation Bible (2005)
neut.	neuter
NewDocs	*New Documents Illustrating Early Christianity*, ed. G. H. R. Horsley and S. Llewelyn (North Ryde, N.S.W., Australia: Macquarie University, 1981–). These will be cited by volume.
NIDNTT	*The New International Dictionary of New Testament Theology*, 3 vols., ed. C. Brown (Grand Rapids: Zondervan, 1975–78)
NIDOTTE	*The New International Dictionary of Old Testament Theology and Exegesis*, 5 vols, ed. W. A. VanGemeren (Grand Rapids: Zondervan, 1997)
NIV	New International Version (2011)
NJB	New Jerusalem Bible (1985)
NKJV	New King James Version
NLT	New Living Translation of the Bible (1996)

nom.	nominative
NovT	*Novum Testamentum*
NRSV	New Revised Standard Version (1990)
NT	New Testament
NTS	*New Testament Studies*
obj.	object(ive)
Omanson	*A Textual Guide to the Greek New Testament* (Stuttgart: Deutsche Bibelgesellshaft, 2006)
orig.	origin, original(ly)
OT	Old Testament
p(p).	page(s)
pace	(from Lat. *pax*, peace) (in stating a contrary opinion) with all due respect to (the person named)
pass.	passive
periph.	periphrastic
pers.	person(al)
pf.	perfect
pl.	plural
Porter	S. E. Porter, *Idioms of the Greek New Testament* (Sheffield: JSOT, 1992)
poss.	possessive, possession
Prasad	J. Prasad, *Foundations of the Christian Way of Life According to 1 Peter 1, 13–25: An Exegetico-Theological Study* (Rome: Pontifical Biblical Institute, 2000)
pred.	predicate, predicative
pref.	prefix
prep.	preposition(al)
Presb	*Presbyterion*
pres.	present
PTR	*Princeton Theological Review*
pron.	pronoun, pronominal
prot.	protasis
ptc.	participle, participial(ly)
R	A. T. Robertson, *A Grammar of the Greek New Testament in the Light of Historical Research*, 4th ed. (Nashville: Broadman, 1934)
rdg(s).	(textual) reading(s)
REB	Revised English Bible (1990)
ref.	reference
refl.	reflexive
Reicke	B. Reicke, *The Disobedient Spirits and Christian Baptism: A Study of 1 Pet. III:19 and Its Context* (Kobenhavn: Ejnar Munksgaard, 1946)

rel.	relative
rev.	revised, reviser, revision
RevExp	*Review and Expositor*
ResQ	*Restoration Quarterly*
Robertson, *Pictures*	A. T. Robertson, *Word Pictures in the New Testament*, 6 vols. (Nashville: Broadman, 1930–33)
RSV	Revised Standard Version (1952)
SBJT	*Southern Baptist Journal of Theology*
SBLSP	*Society of Biblical Literature Seminar Papers*
Scr	*Scripture*
SE	*Studia Evangelica*
Selwyn	E. G. Selwyn, *The First Epistle of St. Peter* (London: Macmillan, 1964)
Sem.	Semitic, Semitism
sg.	singular
sim.	similar(ly)
Sir	Sirach/Ecclesiasticus
SJT	*Scottish Journal of Theology*
Spicq	C. Spicq, *Theological Lexicon of the New Testament*, 3 vols., ET and ed. by J. D. Ernest (Peabody, MA: Hendrickson, 1994)
STJ	*Stulos Theological Journal*
subj.	subject(ive)
subjunc.	subjunctive
subord.	subordinate, subordination
subst.	substantive
suf.	suffix
superl.	superlative
SwJT	*Southwestern Journal of Theology*
T	N. Turner, *A Grammar of New Testament Greek*, by J. H. Moulton, vol. III: *Syntax* (Edinburgh: Clark, 1963)
TBT	*The Bible Today*
TDNT	*Theological Dictionary of the New Testament*, 9 vols., ed. G. Kittel and G. Friedrich, trans. G. W. Bromiley (Grand Rapids: Eerdmans, 1964–74)
temp.	temporal(ly)
Them	*Themelios*
TJ	*Trinity Journal*
TNIV	Today's New International Version (2001)
tr.	translate(d), translator, translation(s)
trans.	transitive
Trench	Richard C. Trench, *Synonyms of the Greek New Testament* (London: Macmillan, 1876; repr., Grand Rapids: Eerdmans, 1975)
TTE	*The Theological Educator*

Turner, *Insights*	N. Turner, *Grammatical Insights into the New Testament* (Edinburgh: Clark, 1965)
Turner, *Style*	N. Turner, *Style*, vol. 4 of *A Grammar of New Testament Greek*, ed. J. H. Moulton (Edinburgh: T&T Clark, 1976)
Turner, *Words*	N. Turner, *Christian Words* (Edinburgh: Clark, 1980)
TynBul	*Tyndale Bulletin*
v(v).	verse(s)
var.	variant (form or reading)
vb.	verb
VE	*Vox evangelica*
viz.	*videlicet* (Lat.), namely
voc.	vocative
vol(s).	volume(s)
VT	*Vetus Testamentum*
Wallace	Daniel B. Wallace, *Greek Grammar Beyond the Basics: An Exegetical Syntax of the New Testament* (Grand Rapids: Zondervan, 1996)
Winer	George Benedict Winer, *A Grammar of the Idiom of the New Testament: Prepared as a Solid Basis for the Interpretation of the New Testament*, ed. Gottlieb Lünemann, 7th ed. (Andover: Draper, 1872)
Wis	Wisdom of Solomon
WTJ	*Westminster Theological Journal*
WW	*Word and World*
Z	M. Zerwick, *Biblical Greek Illustrated by Examples*, trans. J. Smith (Rome: Pontifical Biblical Institute, 1963)
ZG	M. Zerwick and M. Grosvenor, *A Grammatical Analysis of the Greek New Testament*, 5th rev. ed. (Rome: Pontifical Biblical Institute, 1996)
ZNW	*Zeitschrift für die neutestamentliche Wissenschaft und die Kunde der älteren Kirche*

Introduction

AUTHORSHIP

The opening verse of 1 Peter claims that the epistle was authored by Peter the apostle, and in 5:1 the author claims to have been a "witness (μάρτυς) of the sufferings of Christ." The description of Christ's sufferings in 2:21–24 and the ascription "chief shepherd" in 5:4 support eyewitness testimony. While some contend that these references pertain to the gospel tradition rather than indicating eyewitness recollection, 1 Peter doubtless contains a significant number of allusions to the teaching of Jesus (see Achtemeier 10–12).

The Petrine authorship of 1 Peter was never disputed in early church tradition. Apart from the data from 1 Peter itself adduced above, the traditional view is also supported by certain affinities between ideas and terminology found in 1 Peter and those attributed to Peter in Acts. Among these are the cross described as ξύλον, "wood" (2:24; cf. Acts 5:30; 10:39) and the use of the stone text from Psalm 118:22 in 2:7–8 (cf. Acts 4:10–11). Finally, the cryptic reference to Rome in 5:13 is consistent with tradition of Peter's later life in that city.

These strong arguments in support of the Petrine authorship of 1 Peter notwithstanding, in modern times a number of points have been raised against it. Opponents of Petrine authorship commonly argue that the quality of the Greek in this epistle, as well as the rhetorical skills employed, are hardly to be expected from a Galilean fisherman who is described in Acts 4:13 as ἀγράμματος, "unlearned." However, Karen Jobes, in a recent analysis, contends that the quality of the Greek has been overrated and the language in 1 Peter is heavily influenced by Semitic thought and expression ("The Syntax of 1 Peter: Just How Good is the Greek," *BBR* 13 [2003]: 159–73).

Other arguments offered against the traditional view have centered on either a supposed dependence upon Paul's theology or the dating of the persecution that forms the background for the letter. It will be argued below that the latter should probably not be considered a factor in adjudicating Petrine authorship, for it rests on the questionable assumption that the suffering endured by the recipients of the epistle originated from the state. The presumed link to Pauline theology is overstated (1 Peter actually has more in common with James than Paul), and most of the suggested resemblances may be explained by common Christian tradition.

A final consideration regarding authorship centers on the larger question of pseud-onymity. It stands to reason that if the apostle Peter did not write the epistle, then someone wrote it in his name. Although pseudonymous writing may have had a certain amount of currency at the time, serious doubt has been shed on whether this practice was condoned in Christian circles with respect to *epistle writing*. This is especially the case since most pseudonymous writings claim a long-dead hero as their author, not one who has just recently died. Jobes also makes the telling point that Silvanus (if not part of the literary fiction) could hardly fulfill the role of an emissary (his most likely role) for a letter that he knew was falsely written in the name of Peter (Jobes 6).

Recognizing the problems of postulating outright forgery, some are prepared to take the middle ground and posit a Petrine circle, whereby a group of Christians closely linked with Peter wrote to the churches of northern Asia Minor in the name of the preeminent apostle, faithfully preserving and representing the teaching and theological outlook of their mentor (Achtemeier 41–43; Elliott 118–30). However, the existence of such "schools" gathered around and promulgating the teaching of a leading apostle remains speculative.

Overall, it would appear that arguments presented against Petrine authorship are not sufficiently weighty to overcome the traditional view. Although it is now widely recognized that the expression "through Silvanus" in 5:12 relates to him as the letter bearer (see the analysis), this does not preclude him or another acting as an amanu-ensis. Moreover, the burden of proof certainly rests with those who would dispute Petrine authorship, since the letter is explicitly attributed to Peter and ancient episto-lary pseudonymity remains tenuous and unproven. In the remainder of this volume, I will therefore refer to the author as "Peter." In any case, final identification of the writer does not, for the most part, affect the interpretation of individual passages in the letter.

HISTORICAL SETTING AND DATE

First Peter addresses a small persecuted minority, as the theme of suffering is intro-duced at the outset (1:6) and recurs constantly (3:9, 14; 4:1, 12, 16, 19; 5:9–10). It is unclear whether this suffering is actual (4:12, 17; 5:10) or potential (1:6; 3:14), although these options are not mutually exclusive. It is here that we come to the issue of the dating of the epistle. If the state was the source of the conflict the Christian communities were experiencing, then it should be possible to date the letter with some precision.

Assuming that 1 Peter was written in the first century, there are only two possible scenarios for state persecution: Nero or Domitian. In AD 64 Nero blamed Christians for the outbreak of a fire in Rome. This resulted in a brutal attack on the Christians, but this action appears to have been confined to Rome itself. Nevertheless, if Peter was writing from Rome during Nero's persecution, he may well have been preparing his readers for trouble which he felt might soon spread to Asia Minor.

Persecution under Domitian (AD 95) appears to have been more widespread, but does not seem to have been uniform, and its precise extent is unclear. In any event, a date under Domitian would rule out authorship by Simon Peter and for this and other reasons is highly unlikely.

Persecution in this area of Asia Minor is first known from extrabiblical sources in AD 112, where Pliny's letter to Emperor Trajan, and Trajan's subsequent reply, make it clear that Christians faced martyrdom if they refused to acknowledge the emperor as Lord. Nevertheless, Pliny himself regarded Christians as relatively harmless. It is also apparent that there was not an official Roman policy against Christianity at this time, and Trajan seemed reluctant to formulate one.

It should also be noted that "suffering for the name of Christ/suffering as a Christian" (4:14–16) does not necessarily imply state persecution. A similar idea is found in Acts 5:41 (cf. Mark 13:13) in reference to non-Roman persecution. There is no mention of imprisonment, and although legal terminology occurs in 3:15 regarding giving a verbal defense of the faith, this may simply be used of giving a reasoned explanation. As far as other internal evidence is concerned, the positive references to the state in 2:11–17 make it less likely that state oppression is the issue.

A more likely source for the suffering experienced by these readers was general abuse, ill-treatment, and discrimination from the surrounding society as a whole. The church was probably introspective and withdrawn, with its members no longer participating in religious and social practices (4:1–4). As it was deemed improper for one to depart from the religion of one's fathers (for this disrupted the fabric of society), retaliation from the non-Christian populace would hardly have been unexpected. Christians were probably also under suspicion of secret crimes (per Pliny's letter). This scenario best explains Peter's description of his readers as "aliens and exiles" (1:1; 2:11), for they were not only estranged from heaven in a temporal sense, but also from their own society in a social sense (see the exegesis below).

Looking to the external evidence, it is clear that 1 Peter was widely known in the latter part of the second century due to its use by Irenaeus, Clement of Alexandria, and Tertullian. There is also a strong argument to be made that Polycarp was familiar with the epistle in the early second century, although the case of 1 Clement (c. AD 95) is not as conclusive. In this earlier period the supposed parallels are less convincing and may be explained by the use of common Christian tradition, particularly since 1 Peter and 1 Clement share a Roman provenance.

If Peter wrote the epistle, this requires a date prior to his death (mid-60s according to tradition). If, as is unlikely, the letter was penned by later followers, it could have been written anytime between the mid-60s and the end of the first century. One argument in favor of a date toward the latter part of this period is that the spread of Christianity, including the nomenclature "Christian" into the interior of Asia Minor, may have taken some time. But then, growth in southwestern Asia Minor was relatively swift, and so the same could have been the case in the north.

Attempting to date the epistle by examining the state of Christian-Jewish relations reflected in the letter, as mentioned, is also problematic. We find nothing about a separation from Judaism, and the silence on the issue probably has more to do with the composition of the audience rather than constituting evidence of an official separation of church and synagogue.

In the end, if the letter originated with Peter in Rome, a date in the mid-60s is most likely. If the origins of the letter are in a Petrine school or circle in Rome, a date close to the death of the apostle is more likely than a date later in the first century.

THE USE OF THE IMPERATIVE IN 1 PETER

Since the publication of important works by Porter (Stanley E. Porter, *Verbal Aspect in the Greek of the New Testament with Reference to Tense and Mood* [Studies in Biblical Greek 1; New York: Peter Lang, 1989]) and Fanning (Buist M. Fanning, *Verbal Aspect in New Testament Greek* [Oxford: Clarendon, 1990]) a couple of decades ago, the concept of verbal aspect (essentially, the vantage point from which a writer perceives a given action) has played a significant role in the study of the Greek of the NT. Yet rather than give rise to increased certainty regarding the use of verb tense, it has actually led to a period of instability and uncertainty, or at the very least, caution (see Robert E. Picirilli, "The Meaning of the Tenses in New Testament Greek: Where Are We?," *JETS* 48 [2005]: 533–55). In many instances it is a case of not what *can* be said but of what *cannot* be said. This is not the place to engage in an extensive discussion of verbal aspect, as others have done this adequately (see Campbell, *Indicative Mood*, 1–34). Suffice it to say, one of the greatest areas of uncertainty regarding verbal aspect is its impact on the non-indicative moods. Our particular concern is with the imperative.

In previous times grammarians, opting for neatly packaged rules, presented the aorist imperative as a command for a one-time action, whereas the present imperative was viewed as a command to repeated or continual action. While undoubtedly true in some instances, this is a gross oversimplification rightly called into question by more recent studies. The previous approach confused *Aktionsart* ("kind of action") with verbal aspect, with *Aktionsart* properly referring to pragmatic categories rather than basic meaning.

More recent studies have placed the study of the imperative under the umbrella of verbal aspect. There is no consensus on all matters, but it does seem clear that the aorist imperative, with its perfective (i.e. undefined/summary) aspect is generally used for specific commands, while the present imperative, with its imperfective (i.e. unfolding/continuous) aspect is the default tense for general instructions. The specific command is addressed to a definite subject and relates to a specific action at a particular time. The general instruction more readily applies to indefinite subjects and indicates what is to be habitual or normal (and is thus suited to NT parenetic contexts).

What is significant for our study is that the author of 1 Peter invariably uses the aorist imperative for general instructions. Whereas the present imperative appears ten times, the aorist imperative occurs twenty-five times. Imperatives in the second person appear in the aorist 80 percent of the time. Given the nature of the subject matter and the recipients of this epistle, most of the commands are in the category of general instruction. Various explanations have been offered.

Achtemeier considers that the aorist imperatives in 1 Peter should be taken as programmatic, by which a specific command sets a course of action to be followed habitually in the future (Achtemeier 340 n. 60). Elliott regards some of the aorist imperatives as ingressive in force, which is similar to the above in that it pictures entry into a particular state (e.g., Elliott 859). Michaels discusses some aorist imperatives in the epistle as both ingressive and programmatic in the sense that they set a new course of action (Michaels 130, 297). One particular instance of such a programmatic use of the aorist is ἐλπίσατε (1:13), where the readers are exhorted to set their hope on the grace coming to them at the revelation of Jesus Christ. The translation "set your hope" is an attempt to convey this programmatic sense, with a particular resolve to orient one's focus accordingly and work it out as a way of life.

Fanning (370–79), working from the basic assumption that the present imperative is the default tense for general precepts, discusses four possible reasons for the preponderance of the aorist imperative in 1 Peter: (1) *ingressive*: entry into a state, thus focusing on a change of behavior (also Beare 110–11, on ἀγαπήσατε in 1:22); (2) *urgency*: the unexpected aorist imperative carries a sense of forcefulness (also Kelly 66, on ἐλπίσατε in 1:13); (3) *consummative*: focusing on conduct to completion/final point; (4) *use of traditional material*: the aorist (imperative, infinitive, participles) tend to dominate instructions (particularly in Ephesians, Colossians, James, and 1 Peter) regarding putting off evil, submitting oneself, watching/praying, resisting the Devil, and standing firm. This may in turn be explained by the urgency of the subject matter or by focusing on a change of behavior for new Christians (per [1] or [2] above).

We should not overlook the possibility that some cases of the use of the aorist imperative may simply be due to idiomatic usage. For instance, -μι verbs tend to prefer the aorist imperative. For example, in the NT δίδωμι appears in the imperative a total of thirty-five times, four in the present tense and thirty-one in the aorist. Of the thirty-one aorist imperatives, eight are clearly general precepts. Ἵστημι only appears in the aorist imperative, and two out of five of these uses are for general precepts. Τίθημι appears three times as an imperative, two in the aorist and both of these are specific commands (although one of these could be construed as a general precept). Fanning, 354–56, only discusses δίδωμι in this context. But again, this does not explain the volume of aorist imperatives in 1 Peter where only two -μι verbs occur as imperatives (5:9, 12).

McKay (Ken L. McKay, "Aspect in Imperatival Constructions in New Testament Greek," *NovT* 27 [1985]: 208) considers that the aorist imperative can be used to convey a sense of distribution or iteration (a specific action being performed over and over again). Iteration may well explain the final imperative of the letter: ἀσπάσασθε ἀλλήλους ἐν φιλήματι ἀγάπης, "greet one another with a kiss of love" (5:14).

In conclusion, it is important not to force all uses of the aorist imperatives in this epistle into a single paradigm. Some may simply reflect idiomatic usage, some may be drawing on stock early church expressions, some may be ingressive or programmatic, some (given the historical situation of persecution and social ostracism to which 1 Peter was addressed) may convey a sense of urgency. Others are less easily explained. For further comments, see the respective verse analysis.

IMPERATIVAL PARTICIPLES IN 1 PETER

Apart from a conglomeration of imperatival participles in Romans 12:9–19, general opinion is that the epistle of 1 Peter represents the most sustained use of this grammatical form in the NT. Whereas J. H. Moulton (endorsed by R 944–46) argued that the imperatival participle was an increasing phenomenon in Hellenistic Greek during this period, David Daube ("Appended Note: Participle and Imperative in 1 Peter," in Selwyn 467–88) called this into question. Daube concluded that the origins lay in Tannaitic Hebrew rather than being attributable to a development in Hellenistic Greek. Thus the influence is thoroughly Semitic.

In such instances Daube demonstrated that the participles are used in the plural and may not specify a particular subject. They always occur in contexts that concern general rules of conduct, not specific commands. Thus the imperatival use of the participle does not become a substitute for any imperative, but only one particular type. Daube (485) states, "the participle has a flavour of the impersonal, customary, that makes it unfit for spontaneous advice." Furthermore, the imperativial participle is a softer command than the true imperative, more of an appeal than a directive. This finding was then endorsed by examining the participles normally identified as imperatival in Romans 12 and 1 Peter.

With respect to the participles often labelled as imperatival in 1 Peter, Daube considered many of these to be doubtful. He contended that 2:18; 3:1; 3:7–9 (which also contains some imperatival adjectives); and 4:7–10 are genuine instances of participles used imperativally.

Scot Snyder ("Participles and Imperatives in 1 Peter: A Re-examination in the Light of Recent Scholarly Trends," *Filologia Neotestamentaria* 8 [1995]: 187–98) follows Turner (*Insights* 165–68) in rejecting Daube's explanation that the imperatival use of the participle in the NT is due to Hebrew/Aramaic influence. Rather, he contends that "the best explanation for the similarities between Hellenistic Greek and Hebrew or Aramaic is still independent development in each language" (Snyder, "Participles," 188). Nevertheless, he does, for the most part, agree with Daube regarding the limited number of imperatival participles in 1 Peter.

Travis B. Williams ("Reconsidering the Imperative Participle in 1 Peter," *WTJ* 73 [2011]: 59–78) rejects both aspects of Daube's thesis. He argues cogently that the imperatival participle arose in Hellenistic Greek due to the elasticity of its form and the tendency for participles to be linked paratactically with finite imperatives. What is more, there is no justification for the idea that the imperatival participle conveys a milder command or appeal.

Achtemeier (see his excursus, 117) supports Daube's thesis but even consigns participles that Daube considers imperatival to dependency on main verbs in the immediate (and not so immediate) context. For instance, he considers that the participles and adjectives in 3:8–9 are not imperatival, but are dependent on the imperatives of 2:17 and are instrumental in force (Achtemeier 222–23).

A word of clarification is in order at this point. It is one thing to deny that a participle is imperatival on the basis of its dependency on a main verb in the context (even though the context Achtemeier supplies at times seems too remote), but it is another to empty such a participle of any imperatival force whatsoever. For although a participle may not be independent and imperatival, it can be dependent and carry derived imperatival force. This is clearly the case when the main verb on which the participle depends is an imperative, and the participle has either instrumental or modal force, or is attendant circumstance. McKay is surely correct in stating, "In most NT contexts in which participles are associated with imperatives, there can be little doubt that they represent paratactic imperatives" (McKay 225).

A few examples will suffice. In 1:14 μὴ συσχηματιζόμενοι ("not being conformed," i.e., to your previous ignorant desires) is linked paratactically (ἀλλά) to the finite imperatival clause ἅγιοι ἐν πάσῃ ἀναστροφῇ γενήθητε ("be holy all your conduct," 1:15). Thus the participle carries the same semantic weight as the finite form and in fact is the negative counterpart to it.

The participle μηδ' ὡς κατακυριεύοντες ("not lording it over") in 1 Peter 5:3 functions as an adverbial participle of manner (i.e., mode). It is logically dependent on the imperative ποιμάνατε τὸ ἐν ὑμῖν ποίμνιον τοῦ θεοῦ ("tend the flock of God among you") in 5:2 (alternatively, it is dependent on the participle ἐπισκοποῦντες; see the discussion on this verse) and gives the sense "tend the flock, not in the manner of lording it over them." Again, it is difficult to see how the readers would not see two instructions here: tend the flock, and do not lord it over them. An adverbial participle of manner thus has derived imperatival force.

Participles of result (see Wallace 637–39) are not commonly dependent on an imperative, but those that are can function in a similar way to the above. First Peter 5:7 may fall into this category (there are other options; see the discussion on this verse), where πᾶσαν τὴν μέριμναν ὑμῶν ἐπιρίψαντες ἐπ' αὐτόν ("casting all your anxiety upon him") may contain a participle of result dependent upon ταπεινώθητε ("be humbled") in the previous verse. In other words, the result of a humble state under God's mighty hand leads one to cast all one's care upon him. Note, however, that there are two instructions here. First, be humbled. Second, cast all your anxiety upon God. The second is dependent upon the first, but it clearly carries derived imperatival force.

Consequently, throughout the grammatical and exegetical discussion that follows, participles will often be designated as carrying derived imperatival force, thus performing double duty as an adverbial participle of attendant circumstance, means, manner, or result.

OUTLINE

RECOMMENDED COMMENTARIES

Throughout this volume of the *EGGNT*, reference is made to a number of commentaries on 1 Peter. Five of these commentaries, written in English or translated into English, receive special attention as they are based directly on the Greek text.

Achtemeier, Paul J. *1 Peter*. Hermeneia. Minneapolis: Fortress, 1996.

Elliott, John H. *1 Peter*. Anchor Bible. New York: Doubleday, 2001.

Goppelt, Leonhard. *A Commentary on 1 Peter*. Grand Rapids: Eerdmans, 1993.

Jobes, Karen H. *1 Peter*. Baker Exegetical Commentary on the New Testament. Grand Rapids: Baker, 2005.

Michaels, J. Ramsey. *1 Peter*. Word Biblical Commentary. Dallas: Word, 1988.

Frequent use is also made of Mark Dubis, *1 Peter: A Handbook on the Greek Text*. Baylor Handbook on the Greek New Testament (Waco, TX: Baylor University Press, 2010).

If you are considering purchasing a commentary on 1 Peter, Michaels has an even-handed approach, and although he does have a few idiosyncratic interpretations, he constantly relates his exegesis to the situation of the recipients. Achtemeier is the most thorough regarding the Greek text and has a number of helpful excursuses, but the Hermeneia Series is quite expensive. Elliott is very good, but readers may become frustrated with his transliterated Greek. Jobes is rather uneven at times and does not offer a verse-by-verse exposition. Goppelt is also a fine commentary and offers some extremely helpful pastoral and theological insights. My first choice would be Achtemeier, but if cost is an issue, then Michaels. I would also seriously consider Goppelt.

I. Salutation (1:1–2)

STRUCTURE

This is a typical Hellenistic epistolary opening, identifying the author and recipients together with a customary greeting. The basic structure is expanded by three prep. phrases further commenting on the nature and purpose of the elect status of these Christians. The customary Heb. greeting of "shalom" (= Gk. εἰρήνη) is an added feature in line with other NT epistles.

1 Πέτρος
   ἀπόστολος Ἰησοῦ Χριστοῦ   ἐκλεκτοῖς παρεπιδήμοις διασπορᾶς ...
2   κατὰ πρόγνωσιν θεοῦ πατρὸς
                              ἐν ἁγιασμῷ πνεύματος
                              εἰς ὑπακοὴν καὶ ῥαντισμὸν
                                          αἵματος Ἰησοῦ
                                            Χριστοῦ,

χάρις ὑμῖν καὶ εἰρήνη πληθυνθείη.

VERSE 1

Πέτρος ἀπόστολος Ἰησοῦ Χριστοῦ

Proper names in Gk. (here Πέτρος, Ἰησοῦ Χριστοῦ) are often anar. (R 759; T 165–69; BDF §260), even more so in epistolary salutations. Ἀπόστολος is in appos. to Πέτρος. An apostle is an emissary who operates with the full authority of the one by whom he is sent (D. Müller, *NIDNTT* 1.126–35; Turner, *Words* 23–25). In the NT the term is used in three senses: (1) in a general sense of a messenger sent (2 Cor 8:23; Phil 2:25); (2) of those who had received a commission from Jesus Christ or the local church (e.g., 1 Cor 15:7, James; Rom 16:7, Andronicus and Junia); (3) of the Twelve (Matt 10:2; 1 Cor 15:5, 7) and Paul (1 Cor 9:1; Gal 1:11–12) who were commissioned directly by Jesus for the proclamation of the gospel.

Ἰησοῦ Χριστοῦ is a poss. gen., with Χριστοῦ already moving from a title to being part of Jesus' name (Achtemeier 81 n. 26). Peter uses this full title in all nine refs. to

Christ in the epistle (1:1, 2, 3, 7, 13; 2:5; 3:21; 4:11; 5:10), although in the final ref. we find the inverted order Χριστῷ Ἰησοῦ (depending on textual var.).

See below, For Further Study 1, "Peter in the NT," and 2, "Apostleship in the NT."

ἐκλεκτοῖς παρεπιδήμοις διασπορᾶς

Ἐκλεκτός, -ή, -όν, "elect," "chosen" (BDAG 306b; G. Schrenk, *TDNT* 4.181–92). Although it is common for substantives to be anar. in epistolary introductions (R 793; BDF §137, 261 [5]), the indef. sense of the subst. adj. ἐκλεκτοῖς should be retained in the tr. (Michaels 3). Not only does the indef. sense highlight the qualitative aspect of the adj., it is consistent with the idea, clearly stated in 5:9, that these Christians of Asia Minor belong to a much larger group of elect people throughout the world.

Παρεπίδημος, -ου, ὁ, "temporary resident," "refugee," "sojourner" (BDAG 775d; W. Grundmann, *TDNT* 2.64–65; H. Bietenhard, *NIDNTT* 1.690; LN 11.77). See further on 2:11. The dat. may be understood in two ways:

> *1. In appos. to the subst. adj. ἐκλεκτοῖς, giving the rendering "to a chosen people, who are strangers . . ." (most EVV).
> 2. Qualified by ἐκλεκτοῖς, giving the sense "to the chosen strangers" (Dubis 1–2).

The latter option is highlighting the elect out of the larger group of strangers, whereas the former option is labelling the elect as strangers. It is clear from a number of refs. in the epistle that these believers are estranged from their communities because of their distinctive Christian lifestyle (2:11; 4:3–4). Thus, the former option is preferable.

Διασπορά, -ᾶς, ἡ, "dispersion" (BDAG 236d; K. L. Schmidt, *TDNT* 2.98–104; F. S. Rothenberg, *NIDNTT* 1.685–86), a local gen. (T 235) giving "strangers in the dispersion" (REB, NJB), or ". . . scattered throughout . . ." (NASB, NCV, TEV, NIV).

Πόντου, Γαλατίας, Καππαδοκίας, Ἀσίας καὶ Βιθυνίας

Πόντος, -ου, ὁ, "Pontus." Γαλατία, -ας, ἡ, "Galatia." Καππαδοκία, -ας, ἡ, "Cappadocia." Ἀσία, -ας, ἡ, "Asia." Βιθυνία, -ας, ἡ, "Bithynia." The gens. are best taken as in appos. to διασπορᾶς (Jobes 75)—the dispersion which consists in these locations (ZG 703).

VERSE 2

κατὰ πρόγνωσιν θεοῦ πατρός

Πρόγνωσις, -εως, ἡ, "foreknowledge." The noun (cf. the cognate vb. in 1:20) relates not just to divine foreknowledge, but also to divine decision (R. Bultmann, *TDNT* 1.715–16; P. Jacobs and H. Krienke, *NIDNTT* 1.692–93; Turner, *Words* 178–79). This prep. phrase could modify ἀπόστολος, ἐκλεκτοῖς, or παρεπιδήμοις. Some commentators believe that it modifies v. 1 in its entirety (e.g., Jobes 75), although it is best understood as further defining the basis of the elect status of the recipients (NRSV, REB, TEV, NKJV, HCSB, NIV; Dubis 3; ZG 703).

The lack of a def. art. is not uncommon in salutations and also with nouns which are the obj. of a prep. The anar. πατρός, in appos. to θεοῦ, could also be focusing on the quality of God as Father (on anar. substantives see R 127, 793; BDF §137–38; Wallace 243–54).

ἐν ἁγιασμῷ πνεύματος

An instr. (not locat. *pace* T 262) use of ἐν (NJB, TEV, NRSV, REB, NASB) with ἁγιασμός, -οῦ, ὁ, "consecration" (O. Procksch, *TDNT* 1.113–14; Turner, *Words* 83–85; BDAG 10c). Πνεύματος is a subj. gen. The Spirit carries out the role of consecration or setting apart ("through the sanctifying work of the Spirit," NIV), which is the means by which (ἐν) election is actualized.

εἰς ὑπακοὴν καὶ ῥαντισμὸν αἵματος Ἰησοῦ Χριστοῦ

The prep. ἐν denotes goal/purpose, "leading to," "resulting in" (R 594–95; Harris 88–90; BDAG 290d; Dubis 3, Wallace 369–71). Ὑπακοή, -ῆς, ἡ, "obedience," a key term in this epistle. Ῥαντισμός, -οῦ, ὁ, "sprinkling," is unattested outside of BGk. (BDAG 903d; Turner, *Words* 55–56; Hunzinger, *TDNT* 6.976–84). This is a metaphor drawn from covenant ratification (Exod 24:7–8) where, following a pledge of obedience, the people were sprinkled with sacrificial blood (ZG 703). Αἵματος is an obj. gen. signifying that which is sprinkled.

Ἰησοῦ Χριστοῦ modifies αἵματος. Renderings that link the name primarily to ὑπακοήν (as do most EVV, e.g., NRSV, NASB, NIV; also Dubis 3–4) are problematic as this forces Ἰησοῦ Χριστοῦ to have two different senses with respect to the two different nouns (i.e., obedience *to* Jesus—an obj. gen., and sprinkling with his blood—poss. gen.). On the two other occasions in which ὑπακοή is used in 1 Peter (1:14, 22), it is not linked to Jesus. The preferred rendering is "for obedience, and sprinkling with the blood of Jesus Christ" (cf. Weymouth—"with a view to their obedience and to their being sprinkled with the blood of Jesus Christ;" sim. Moffatt).

This v. lays the theological foundation for the epistle by outlining the nature and origin of the salvation that believers have experienced. God is the ultimate source, activated by the Spirit, for the express purpose of obedience.

χάρις ὑμῖν καὶ εἰρήνη πληθυνθείη

"Grace and peace" is the customary NT greeting and represents an expansion of the Jewish greeting *shalom*. Πληθυνθείη is 3 sg. aor. pass. opt. of πληθύνω, "increase," "multiply" (BDAG 826a). The volitive opt. (R 939; Z §355; Wallace 481–93) is used to express a polite request (cf. 1 Thess 3:11; 2 Tim 1:16; 2 Pet 1:2; ZG 703).

FOR FURTHER STUDY

1. Peter in the NT (1:1)

Brown, Raymond E., Karl P. Donfried, and John Reuman, eds. *Peter in the New Testament.* Minneapolis: Fortress, 1973.

Bruce, F. F. *Peter, Stephen, James and John: Studies in Non-Pauline Christianity.* Grand Rapids: Eerdmans, 1979.

Donfried, Karl P. *ABD* 5.251–63.

Perkins, Pheme. *Peter: Apostle for the Whole Church*. Columbia: University of South Carolina Press, 1994.

Smith, Terrence V. *Petrine Controversies in Early Christianity*. Tübingen: Mohr, 1985.

*Witherington, Ben, III. *What Have They Done with Jesus?* San Francisco: Harper, 2006. See pages 55–94.

2. Apostleship in the NT (1:1)

Agnew, F. H. "On the Origin of the Term *Apostolos*." *CBQ* 38 (1976): 49–53.

_____. "The Origin of the NT Apostle-Concept: A Review of Research." *JBL* 105 (1986): 75–96.

*Barnett, Paul W. *DPL* 45–51.

Barrett, C. K. *The Signs of an Apostle*. Philadelphia: Fortress, 1972.

Bühner, Jan–Adolf. *EDNT* 1.142–46.

Kirk, J. Andrew. "Apostleship Since Rengstorf: Towards a Synthesis." *NTS* 21 (1974–75): 249–64.

*Kruse, Colin G. *DJG* 27–33.

Müller, Dietrich. *NIDNTT* 1.126–35.

Rengstorf, Karl H. *TDNT* 1.407–47.

Schmithals, Walter. *The Office of Apostle in the Early Church*. Nashville: Abingdon, 1969.

Schnackenburg, Rudolf. "Apostles before and during Paul's Time." Pages 287–303 in *Apostolic History and the Gospel*. Edited by W. W. Gasque and R. P. Martin. Grand Rapids: Eerdmans, 1970.

Spicq 1:186–94.

3. Election (1:1–2)

*Basinger, David, and Randall Basinger, eds. *Predestination and Free Will: Four Views of Divine Sovereignty and Human Freedom*. Downers Grove: InterVarsity, 1986.

Carson, D. A. *Divine Sovereignty and Human Responsibility: Biblical Themes in Tension*. Atlanta: John Knox, 1981.

Erickson, Millard E. *Christian Theology*. Grand Rapids: Baker, 1985. See pages 907–28.

Klooster, Fred H. *EDT* 348–49.

MacDonald, W. G. "The Biblical Doctrine of Election." Pages 207–29 in *The Grace of God, The Will of Man*. Edited by C. H. Pinnock. Grand Rapids: Zondervan, 1989.

McGrath, Alister E. *Christian Theology: An Introduction*. Oxford: Blackwell, 1994. See pages 394–404.

Schreiner, Thomas R. *NDBT* 450–54.

Shogren, Gary S. *ABD* 2.441–44.

4. God's People as Aliens/Strangers (1:1)

*Chin, Moses. "A Heavenly Home for the Homeless: Aliens and Strangers in 1 Peter." *TynBul* 42 (1991): 96–112.

Coughenour, Robert A. *ISBE* 4.561–64.

*Dunning, Benjamin H. *Aliens and Sojourners: Self as Other in Early Christianity*. Philadelphia: University of Pennsylvania Press, 2009.

Elliott, John H. *A Home for the Homeless: A Sociological Exegesis of 1 Peter, Its Situation and Strategy*. Philadelphia: Fortress, 1981.

Green, Joel B. "Living as Exiles: The Church in the Diaspora in 1 Peter." Pages 311–25 in *Holiness and Ecclesiology in the New Testament*. Edited by K. E. Brower and A. Johnson. Grand Rapids: Eerdmans, 2007.

_____. *1 Peter*. Grand Rapids: Eerdmans, 2007. See pages 191–97.

Hauerwas, Stanley, and William H. Willimon. *Resident Aliens: Life in the Christian Colony*. Waterloo, ON: Wilfrid Laurier University Press, 2006.

Horrell, David G. *1 Peter*. London: T&T Clark, 2008.

Seland, T. "Πάροικος καὶ παρεπίδημος: Proselyte Characterisations in 1 Peter?" *BBR* 11 (2001): 239–68.

Talbert, Charles H., ed. *Perspectives on 1 Peter*. Macon, GA: Mercer University Press, 1986.

Winter, Bruce. "Seek the Welfare of the City: Social Ethics according to 1 Peter." *Them* 13 (1988): 91–94.

5. Dispersion (1:1)

Barclay, John M. G. *Jews in the Mediterranean Diaspora: From Alexander to Trajan (323 BCE—117 CE)*. Edinburgh: T&T Clark, 1996.

Ellison, H. L. *From Babylon to Jerusalem: The People of God between the Testaments*. Grand Rapids: Baker, 1976.

Feldman, Louis H., and Meyer Reinhold. *Jewish Life and Thought among Greeks and Romans*. Edinburgh: T&T Clark, 1996.

Lieu, Judith, John North, and Tessa Rajak, eds. *The Jews among Pagans and Christians in the Roman Empire*. London: Routledge, 1992.

Safrai, S., and M. Stern, eds. *The Jewish People in the First Century*. 2 vols. Philadelphia: Fortress, 1974–76.

*Skarsaune, Oskar. *In the Shadow of the Temple: Jewish Influences on Early Christianity*. Downers Grove: InterVarsity, 2002. See pages 67–85.

Smallwood, E. Mary. *The Jews under Roman Rule: From Pompey to Diocletian*. Second edition. Leiden: Brill, 1981.

Trebilco, Paul R. *DLNT* 287–300.

6. Divine Foreknowledge (1:2)

Bromiley, Geoffrey W. *EDT* 419–21.

Bultmann, Rudolf. *TDNT* 1.715–16.

Cook, Robert R. "Divine Foreknowledge: Some Philosophical Issues." *Vox Evangelica* 20 (1990): 57–72.

Craig, William Lane. *Divine Foreknowledge and Human Freedom*. Leiden: Brill, 1991.

*Erickson, Millard E. *Christian Theology*. Grand Rapids: Baker, 1985. See pages 345–63.

Fischer, John Martin. "Divine Foreknowledge and Human Freedom." *Religious Studies* 28 (1992): 269–74.

Hammett, John S. "Divine Foreknowledge and Open Theism." *Faith and Mission* 21 (2003): 18–31.

Jewett, Paul K. *God, Creation and Revelation: A Neo-Evangelical Theology*. Grand Rapids: Eerdmans, 1991. See pages 369–81.

Pinnock, Clark H., ed. *The Grace of God, the Will of Man: A Case for Arminianism*. Grand Rapids: Zondervan, 1989.

Sand, Alexander. *EDNT* 3.153–54.

7. Consecration/Work of the Holy Spirit in 1 Peter (1:2)

Green, Joel B. "Faithful Witness in Diaspora: The Holy Spirit and the Exiled People of God According to 1 Peter." Pages 282–95 in *The Holy Spirit and Christian Origins: Essays in Honor of James D. G. Dunn*. Edited by G. Stanton, B. Longenecker, and S. Barton. Grand Rapids: Eerdmans, 2004.

8. Letter Writing in Antiquity (1:1–2)

Aune, David E. *The New Testament in its Literary Environment*. Philadelphia: Westminster, 1987. See pages 158–82.

Bahr, Gordon J. "Paul and Letter Writing in the First Century." *CBQ* 28 (1966): 467–77.

Dahl, Nils A. *IDB* 5.538–41.

Doty, William G. *Letters in Primitive Christianity*. Philadelphia: Fortress, 1973.

Elsom, Helen. "The New Testament and Greco-Roman Writing." Pages 561–78 in *The Literary Guide to the Bible*. Edited by R. Alter and F. Kermode. Cambridge, MA: Harvard University Press, 1987.

NewDocs 8.127–28.

*Stowers, Stanley K. *Letter Writing in Greco-Roman Antiquity*. Philadelphia: Westminster, 1986.

White, J. L. *The Form and Function of the Body of the Greek Letter*. Missoula, MT: Scholars, 1972.

_____. "Ancient Greek Letters." Pages 85–105 in *Greco-Roman Literature and the New Testament*. Edited by D. E. Aune. Atlanta: Scholars, 1988.

HOMILETICAL SUGGESTIONS

Salutation (1:1–2)

1. The author: Peter (v. 1a)
2. The recipients: Christians in northern Asia Minor (v. 1b)
3. Statement of election (v. 2a)
   (a) Its basis/origin (κατά): the foreknowledge of God
   (b) Its effecting (ἐν): the sanctifying work of the Spirit
   (c) Its purpose (εἰς): obedience
4. The greeting: grace and peace (v. 2b)

II. The Christian Hope (1:3–12)

A. THE LIVING HOPE (1:3–5)

STRUCTURE

This section begins with a liturgical blessing to God then proceeds to describe what God has done for the recipients in granting new birth to a living hope (v. 3). The repetition of εἰς in v. 4 provides further detail regarding this hope, expressed in terms of a grand, safely kept inheritance. The three alpha privatives provide an alliterative effect. The shift to the second person pl. ὑμᾶς at the end of v. 4 provides a transition to show, by means of three prep. phrases, how and why believers are being protected.

3   Εὐλογητὸς ὁ θεὸς
        καὶ πατὴρ
            τοῦ κυρίου ἡμῶν Ἰησοῦ Χριστοῦ

       ὁ
       ⋮ κατὰ τὸ πολὺ αὐτοῦ ἔλεος
      ἀναγεννήσας ἡμᾶς
        εἰς ἐλπίδα ζῶσαν
        δι᾽ ἀναστάσεως Ἰησοῦ Χριστοῦ ἐκ νεκρῶν,

4   εἰς κληρονομίαν ἄφθαρτον
             καὶ ἀμίαντον
             καὶ ἀμάραντον
               τετηρημένην ἐν οὐρανοῖς εἰς ὑμᾶς

5   τοὺς   ἐν δυνάμει θεοῦ
            ⋮ φρουρουμένους
              διὰ πίστεως
              εἰς σωτηρίαν
                 ἑτοίμην ἀποκαλυφθῆναι
                     ἐν καιρῷ
                       ἐσχάτῳ

VERSE 3

Εὐλογητὸς ὁ θεὸς καὶ πατὴρ τοῦ κυρίου ἡμῶν Ἰησοῦ Χριστοῦ

The adj. εὐλογητός is pred. and the opt. form of εἰμι should be understood in this prayer wish (cf. v. 2). The single def. art. governs both θεός and πατήρ and is an example of the Granville Sharp Rule (see Wallace 270–90; R 785). Thus, while "God" and "Father" relate to the same Person, the rule does not indicate whether we are to understand that (1) God is both God of Jesus and Father of Jesus; or (2) God is Father of Jesus. The same grammatical formula occurs in 2 Cor 1:3; 11:31; Eph 1:3; cf. Rom 15:6, and is a Christianized version of the Jewish liturgical blessing that requires the art. to be in this position, i.e., with θεός (e.g., LXX Gen 14:20; Ps 17:47; Tob 11:17; 13:1, 18). Given that most commentators agree that the Christian version of the formula has revelation rather than subordination as its focus (i.e., God is revealed as God through Jesus—Goppelt 80; Achtemeier 94; Michaels 17), a more accurate tr. would be "blessed be God, who is Father of our Lord Jesus Christ" (cf. Col 1:3). Most EVV (e.g., NRSV, NEB, NASB, NIV) follow the more lit. trans. "blessed be the God and Father of our Lord Jesus Christ."

ὁ κατὰ τὸ πολὺ αὐτοῦ ἔλεος ἀναγεννήσας ἡμᾶς

Ἀναγεννήσας nom. sg. masc. of aor. act. ptc. of ἀναγεννάω, "give new life" or "new birth" (BDAG 59d; F. Büchsel, *TDNT* 1.673–75; A. Ringwald, *NIDNTT* 1.176–80; LN 13.55). The vb. appears only here and in v. 23 in the NT, although the uncompounded form γεννάω appears in the Johannine literature (John 3:3, 5; 1 John 2:29; 3:9) with the same sense. Elsewhere in the NT the same idea is conveyed by the use of different verbs (Titus 3:5 ἀνακαίνωσις; Jas 1:18 ἀποκυέω). The art. ὁ belongs with ἀναγεννήσας, with κατὰ τὸ πολὺ αὐτοῦ ἔλεος qualifying this art. ptc. Here κατά expresses cause (ZG 703) or conformity (BDAG 512c). Peter's use of ἔλεος ("mercy") parallels Paul's use of χάρις ("grace"), highlighting the undeserved nature of salvation.

εἰς ἐλπίδα ζῶσαν

The adj. ptc ζῶσαν expresses the quality of the hope ("living," "vibrant"), not its obj. ("life"; cf. Cassirer "life-giving hope").

δι' ἀναστάσεως Ἰησοῦ Χριστοῦ ἐκ νεκρῶν

For anar. nouns used with a prep., see v. 2. Ἰησοῦ Χριστοῦ is an obj. gen. Ἐκ νεκρῶν (lit. "from among dead people") is a NT idiom (BDF §254).

VERSE 4

εἰς κληρονομίαν ἄφθαρτον καὶ ἀμίαντον καὶ ἀμάραντον

Κληρονομία, -ας, ἡ, "inheritance." Given the lack of a connective καί, the inheritance that is now depicted should not be understood as a further result of new birth in

addition to the living hope (as NRSV, NJB, NIV; Achtemeier 95; Elliott 335), but a
further definition of the living hope (Weymouth, REB; Dubis 7). The use of the three
alpha privatives creates an alliterative effect. The first, ἄφθαρτος, -ον, "imperishable,"
refers to that which death cannot ravage (BDAG 156a; G. Harder, *TDNT* 9.93–106),
the second, ἀμίαντος, -ον, "undefiled," to that which is unstained by evil (BDAG 54a;
F. Hauck, *TDNT* 4.644–47), and the third, ἀμάραντος, -ον, "unfading," to that which is
not affected by the passing of time (BDAG 49d). On the lack of fem. form for these
adjs., see R 272–73; MH 156–68. The inheritance is a natural corollary of the father-
child relationship (1:3, 17).

τετηρημένην ἐν οὐρανοῖς εἰς ὑμᾶς

The ptc. τετηρημένην (acc. sg. fem. of perf. pass. ptc. of τηρέω) is in agreement with
κληρονομίαν. The pf. tense highlights the secure nature of the inheritance, while the
pass. indicates the activity of God. The prep. εἰς is referential ("for us") and equates
to "for our benefit" (BDAG 291a; R 535, 594). Opponents may ridicule and slander
(2:12; 3:14; 4:3–4), but they cannot deprive believers of their inheritance.

VERSE 5

τοὺς ἐν δυνάμει θεοῦ φρουρουμένους διὰ πίστεως

Φρουρουμένους acc. pl. masc. of pres. pass. ptc. of φρουρέω, "guard," "protect"
(BDAG 1067a). With its accompanying art. τούς this ptc. is in appos. to ὑμᾶς.

The guarding has both an obj. and subj. sense. On the obj. side, the instr. dat.
ἐν δυνάμει θεοῦ shows that believers are under divine protection. Thus the ptc.
φρουρουμένους should be taken as pass. rather than mid. (so most EVV, Feldmeier
78). On the subj. side, the blessings that God has in store and the protection he offers,
can be appropriated only διὰ πίστεως "through faith" (instr. use of prep., see R 582;
Harris 70–72).

εἰς σωτηρίαν ἑτοίμην ἀποκαλυφθῆναι ἐν καιρῷ ἐσχάτῳ

The repetition of εἰς gives another perspective on the living hope, described here as
simply "salvation." Thus the three uses of εἰς in vv. 3–5 discuss the same reality utilizing different images: "living hope" (v. 3), "inheritance" (v. 4), and "salvation" (v. 5).

The adj. ἕτοιμος, -η, -ον, "ready," with its accompanying infin. of purpose
ἀποκαλυφθῆναι (R 1076–77; T 139; BDF §393[4]) is epex. of σωτηρίαν—it is a salvation that is "ready to be revealed," thus conveying a sense of imminence.

Ἐν καιρῷ ἐσχάτῳ only here in the NT. Here καιρός refers to a specific time (i.e., the
end; cf. 4:7), rather than a period of time (Michaels 23; Elliott 338). In 1:20 ἐσχάτου
τῶν χρόνων is used to refer to the last days as the current epoch.

Here we see an example of the theological diversity of the early church. For Paul,
the things which were kept hidden have already been revealed (Rom 1:17; 3:21; Col
1:27; Eph 3:9). This is not a contradiction, but an example of the tension between the
now and the not yet in which believers find themselves.

FOR FURTHER STUDY

9. The Resurrection of Jesus Christ (1:3)

Avis, Paul, ed. *The Resurrection of Jesus Christ*. London: Darton, Longman and Todd, 1993.

Copan, Paul, and Ronald K. Tacelli, eds. *Jesus' Resurrection: Fact or Figment?* Downers Grove: InterVarsity, 2000.

Green, Michael. *The Empty Cross of Jesus*. London: Hodder and Stoughton, 1984.

Habermas, Gary R. *EDT* 938–41.

Harris, Murray J. *Raised Immortal: Resurrection and Immortality in the New Testament*. Grand Rapids: Eerdmans, 1985.

*_____. *From Grave to Glory: Resurrection in the New Testament*. Grand Rapids: Zondervan, 1990.

Jansen, J. F. *The Resurrection of Jesus Christ in New Testament Theology*. Philadelphia: Westminster, 1980.

Morris, Leon. *ISBE* 4.150–54.

Moule, Charles F. D., ed. *The Significance of the Message of the Resurrection for Faith in Jesus Christ*. London: SCM, 1968.

Nickelsburg, George W. E. *ABD* 5.684–91.

Osborne, Grant R. *DJG* 673–88.

Wright, N. T. *The Resurrection of the Son of God*. London: SPCK, 2003.

10. The Inheritance of Believers (1:4)

Eichler, Johannes. *NIDNTT* 2.295–303.

Foerster, Werner. *TDNT* 3.758–69.

Fuller, Ruth M. *DPL* 819–20.

*_____. *DLNT* 1038–41.

Hirsch, Frank E., and Donald K. McKim. *ISBE* 2.823–25.

11. Salvation in the NT and 1 Peter (1:5, 9)

Barnett, Paul W. *DLNT* 1072–75.

Foerster, Werner. *TDNT* 7.965–69.

*Green, Joel B. *1 Peter*. Grand Rapids: Eerdmans, 2007. See pages 258–79.

Hanson, Anthony T. "Salvation Proclaimed, pt 1: 1 Peter 3:18–22." *ExpTim* 93 (1982): 100–105.

Jobes 48–49.

Liefeld, Walter L. *ISBE* 4.287–95.

Michaels lxx–lxxiv.

O'Collins, Gerald G. *ABD* 5.907–14.

Ryken, Philip Graham. *The Message of Salvation*. Leicester: InterVarsity, 2001.

Schneider, Johannes. *NIDNTT* 3.211–16.

Stott, John. *The Cross of Christ*. Leicester: InterVarsity, 1986. See pages 167–203.

White, R. E. O. *EDT* 967–69.

Williams, Martin. *The Doctrine of Salvation in the First Letter of Peter*. Cambridge: Cambridge University Press, 2011.

12. The Last Day/Days (1:5)

Allison, Dale C. *The End of the Ages Has Come*. Philadelphia: Fortress, 1985.

Aune, David E. *ABD* 2.594–609.

*Beale, Gregory K. *DLNT* 330–45.

Brown, Colin. *NIDNTT* 2.901–35.

Daley, Brian E. "Eschatology." Pages 309–14 in *Encyclopedia of Early Christianity*. 2nd ed. Edited by Everett Ferguson. New York: Garland, 1990.

Davies, W. D., and David Daube, eds. *The Background of the New Testament and Its Eschatology: Studies in Honor of C. H. Dodd*. Cambridge: Cambridge University Press, 1956.

Dumbrell, William J. *The Search for Order: Biblical Eschatology in Focus*. Grand Rapids: Baker, 1994.

Hoekema, Anthony A. *The Bible and the Future*. Grand Rapids: Eerdmans, 1979.

Ladd, George Eldon. "Eschatology and the Unity of New Testament Theology." *ExpTim* 68 (1957): 268–78.

————. *The Presence of the Future*. Grand Rapids: Eerdmans, 1974.

Lewis, J. P., ed. *The Last Things: Essays Presented to W. B. West Jr*. Austin, TX: Sweet, 1972.

Russell, Ronald. "Eschatology and Ethics in 1 Peter." *EvQ* 47 (1975): 78–84.

Wright, N. T. *Climax of the Covenant*. Minneapolis: Fortress, 1991.

HOMILETICAL SUGGESTIONS

The Living Hope (1:3–5)

1. Basis of the living hope (v. 3)
   (a) the mercy of God
   (b) the resurrection of Jesus Christ
2. Content of the hope (1:4–5)
   (a) An inheritance of great quality (vv. 4–5a)
      (i) Not ephemeral
      (ii) Kept in heaven
      (iii) Guarded by God through faith
   (b) Salvation (v. 5b)

B. JOY IN THE MIDST OF TRIALS (1:6–9)

STRUCTURE

The rel. clause ἐν ᾧ ἀγαλλιᾶσθε that begins v. 6 facilitates a further discussion regarding "the last time" (v. 5). This will be an occasion for great rejoicing, although, by means of a concessive cstr. (ὀλίγον ἄρτι, εἰ δέον) the sober reality and purpose (ἵνα clause) of the present time of suffering is enumerated. The ἵνα clause is quite complex due to the inclusion of a parenthesis within a parenthesis (see Gk. below). The conclusion of v. 7 introduces the future "revelation of Jesus Christ" (cf. 1:13; 4:13), with Jesus Christ functioning as the antecedent of the rel. pron. that introduces v. 8. By means of the two concessive ptcs. ἰδόντες and ὁρῶντες, this v. shows that love for Christ and faith in him are not dependent on his personal presence. The ptc. that introduces the final v. of the section (v. 9) again links the theme of great rejoicing (v. 8b) with the final day of salvation.

6   ἐν ᾧ <u>ἀγαλλιᾶσθε</u>
                    ὀλίγον ἄρτι,
                    εἰ δέον ἐστὶν,
            λυπηθέντας
                    ἐν ποικίλοις πειρασμοῖς,
7   ἵνα τὸ <u>δοκίμιον</u>
                    ὑμῶν τῆς πίστεως
            —πολυτιμότερον χρυσίου
                            τοῦ ἀπολλυμένου,
                            διὰ πυρὸς δὲ <u>δοκιμαζομένου</u>—
                    εὑρεθῇ
                            εἰς ἔπαινον
                            καὶ δόξαν
                            καὶ τιμὴν
                                    ἐν ἀποκαλύψει Ἰησοῦ Χριστοῦ

8   ὃν ‾‾‾‾‾‾‾ οὐκ ἰδόντες
            <u>ἀγαπᾶτε</u>,
    εἰς ὃν   ἄρτι μὴ ὁρῶντες,
                    πιστεύοντες δὲ
            <u>ἀγαλλιᾶσθε</u>
                    χαρᾷ ἀνεκλαλήτῳ
                    καὶ δεδοξασμένῃ
9   κομιζόμενοι τὸ τέλος τῆς πίστεως ὑμῶν
                            σωτηρίαν ψυχῶν.

VERSE 6

ἐν ᾧ ἀγαλλιᾶσθε

The antecedent of the rel. pron. ᾧ is unclear, with options in order of likelihood being:

*1. ἐν καιρῷ ἐσχάτῳ (Weymouth, CEV; Michaels 27; Goppelt 89; Dubis 9);
2. the general thought of vv. 3–5 (rel. is neut.—so RSV, Barclay, NKJV, NASB, NIV; Achtemeier 100; Elliott 339; Jobes 92);
3. θεός or Χριστοῦ (from v.3); or
4. ἐν ᾧ is causal, "and so you rejoice . . ." (ZG 703).

Questions also arise with ἐν ᾧ elsewhere in this epistle. In 2:12 and 3:16 the cstr. appears to be used as a temp. adv. conj. "when," whereas in 4:4 it has circumstantial force "in this connection." The use in 3:19 is disputed (see BDF §219[2], 383[1], 455[3]; R 978).

Ἀγαλλιᾶσθε 2 pl. pres. mid. indic.*/impv. of ἀγαλλιάω, "be full of joy" (BDAG 4c–d; Turner, *Words* 148–50; E. Beyreuther, *NIDNTT* 2.352–56). The form ἀγαλλιᾶσθε (also v. 8b) is ambiguous (R 941) and could be taken as:

1. Impv.: "be full of joy" (Barclay, TEV; R 949);
2. Indic.: descriptive pres. "you are full of joy" (Dubis 10; most EVV); or
*3. Indic.: futuristic pres. "you will be full of joy" (CEV).

The impv. option should be ruled out on the following grounds: (1) impvs. begin in 1:13, with 1:3–12 laying a theological foundation for the ethics that follow; (2) when impvs. are used they are usually in the aor. (25/35 uses); (3) the same vb. in 1:8 is extremely awkward as an impv. (Michaels 28; Jobes 93).

Elsewhere in the NT this vb. is used a number of times to refer to rejoicing in the present in light of eschatological blessings that have either arrived (Luke 1:47; Rev 19:7), or are imminent or certain (Matt 5:12; John 8:56; Acts 2:26). It is not used with respect to future rejoicing. On the other hand, the cognate noun ἀγαλλίασις is used with a future orientation in Luke 1:14 and Jude 24, although only the latter refers to the end as such. The vb. is also employed in 4:13, where in the first part of this v. another word for rejoice is used (χαίρω); here Peter clearly exhorts his readers to rejoice in the present time because they share the sufferings of Christ. The purpose of this present attitude of rejoicing is given by what follows, namely that rejoicing under adverse circumstances in the present will lead to even greater rejoicing when Christ's glory is revealed at the end. This greater rejoicing is portrayed by the juxtaposition of both vbs. χαίρω and ἀγαλλιάω. This use of ἀγαλλιάω seemingly relates to a future rejoicing, so the vb. is best taken as a futuristic pres. here in 1:6 (see further argument below).

ὀλίγον ἄρτι εἰ δέον ἐστιν λυπηθέντας ἐν ποικίλοις πειρασμοῖς [λυπηθέντας reflects the text of the forthcoming fifth edition of the UBS *Greek New Testament*. The fourth edition reads λυπηθέντες.]

The neut. form of the adj. ὀλίγος, -η, -ον is used adv. to indicate duration of time (BDAG 703a; ZG 703; Achtemeier 101; Michaels 28; Goppelt 89). Together with the adv. ἄρτι the ref. is to the present time. The use of the temp. adv. ἄρτι clearly indicates that suffering is a present experience (Michaels 28). Δέον nom. sg. neut. of pres. act. ptc. of δεῖ, "be necessary." The ptc. is supplementary, here needing the ptc. λυπηθέντας to complete its mng. (R 1119). The cond. εἰ δέον functions in somewhat of a concessive sense (R 919–20; ZG 703) and in no way implies that suffering is a remote possibility.

Λυπηθέντας acc. pl. masc. of aor. pass. ptc. of λυπέω, in agreement with ὑμᾶς in v. 4. This is the preferred reading of the forthcoming UBS[5], following the *Editio Critica Maior*, and is supported by ℵ* L and several minuscules. The vb. λυπέω can refer to emotional pain and grief, as well as physical pain (BDAG 604c; Spicq 2.417–22; H. Haarbeck and H.-G. Link, *NIDNTT* 2.419–21). Whereas the suffering that Peter's readers are experiencing could well be physical (2:20), they are clearly the victims of slander and verbal abuse (2:11–12; 3:9; 4:14). The ptc. λυπηθέντας is aor., traditionally seen as expressing time antecedent to the main vb., but this is an overgeneralization (see Fanning, 416–19 on the temporal value of ptcs).

Ποικίλος, -η, -ον, "varied" (BDAG 842b–c). Πειρασμός, -οῦ, ὁ, "trial." The dat. ἐν ποικίλοις πειρασμοῖς can either be cstr. as instr. ("by means of various trials," NKJV, NASB) or as locat. ("in the midst of various trials," Weymouth, NIV).

VERSE 7

ἵνα τὸ δοκίμιον ὑμῶν τῆς πίστεως

Δοκίμιον, -ου, τό can refer to the testing process itself (as in Jas 1:3; see Turner, *Insights* 168–69), or to the result of testing, i.e., "genuineness" (as here; BDAG 256b; Spicq 1.353–61; Turner, *Words* 444–46; H. Haarbeck, *NIDNTT* 3.808–11; LN 73.3; Dubis 12; R 654). Τῆς πίστεως is an obj. gen., signifying that which is tested.

πολυτιμότερον χρυσίου τοῦ ἀπολλυμένου διὰ πυρὸς δὲ δοκιμαζομένου

A parenthesis (containing another parenthesis), commenting on the precious nature of genuine faith. The comp. adj. πολυτιμότερον (from πολύτιμος, "costly," "of great value" [BDAG 850c]) agrees with δοκίμιον, thus stressing that it is the genuine quality of faith that is most precious. The explicit point is that genuine faith is more precious than gold. There are two implicit points. The first is that genuine faith is more precious than gold because gold is perishable, with τοῦ ἀπολλυμένου (gen. sg. neut. of pres. mid. ptc. of ἀπόλλυμι, "perish," [BDAG 116a]; for art. ptc. following anar. noun, see Z §192; R 778, 1107; T 152–53) standing in appos. to χρυσίου (gen. of comparison). The second is that faith must be refined and tested as is gold. Δέ is postscriptive with διὰ πυρός and is most likely adversative which gives the ptc. τοῦ ἀπολλυμένου concessive force—"more precious than gold which, though perishable, is tested through fire" (Dubis 13–14).

εὑρεθῇ εἰς ἔπαινον καὶ δόξαν καὶ τιμήν

Although it is possible to cstr. πολυτιμότερον as the pred. of εὑρεθῇ, "may be found to be more precious than gold" (as Hort 42; Selwyn 130; Kelly 54), the word order makes this less likely; it is preferable to understand εὑρεθῇ (subjunc. with ἵνα) with εἰς indicating result ("may be found to result in," NASB; "may result in," NIV).

῎Επαινος, -ου, ὁ, "praise." Given the further ref. to the revelation of Jesus Christ in 1:13 and the grace (χάριν) destined for believers, "praise, glory and honor" most likely refers to that which God bestows rather than what is directed toward God ("may result in you receiving praise, glory and honor. . . .," sim. Moffatt, CEV, NLT).

ἐν ἀποκαλύψει Ἰησοῦ Χριστοῦ

᾿Εν is locat. of time. The ref. is to the Parousia, and the term ἀποκαλύψει may imply a current hidden presence (Michaels 32). Ἰησοῦ Χριστοῦ is an obj. gen—it is Jesus Christ who will be revealed (cf. 1:13; 4:13). The revelation of Jesus Christ is an important concept in this epistle (cf. 1:13; 4:13) and underlines its eschatological tone. Peter possibly avoids the use of the word παρουσία (a term that implies a current absence) because he wants to emphasize the ongoing presence of Jesus with his followers. This is part of the language of encouragement to a persecuted minority.

VERSE 8

ὃν οὐκ ἰδόντες ἀγαπᾶτε

᾿Ιδόντες nom. pl. masc. of aor. act. ptc. of ὁράω, "see." The ptc. is concessive in force (i.e., "although you have not seen him"). Ἀγαπᾶτε 2 pl. pres. act. indic.*/impv. ἀγαπάω, "love." Best taken as indic. rather than impv. given that it parallels πιστεύοντες, which is hardly impv. The particle οὐ/οὐκ does not normally negate the ptc., but such usage is not infrequent in the NT (R 1136–39; BDF §430[3]; Z §440 n. 2). See further below.

εἰς ὃν ἄρτι μὴ ὁρῶντες πιστεύοντες δέ

The switch from οὐ to μή with the ptc. is striking. R (1138) contends that we should understand the former in terms of "an actual experience, while μή with ὁρῶντες is in accord with the concessive idea in contrast with πιστεύοντες" (see also BDF §430[3]; Dubis 15).

It is unclear whether the two ptc. clauses ὃν οὐκ ἰδόντες ἀγαπᾶτε and εἰς ὃν ἄρτι μὴ ὁρῶντες are meant to:

1. refer to two distinct time periods—i.e., not seeing the historical Jesus during his earthly ministry nor the risen Jesus at present (Achtemeier 103 possibly); or

2. reinforce the point that they do not see Jesus at present (Elliott 342–43).

The change in tense, combined with the temp. adv. ἄρτι, should not be overlooked. However, it is best to opt for a more general version of option 1—that the recipients have never seen Jesus in the past or in the present.

ἀγαλλιᾶσθε χαρᾷ ἀνακλαλήτῳ καὶ δεδοξασμένῃ

Ἀγαλλιᾶσθε is 2 pl. pres. mid. indic. of ἀγαλλιάω, "be overjoyed" (see v. 6). Ἀνεκλάλητος, -ον, "inexpressible" ("unspeakable," Weymouth). The entire cstr. εἰς ὃν ἄρτι μὴ ὁρῶντες πιστεύοντες δὲ ἀγαλλιᾶσθε χαρᾷ ἀνακλαλήτῳ καὶ δεδοξασμένῃ can be cstr. in several ways:

1. "Though you do not see him now you believe in him and (will) rejoice." (NRSV, NJB, ESV, NIV, Michaels [with some variation] 25). This rendering takes εἰς ὃν with πιστεύοντες, and the ptc. μὴ ὁρῶντες as concessive. The main problem is that δέ then connects πιστεύοντες and ἀγαλλιᾶσθε, whereas given its normal postscriptive position it more likely functions as an adversative contrasting μὴ ὁρῶντες and πιστεύοντες (as it does in v.12—ἑαυτοῖς ὑμῖν δέ);
2. "Although you do not see him now but believe in him you (will) rejoice . . ." Here the problem with δέ in rendering 1. above is overcome (NASB);
3. "Although you do not see him now but believe, you (will) rejoice in him" (Achtemeier, with some variation, 103). Here εἰς ὃν is taken with ἀγαλλιᾶσθε rather than πιστεύοντες, with the intervening words functioning as a parenthesis; or
*4. "You do not see him now but because you believe in him you (will) rejoice." πιστεύοντες is here dependent upon ἀγαλλιᾶσθε and taken as causal (Cassirer: "Though you still do not see him, you exult by reason of your believing in him").

In weighing the above options, the first should be rejected due to its use of δέ. Given that εἰς ὃν more naturally goes with πιστεύοντες, option 3 is unlikely. The rhythm of the first two ptc. clauses makes it probable that they both have the same concessive force, thus favoring option 2. However, given that πιστεύοντες is a ptc. whereas both ἀγαπᾶτε and ἀγαλλιᾶσθε are indic., this tends to favor option 4. In the end, options 2 or 4 are the most likely, with the balance slightly favoring the latter.

Ἀγαλλιᾶσθε is a futuristic pres. in line with the interpretation given in v. 6 (*pace* most modern commentators, though see Goppelt 94; Michaels 34). The dats. χαρᾷ ἀνεκλαλήτῳ καὶ δεδοξασμένῃ are instr. of manner (R 531), and the pf. ptc. δεδοξασμένῃ is intensive in force (Campbell, *Indicative Mood* 161–211), adding to the passionate language already employed.

VERSE 9

κομιζόμενοι τὸ τέλος τῆς πίστεως ὑμῶν σωτηρίαν ψυχῶν

Κομιζόμενοι nom. pl. masc. of pres. mid. ptc. of κομίζω, "obtain" (BDAG 557d). In line with the interpretation given in v. 6, κομιζόμενοι is taken as a temp. ptc. that has a fut. time ref. in its dependence on the futuristic pres. ἀγαλλιᾶσθε. Most EVV and commentators, however, regard ἀγαλλιᾶσθε as a descriptive pres., thus making κομιζόμενοι most likely to be causal, that is rejoicing now because of the salvation to come (NRSV, TEV, HCSB, NIV; Achtemeier 104; Dubis 16).

Τέλος is used here in the sense of final result or outcome. The gen. τῆς πίστεως is partitive, in the sense that it is one segment of faith, "the outcome of your faith," (*pace* Dubis 17, who takes it as a gen. of producer [see Wallace 104–6]).

Σωτηρίαν ψυχῶν is an "explanatory apposition" to τὸ τέλος (Achtemeier 104; Dubis 17). ψυχή (here an obj. gen.) should not be understood in terms of a body-soul dualism. The word is used six times in 1 Peter (1:9, 22; 2:11, 25; 3:20; 4:19). In two of those uses (3:20; 4:19) it clearly relates to the entire person (BDAG 1099d; ZG 704; Achtemeier 104). The usage corresponds to that of the Hebrew term *nephesh*.

For 1 Peter (1:5, 9; 2:2) and Hebrews (1:14; 9:28) the term "salvation" relates primarily to the future. For Paul, salvation can have a past (Eph 2:8–9), present (Phil 2:12), and future sense (Rom 13:11). See further, Martin Williams, *The Doctrine of Salvation in the First Letter of Peter* (Cambridge: Cambridge University Press, 2011).

FOR FURTHER STUDY

13. Christian Suffering (1:6)

Bechtler, Steven R. *Following in His Steps: Suffering, Community and Christology in 1 Peter.* Atlanta: Scholars, 1998.

Beker, J. C. *Suffering and Hope: The Biblical Vision and the Human Predicament.* Grand Rapids: Eerdmans, 1994.

*Carson, D. A. *How Long, O Lord? Reflections on Suffering and Evil.* Grand Rapids: Baker, 1990.

Elliott, John H. *A Home for the Homeless: A Social-Scientific Criticism of 1 Peter, Its Situation and Strategy.* Minneapolis: Fortress, 1981.

Green, Joel B. *1 Peter.* Grand Rapids: Eerdmans, 2007. See pages 225–28.

Hicks, Peter. *The Message of Evil and Suffering: Light into Darkness.* Nottingham: InterVarsity, 2006.

Horbury William, and Brian McNeil, eds. *Suffering and Martyrdom in the New Testament.* Cambridge: Cambridge University Press, 1981.

Simundson, Daniel J. *Faith under Fire: Biblical Interpretation of Suffering.* Minneapolis: Fortress, 1980.

_____. *ABD* 6.219–25.

Sproul, R. C. *Surprised by Suffering.* Downers Grove: Tyndale, 1989.

Talbert, Charles H. *Learning through Suffering: The Educational View of Suffering in the New Testament and its Milieu.* Collegeville, MN: Liturgical Press, 1991.

Webb, William J. *DLNT* 1135–41.

14. Parousia of Christ (1:7)

Carroll, John T. *The Return of Jesus in Early Christianity.* Peabody, MA: Hendrickson, 2000.

Erickson, Millard J. *Christian Theology*. Grand Rapids: Baker, 1985. See pages
    1185–1204.
*Kreitzer, Larry J. *DLNT* 856–75.
Moore, Arthur L. *The Parousia in the New Testament*. Leiden: Brill, 1966.
Oepke, Albrecht. *TDNT* 5.858–71.
Osborne, Grant R. "The 'Rapture' Question." *Them* 2 (1977): 77–80.
Perriman, Andrew. *The Coming of the Son of Man: New Testament Eschatology for an
    Emerging Church*. Bletchley: Paternoster, 2005.
Rowland, Christopher. *ABD* 5.166–70.
Travis, Stephen. *I Believe in the Second Coming of Jesus*. Grand Rapids: Eerdmans, 1982.
Witherington, Ben III. *Jesus, Paul and the End of the World*. Downers Grove: InterVarsity,
    1992.

HOMILETICAL SUGGESTIONS

Joy in the Midst of Trials (1:6–9)

1. The nature of trials (v. 6)
2. The refining of faith (v. 7)
3. Love for, and faith in, Jesus in the midst of trial (v. 8)
4. Salvation as the outcome of faith (v. 9)

The Role of Suffering in Refining Faith (1:6–7)

1. Definition of Christian suffering
   (a) Suffering for the Christian faith
   (b) The tendency to import illness/other hardships into the biblical terminology
2. Suffering promotes endurance and perfection of character (cf. Rom 5:3–4;
   Jas 1:3–4)
   (a) The Christian life is a work in progress (Phil 1:6; 1 Pet 2:4–5)
   (b) Suffering as refining/judgment (1 Pet 1:6; 4:12–17)
   (c) Momentary suffering compared to eternal glory (1 Pet 1:6; 2 Cor 4:17)
3. Christians do not suffer alone
   (a) Christ also suffered (1 Pet 2:21–25)
   (b) Christ the model for suffering (1 Pet 2:21–25)
   (c) Suffering is the common lot of Christians worldwide (1 Pet 5:9; 1 Thess 2:14)

C. THE PROPHETIC WITNESS TO THE CHRISTIAN HOPE (1:10–12)

STRUCTURE

The rel. clause that begins this section picks up the theme of σωτηρία from the previous v. This salvation is then depicted by the umbrella term τῆς εἰς ὑμᾶς χάριτος ("the grace destined for you"). The opening ptc. ἐραυνῶντες in v. 11 summarizes the two indic. vbs. ἐξεζήτησαν and ἐξηραύνησαν in v. 10 and introduces the concern of the prophets to further understand the nature of their prophecies with respect to the sufferings and subsequent glory of the Messiah. A further rel. clause opens v. 12 which itself contains a content (ὅτι) clause explaining what was revealed to the prophets. The final two rel. clauses (ἃ . . . εἰς ἅ . . .) pick up the antecedent αὐτά, describing these matters as first the gospel message proclaimed to the recipients, and second as matters that the angels desire to examine.

```
10      περὶ ἧς σωτηρίας
               ἐξεζήτησαν καὶ ἐξηραύνησαν
  προφῆται
   οἱ     περὶ τῆς εἰς ὑμᾶς χάριτος
   ⋮  προφητεύσαντες
11      │   ἐραυνῶντες εἰς τίνα
        │       ἢ ποῖον καιρὸν                              ἐδήλου
        │              τὸ ἐν αὐτοῖς πνεῦμα Χριστοῦ    προμαρτυρόμενον
        │
        │            τὰ εἰς Χριστὸν παθήματα
        │          καὶ τὰς μετὰ ταῦτα δόξας
12  οἷς ἀπεκαλύφθη
        ὅτι          οὐχ ἑαυτοῖς
                     ὑμῖν δὲ
               διηκόνουν αὐτὰ
                   ἃ νῦν ἀνηγγέλη ὑμῖν
                         διὰ τῶν εὐαγγελισαμένων ὑμᾶς
                               ἐν πνεύματι ἁγίῳ
                                     ἀποσταλέντι ἀπ' οὐρανοῦ,
                     εἰς ἃ ἄγγελοι ἐπιθυμοῦσιν παρακύψαι.
```

VERSE 10

περὶ ἧς σωτηρίας

The use of rel. pronouns, often with a prep., as linking mechanisms is a typical stylistic feature of this letter (Elliott 345). Περὶ ἧς σωτηρίας picks up the salvation mentioned in v. 9 and is virtually synonymous with περὶ τῆς εἰς ὑμᾶς χάριτος below. For the incorporation of the antecedent into the rel. clause, see R 719–721.

ἐξεζήτησαν καὶ ἐξηραύνησαν

'Εξεζήτησαν 3 pl. aor. act. indic. of ἐκζητέω, "search diligently" (BDAG 302d; H.-G. Link, *NIDNTT* 3.530–32). 'Εξηραύνησαν 3 pl. aor. act. indic. of ἐξεραυνάω, "seek diligently" (BDAG 347c; M. Seitz, *NIDNTT* 3.532–33; LN 27.35). The two vbs. form a hendiadys (the latter vb. is a NT *hapax*) and the preps. ἐξ- in compound here are intensive, thereby denoting a diligent search (R 563–65, 597). Both vbs. are summed up by the ptc. ἐραυνῶντες in the following v.

προφῆται οἱ . . . προφητεύσαντες

Προφητεύσαντες nom. pl. masc. of aor. act. ptc. of προφητεύω, "prophesy." Here the aor. ptc. indicates past prophecy and most naturally refers to the OT prophets (*pace* Selwyn 259–68, who regards them as Christian prophets). For the art. ptc. following anar. noun, see Z §192; R 778, 1107; T 152–53.

περὶ τῆς εἰς ὑμᾶς χάριτος

The prep. phrase gives the content of the prophecy. In this epistle χάρις is a general term denoting all that God gives to believers (see Elliott 345; Michaels 41). It is an umbrella term for what Peter has elsewhere described as a "living hope" (1:3), "an inheritance" (1:4), and "salvation" (1:5, 9). The prep. εἰς is used here of destination (BDAG 291a; R 594), "the grace that was to come to you" (NIV).

VERSE 11

ἐραυνῶντες εἰς τίνα ἢ ποῖον καιρόν

'Εραυνῶντες nom. pl. masc. of pres. act. ptc. of ἐραυνάω, "search," "examine" (BDAG 389a; M. Seitz, *NIDNTT* 3.532–33). A ptc. of manner that gathers up the previous two indic. vbs. (see Moulton 115 on non-compound forms following a compound vb. with the same sense).

Τίνα could be an interr. adj. modifying καιρόν giving "what or what sort of time" (KJV, NKJV; Achtemeier 109; Michaels 41) or an interr. pron. If masc., this would give "what person or what sort of time" (Barclay, NRSV, CEV, NASB; Elliott 345–46; Dubis 19), if neut. pl. "what circumstances or what sort of time" (JB, Cassirer, NEB, NLT, HCSB, NIV; ZG 704; Jobes 102–3). Although both uses are found in the NT, it is far more common as a pron. This, together with the fact that the author uses the interr. τίς as a pron. in all its other uses (3:13; 4:17; 5:8 [depending on textual variant]), makes the pronominal use preferable here. It is difficult to determine whether the pron. is masc. or neut. The objection of Michaels 41–42, that there was no doubt regarding the identity of the person, refers to Peter's perspective, not that of the prophets. On combination of τίς with ποῖος, see BDF §298(2); R 735, 740, 1176; T 48.

ἐδήλου τὸ ἐν αὐτοῖς πνεῦμα Χριστοῦ

᾽Εδήλου 3 sg. impf. act. indic. of δηλόω, "show," "indicate" (BDAG 222c–d). Αὐτοῖς could be either "in them" (most EVV; Davids 62) or "among them" (Achtemeier 109; Michaels 43).

The "Spirit of Christ" is not an unusual designation in the NT (Acts 16:7 [Spirit of Jesus]; Rom 8:9), although it is unclear in what sense the Spirit of Christ was resident in the OT prophets. Some commentators soften this by speaking of the same Spirit who empowered Jesus (Beare 92) or the Spirit that witnesses to Christ (Davids 62). However, the language here in 1 Peter does seem to imply pre-existence (see 1 Cor 10:4 for a similar idea in Paul). Note also that in 2 Pet 1:21 prophecy is said to be instigated by the Holy Spirit.

προμαρτυρόμενον τὰ εἰς Χριστὸν παθήματα

Προμαρτυρόμενον nom. sg. neut. of pres. mid. ptc. of προμαρτύρομαι, "foretell," "predict" (Turner, *Words* 443–44). Together with the impf. ἐδήλου this ptc. signifies "a process of revelation" (Michaels 43). The ptc. is temp. and, together with the dir. objs. that follow, gives the content for ἐδήλου ("the Spirit of Christ in them was pointing when he predicted," NIV).

Despite most EVV rendering the prep. εἰς as equivalent to the genitival phrase τὰ παθήματα τοῦ Χριστοῦ ("the sufferings of Christ"; cf. 4:13; 5:1), it is better cstr. here as destination (BDAG 291a; R 594), "the sufferings destined for Christ," "the sufferings that were to come up on Christ" (Weymouth), and underlines the divine purpose. Note the sim. use of the prep. in v. 10—τῆς εἰς ὑμᾶς χάριτος, "the grace that was coming to you." Although not explicitly stated here, the obvious parallelism, in addition to other more explicit statements in the letter (3:18; 4:13), show that believers are the recipients of grace precisely because Christ was the recipient of suffering. Χριστόν could be taken as a title "the Messiah/Christ" (NIV) or as a name "Christ" (NASB).

καὶ τὰς μετὰ ταῦτα δόξας

The pl. δόξαι only occurs three times in the NT. The other two uses (2 Pet 2:10; Jude 8) refer to majestic beings (BDAG 258a), but here the pl. is a summary of the majesty and privileges that were in store for Christ after his suffering. This would include his resurrection (1:3, 21; 3:18, 21), ascension and universal authority (3:22), and future revelation (1:7, 13; 4:13). The antecedent of ταῦτα is παθήματα, and τὰς μετὰ ταῦτα δόξας clearly indicates that glory follows suffering ("subsequent glories," ESV), a pattern that is applicable to both Christ and his followers (see 1:6–7; 4:12–13; Rom 8:18–25; 2 Cor 4:17; 2 Tim 2:12; Rev 2:10–11; 20:4 with respect to believers). Εἰς Χριστόν from the previous phrase is the main focus of the "subsequent glories" here, although believers are obvious recipients as well (Harris 162).

VERSE 12

οἷς ἀπεκαλύφθη ὅτι οὐχ ἑαυτοῖς ὑμῖν δὲ διηκόνουν αὐτά

The pass. ἀπεκαλύφθη is divine. The antecedent of the rel. pron. οἷς is προφῆται. This ὅτι clause gives the content of what was revealed to the prophets (BDAG 731d; R 1032–36). Αὐτά is an acc. of respect, whereas ἑαυτοῖς ὑμῖν δέ is the dir. obj. of διηκόνουν (3 pl. impf. act. indic. of διακονέω, "serve") which takes the dat., "they were not serving themselves but you in the things" (though note BDAG 229c which takes ἑαυτοῖς ὑμῖν δέ as the indir. obj. in the sense of "they were not acting as agents in their own behalf but for yours in the things"). For change of tense in indir. discourse see R 1029.

ἃ νῦν ἀνηγγέλη ὑμῖν

Ἀνηγγέλη 3 sg. aor. pass. indic. of ἀναγγέλλω, "proclaim," "announce" (BDAG 59d). The rel. pron. ἃ picks up αὐτά from the previous clause, and, although loosely relating to the content of the εὐαγγέλιον, it more precisely relates to the sufferings and glories destined for the Messiah (v. 11).

διὰ τῶν εὐαγγελισμένων ὑμᾶς

On the form of εὐαγγελίζω see R 332–33; Wallace 414–30. Διά is used here of intermediate agency (R 581–83; Harris 70–72), the ultimate agent being God himself (Dubis 21).

This has important theological and canonical ramifications. The proclamation of the gospel is identical with the predictions of the OT prophets; consequently, the unity and continuity of the Old and New Testaments are demonstrated (Harris 162–63). See below, For Further Study 15, "NT Fulfilment of the OT."

ἐν πνεύματι ἁγίῳ ἀποσταλέντι ἀπ᾽ οὐρανοῦ

The dat. πνεύματι (with or without ἐν—an evenly balanced textual variant) is instr. of means. The apostles were the human agents, but the Holy Spirit was the means by which the gospel was activated and empowered. The fact that the Spirit was sent from heaven indicates that God was the ultimate author of the message itself. Ἀποσταλέντι is attrib. with πνεύματι and the pass. is again divine, possibly referring to the Pentecost experience.

εἰς ἃ ἐπιθυμοῦσιν ἄγγελοι παρακύψαι

Ἐπιθυμοῦσιν (3 pl. pres. act. indic. of ἐπιθυμέω, "long for," "desire") denotes an eager longing (BDAG 371d–372a; H. Schönweiss, NIDNTT 1.456–58; F. Büchsel, TDNT 3.168–72), which by implication is unfulfilled. Παρακύψαι (aor. act. inf. of παρακύπτω, "stoop," "peer into" [BDAG 767c]; in a literal sense, John 20:5, 11) is a complimentary inf. The word implies a stooping forward to look into something (W. Michaelis, TDNT 5.814–16), and in 1 Enoch 9:1 is also used of the four archangels viewing the violence of humanity from heaven. *Pace* ZG (704), it is highly unlikely that the anar. ἄγγελοι connotates "even such exalted beings as angels."

This cryptic statement regarding the angels is understood in different ways:

1. The angels do not have a detailed or complete understanding of redemption, even in the present time. This builds on a widespread tradition of the inferiority of angelic knowledge reflected in such texts as *1 Enoch* 16:3; *2 Enoch* 24:3; Mark 13:32; Ig. *Eph* 19:1 (Achtemeier 112; Michaels 48);

2. The angels were similar to the OT prophets in that they desired to understand more about the nature and sufferings of the Messiah ahead of time (Jobes 104–5); or

*3. The reference is to the eagerness of the angels with respect to matters of redemption and its fulfillment, rather than their curiosity or ignorance as such (Davids 64; NLT: "even the angels are eagerly watching these things happen").

The use of the pres. tense ἐπιθυμοῦσιν makes option 2 unlikely. Option 1 is often supported on the basis that it highlights the exalted position of believers, but this is still the case with option 3, albeit in a reduced sense. In the end 3 is the most likely option, especially given that in other NT texts the gospel events have been made known to the rulers and authorities in the heavenly realms (Eph 3:10; cf. 1 Pet 3:18–19), and angels are involved in announcements to humanity regarding key salvific events (Luke 1:8–20; 2:8–14; Matt 28:5–7).

FOR FURTHER STUDY

15. NT Fulfilment of the OT (1:10–12)

Beale, G. K., and D. A. Carson, eds. *Commentary on the New Testament Use of the Old Testament*. Grand Rapids: Baker, 2007.

Beale, G. K. *A New Testament Biblical Theology: The Unfolding of the Old Testament in the New*. Grand Rapids: Baker Academic, 2011.

_____, ed. *The Right Doctrine from the Wrong Texts? Essays on the Use of the Old Testament in the New*. Grand Rapids: Baker, 1994.

Berding, Kenneth, and Jonathan Lunde, eds. *Three Views on the New Testament Use of the Old Testament*. Grand Rapids: Zondervan, 2008.

Bruce, F. F. *New Testament Development of Old Testament Themes*. Grand Rapids: Eerdmans, 1968.

Dumbrell, William J. *The End of the Beginning*. Homebush West: Lancer, 1985.

Ellis, E. Earle. *The Old Testament and Early Christianity*. Tübingen: Mohr, 1991.

Enns, Peter. "Apostolic Hermeneutics and an Evangelical Doctrine of Scripture: Moving Beyond a Modernist Impasse." *WTJ* 65 (2003): 263–87.

Evans, Craig A., and W. R. Stegner. *The Gospels and the Scriptures of Israel*. Sheffield: JSOT, 1994.

Evans, Craig A. "The Function of the Old Testament in the New." Pages 163–93 in *Introducing New Testament Interpretation*. Edited by S. McKnight. Grand Rapids: Baker, 1989.

*_____, ed. *From Prophecy to Testament: The Function of the Old Testament in the
   New*. Peabody, MA: Hendrickson, 2004. See pages 1–22, 206–18.
*Hays, Richard B., and Joel B. Green. "The Use of the Old Testament by New Testament
   Writers." Pages 222–38 in *Hearing the New Testament*. Edited by J. B. Green. Grand
   Rapids: Eerdmans, 1995.
Martin, Francis, ed. *Narrative Parallels to the New Testament*. Atlanta: Scholars, 1988.
Moo, Douglas J. "The Problem of Sensus Plenior." Pages 179–211 in *Hermeneutics,
   Authority, and Canon*. Edited by D. A. Carson and J. D. Woodbridge. Grand Rapids:
   Zondervan, 1986.
Osborne, Grant R. *The Hermeneutical Spiral*. Downers Grove: InterVarsity, 1991. See
   pages 263–85.
Porter, Stanley E., ed. *Hearing the Old Testament in the New Testament*. Grand Rapids and
   Cambridge: Eerdmans, 2006.
Pryor, Neale. "The Use of the Old Testament in the New." Pages 276–86 in *Biblical
   Interpretation: Principles and Practice*. Grand Rapids: Baker, 1986.
Snodgrass, Klyne. "The Use of the Old Testament in the New." Pages 209–29 in
   Interpreting the New Testament: Essays on Methods and Issues. Edited by D. A. Black
   and D. S. Dockery. Nashville: B&H, 2001.

16. Angelic Beings (1:12)

Newsom, Carol A. *ABD* 1.248–53.
Watson, Duane F. *ABD* 1.253–55.
Wilson, J. Macartney. *ISBE* 1.124–27.

HOMILETICAL SUGGESTIONS

The Prophetic Witness to the Christian Hope (1:10–12)

1. With respect to the grace destined for believers (v. 10)
2. With respect to their inspiration by the preexistent Christ (v. 11)
3. With respect to the sufferings and the subsequent glory of the Messiah (v. 11b)
4. With respect to serving believers as recipients of the gospel (v. 12)

Christ as the Fulfillment of the OT Prophetic Hope (1:10–12)

1. The role of OT prophecy
   (a) Its historical dimension (1:10)
   (b) Its eschatological dimension (1:10)
   (c) Messianic prophecy (1:11)
2. The pre-existence of Christ and his role in the inspiration of the prophetic word (1:11; cf. 2 Pet 1:20–21)
3. The gospel as the culmination of the prophetic hope (1:12)
   (a) The divine origin of the gospel (cf. Gal 1:11–24)
   (b) The human agents of the proclamation of the gospel
   (c) The role of the Holy Spirit in the proclamation of the gospel

4. The privilege and status of believers compared to the angels (1:12c; cf. Heb 1:5–14)

The Privileged Status of Believers

1. The recipients of 1 Peter
   (a) Nature of their suffering
   (b) Their need for identity
2. Believers in the twenty-first century
   (a) Postmodern de-centeredness
   (b) The cry for identity
3. The pastoral response of the author
   (a) Believers exist in the age of fulfillment (1:10–12)
   (b) The OT prophets served the church (1:12)
   (c) Believers are more privileged than the angels (1:12; cf. Heb 1:14; 2:16; 1 Cor 6:3)
   (d) Believers are God's own possession and are part of the people of God stretching throughout history (2:9–10)

III. A Call to Holy Living (1:13–2:3)

A. EMULATING THE HOLINESS OF GOD (1:13–16)

STRUCTURE

The first subsection of this unit comprises vv. 13–16 and embodies two main thoughts: (1) hope is to be focused on the future revelation of Jesus, and (2) believers are to emulate the holiness of God. The call to holiness is first framed in neg. terms using the ptc. μὴ συσχηματιζόμενοι ("do not be conformed"), then in positive terms utilizing the impv. ἅγιοι γενήθητε ("be holy") and the emphatic καὶ αὐτοί ("you yourselves also"). The subsection then concludes with the scriptural citation.

```
13  διὸ         ἀναζωσάμενοι τὰς ὀσφύας τῆς διανοίας ὑμῶν
                      νήφοντες
                 τελείως
         ἐλπίσατε
                 ἐπὶ τὴν φερομένην ὑμῖν χάριν
                         ἐν ἀποκαλύψει Ἰησοῦ Χριστοῦ.

14                    ὡς τέκνα ὑπακοῆς
                 μὴ συσχηματιζόμενοι
                      ταῖς πρότερον ἐν τῇ ἀγνοίᾳ ὑμῶν ἐπιθυμίαις
15               ἀλλὰ κατὰ τὸν καλέσαντα ὑμᾶς ἅγιον
         καὶ αὐτοὶ ἅγιοι
                         ἐν πάσῃ ἀναστροφῇ
                 γενήθητε,
16  διότι γέγραπται· ἅγιοι ἔσεσθε, ὅτι ἐγὼ ἅγιός
```

VERSE 13

διὸ ἀναζωσάμενοι τὰς ὀσφύας τῆς διανοίας ὑμῶν

Ἀναζωσάμενοι nom. pl. masc. of aor. mid. ptc. of ἀναζώννυμι, "bind up," "gird up" (a NT *hapax*, though the root ζώννυμι is used with a περί compound in Luke 12:35 with the same metaphorical intent; see R 314). The ptc. is dependent on the impv. (attendant circumstance) ἐλπίσατε and therefore takes on derived impv. force (see the discussion on "Imperatival Participles in 1 Peter" in the Introduction). The vb. commonly referred to the gathering up of garments, which were worn loose around the home in preparation for some activity (BDAG 62d; F. Selter, *NIDNTT* 3.120–21; ZG 704).

Ὀσφῦς, -ύος, ἡ, "waist" (BDAG 730c–d). Διάνοια, -ας, ἡ, "mind" (BDAG 234b–c). The entire expression is a graphic metaphor for mental alertness ("gird up the loins of your mind"), appropriately rendered as "roll up the sleeves of your mind" (Elliott 355).

νήφοντες τελείως ἐλπίσατε ἐπὶ τὴν φερομένην ὑμῖν χάριν ἐν ἀποκαλύψει Ἰησοῦ Χριστοῦ

Νήφοντες nom. pl. masc. of pres. act. ptc. of νήφω, "be sober." The ptc. also has impv. force due to its dependence on ἐλπίσατε (see above on ἀναζωσάμενοι). The word is commonly used in Gk. literature for sobriety, but in the NT it is only used in a metaphorical sense of self-controlled and attentive behavior (cf. 5:8; 2 Tim 4:25; 1 Thess 5:6, 8; *NewDocs* 2.21; BDAG 672d; P. J. Budd, *NIDNTT* 1.514–15; O. Bauernfeind, *TDNT* 4.936–39). Given that the two other uses of this word (as impvs.) in 1 Peter are in the aor. (4:7; 5:8), it is interesting to note the change from the preceding aor. ptc. to the pres. ptc. here. The aspect of the aor. ptc. presents matters in summary form, whereas the aspect of the pres. ptc. indicates unfolding action (Fanning 406–19). Consequently, this second ptc. is stressing something that is to be a characteristic feature of one who is prepared for action and has his or her hope set on Jesus Christ.

The adv. τελείως can be taken with either νήφοντες, "be completely vigilant" (NIV; Goodspeed "with perfect calmness" misses the point) or ἐλπίσατε, "set your hope fully" (most EVV; Selwyn 140; Achtemeier 119; Elliott 356; Goppelt 107 n. 20). The former is favored by the fact that the author elsewhere uses advs. ending in -ως following the word they modify (1:22; 2:19, 23; see Michaels 55), whereas the latter emphasizes the need to orientate hope eschatologically in light of the the present time of trial. Given that the latter is a major theme of the epistle, this is probably the intended sense.

Ἐλπίσατε is the first of a number of aor. impvs. used in this epistle for general precepts (the pres. impv. is the default tense for general precepts; see discussion on "The Use of the Imperative in 1 Peter" in the Introduction; BDF §337[2]). In this case, the aor. appears to have a programmatic sense, where the readers are exhorted to "set their hope" (NRSV, HCSB, NIV) on the grace coming to them at the revelation of Jesus Christ. The tr. "set your hope" is an attempt to convey this programmatic sense, with a particular resolve to orientate one's life accordingly when worked out as a way of life. Hope is a dominant theme of this letter (1:21; 3:5, 15), and for Peter it is almost synonymous with faith, as it represents part of the human side of the salvation equation. On the prep. ἐπί used with vbs. of emotion, see R 602.

Χάριν sums up "praise, glory, and honor" from v. 7—the eschatological blessings in store for faithful followers of Jesus. Thus φερομένην is a pres. ptc. with a fut. ref. (Michaels 56; Achtemeier 119; Dubis 24). Ἀποκάλυψις, -εως, ἡ, "revelation" (BDAG 112b). On ἐν ἀποκαλύψει Ἰησοῦ Χριστοῦ, see v. 7.

VERSE 14

ὡς τέκνα ὑπακοῆς, μὴ συσχηματιζόμενοι

The particle ὡς can be comp. "like," but here Peter probably intends this to be more than a metaphor. Believers are not to be like obedient children; they are to be obedient children—children of God (1:2, 17). Thus the particle functions as a marker, introducing the perspective from which someone is viewed (BDAG 1104d).

Ὑπακοή, -ῆς, ἡ, "obedience" (BDAG 1028c). The gen. is descriptive and reflects a Sem. idiomatic cstr. where the gen. signifies a typical quality of the previous noun ("children characterized by obedience," i.e., "obedient children"; cf. Luke 18:6; Eph 2:2; 1 Thess 5:5; MH 440–41; Moule 175; R 496–97; Z §43; ZG 704).

Συσχηματιζόμενοι nom. pl. masc. of pres. mid. ptc. of συσχηματίζω, "mold" (BDAG 979b; G. Braumann, NIDNTT 1.708–10; LN 41.29). The ptc. is linked paratactically with the impv. γενήθητε in v. 15 and therefore takes on the same impv. force (see discussion on "Imperatival Participles in 1 Peter" in the Introduction). However, in reality it is not an additional command but the neg. counterpart of the command to be holy (Achtemeier 120). In this sense it can also be cstr. as instr., for at least part of what it means to be holy is to no longer be molded by sinful desires. Examples of such sinful desires are given in 2:1; 4:2–4.

The sense of the mid. voice with the neg. could be brought out in a tr. such as "do not allow yourselves to be molded" (NJB, CEV; Elliott 357). The vb. is also used in Rom 12:2 in a metaphorical sense (BDAG 979b).

ταῖς πρότερον ἐν τῇ ἀγνοίᾳ ὑμῶν ἐπιθυμίαις

Πρότερον is the neut. form of the adj. πρότερος, -α, -ον, "former," "previous" (BDAG 888d) that is normally used as an adv. Here, though, it functions adj. (BDF §62; BDAG 889a).

Ἄγνοια, -ας, ἡ, "ignorance" (BDAG 13b; E. Schütz, NIDNTT 2.406–8). The dat. ἐν τῇ ἀγνοίᾳ could be understood as a locat. of time ("the desires you had during your previous time of ignorance;" ASV, NIV; Achtemeier 120 n. 5) but equally as an instr. of cause ("the desires that you had previously because of ignorance"). In the NT the term is used of ignorance of God, which is not only an intellectual problem but a moral one (Acts 3:17; 17:30; Eph 4:18; BDAG 13c; R. Bultmann, TDNT 1.116–19).

Ἐπιθυμία is a neutral term for desire (LSJ 634d), but in the NT it is predominately neg. (BDAG 372c). It is based on the Jewish concept of the evil impulse yēṣer ra', and refers not just to sexual lust but to all kinds of self-indulgence and cravings (see H. Schönweiss, *NIDNTT* 1.456–58; F. Büchsel, *TDNT* 3.167–72; Davids 68 esp. n. 5).

The statement here regarding previous ignorant desires, together with a similar comment in 1:18 and the vice list in 4:2–4, is compelling evidence for a largely Gentile readership.

VERSE 15

ἀλλὰ κατὰ τὸν καλέσαντα ὑμᾶς ἅγιον

The prep. κατά is used here as a marker of norm or similarity giving the sense "in conformity with," "as" (BDAG 512c; Harris 152–54). Ἅγιον is most likely a pred. adj. (ἐστίν is implied) in agreement with τὸν καλέσαντα, given that the latter almost functions as a title in this epistle (2:9; 5:10) and the NT, giving the rendering "but as the one who called you is holy" (NRSV, HCSB, ESV, NIV). Alternatively, ἅγιον is a subst. giving the rendering "but in conformity with the Holy One who called you" (NASB, NJB, NKJV, NET; Michaels 51, 58; Elliott 360, who notes the regular use of this expression in the OT [Pss 70:22; 88:19; Isa 40:25; 43:3; Hos 11:9; etc]). Also supporting the latter view is the unlikelihood of an implied vb. in a prep. phrase (Dubis 27; Michaels 51, 58).

καὶ αὐτοὶ ἅγιοι ἐν πάσῃ ἀναστροφῇ γενήθητε

Ἅγιοι is pred. with γενήθητε "be holy," with αὐτοί an intensive pron. (Porter 130–31; R 287), i.e., "you yourselves" (ZG 705). Here καί is adv. "also."

Ἀναστροφή, -ῆς, ἡ, "conduct," "manner of life" (BDAG 73b; G. Bertram, *TDNT* 7.715–17; Spicq 1.111–14). The dat. ἐν πάσῃ ἀναστροφῇ is a locat. of sphere ("in all [your] conduct"). The noun is characteristic of this epistle (6/13 NT uses).

The impv. γενήθητε should not be tr. "become" as this could give the erroneous impression that holiness is something dependent on human behavior. On the contrary, believers are already holy because of their relationship with God (1:2; 2:5, 9; cf. 1 Cor 6:11; Titus 3:5; Heb 10:10). The command here, therefore, is to demonstrate this reality in terms of ethical behavior (cf. 2 Cor 7:1; Heb 12:14).

VERSE 16

διότι γέγραπται Ἅγιοι ἔσεσθε, ὅτι ἐγὼ ἅγιός [This reflects the text of the forthcoming fifth edition of the UBS *Greek New Testament*. The fourth edition reads [ὅτι] after γέγραπται and [εἰμι] after ἅγιός]

The conj. διότι is a contraction of διὰ τοῦτο ὅτι (BDAG 251c) and regularly introduces scriptural citations in this epistle (also 1:24; 2:6). Γέγραπται is part of a standard introductory formula for OT quotations in the NT, here Lev 11:44-45 (see Beale and Carson 1017–18). The perfect is intensive in nature (Campbell, *Indicative Mood* 161–211) and gives the sense "it stands written" (ZG 705; Wallace 576).

The fut. tense (here ἔσεσθε) used as an impv. is a Hebraism (Z §280; BDF §362; R 942–43; Wallace 569). Ὅτι ἐγὼ ἅγιός provides the rationale for the impv. The concluding εἰμι (square brackets in UBS⁴) has been omitted in the text of the forthcoming UBS⁵ following the *Editio Critica Maior*. In any case, it can be easily implied from the context.

FOR FURTHER STUDY

17. Christian Holiness (1:14–16)

Barton, Stephen C., ed. *Holiness Past and Present*. London, New York: T&T Clark, 2003.

Dempsey, C. J. "Be Holy for I Am Holy: Clothing Ourselves in Our Biblical Identity—1 Peter 1:13–2:10." Pages 34–44 in *Catholic Identity and the Laity*. Edited by T. Muldoon. Maryknoll, NY: Orbis, 2009.

Elliott, John H. *The Elect and the Holy: An Exegetical Examination of 1 Peter 2:4–10 and the Phrase basileion hierateuma*. Leiden: Brill, 1966.

Hanigan, James P. "Conversion and Christian Ethics." *Theology Today* 40 (1983): 25–35.

Harrison, Everett F. *ISBE* 2.725–29.

*Hawthorne, Gerald F. *DLNT* 485–89.

Johnson, W. Stanley. "Christian Perfection as Love for God." Pages 97–113 in *Christian Ethics*. Edited by L. O. Hynson and L. A. Scott. Anderson: Warner Press, 1983.

Mullen, L. K. "Holy Living: The Adequate Ethic." *Wesleyan Theological Journal* 14 (1979): 82–95.

Neil, Stephen. *Christian Holiness*. New York: Harper, 1960.

Procksch, Otto, and Karl G. Kuhn. *TDNT* 1.88–115.

Williams, J. Rodman. *EDT* 514–16.

See also For Further Study §§ 14, 20, 22.

HOMILETICAL SUGGESTIONS

Emulating the Holiness of God (1:13–16)

1. Be mentally prepared (v. 13a)
2. Hope must be centered on Jesus (v. 13b)
3. Leave behind past lifestyle (v. 14)
4. Mirror the holiness of God (vv. 15–16)

B. PRECIOUS REDEMPTION THROUGH CHRIST (1:17–21)

STRUCTURE

The call to holiness is repeated here using a different impv. ἀναστράφητε ("conduct yourselves") in the opening v., with the next three vv. depicting salvation in terms of ransom/redemption. The subsection concludes with a statement about the orientation of faith through Christ who is risen and glorified.

17 καὶ εἰ   πατέρα
            ἐπικαλεῖσθε τὸν ἀπροσωπολήμπτως κρίνοντα κατὰ τὸ ἑκάστου ἔργον,
            ἐν φόβῳ
                  τὸν τῆς παροικίας ὑμῶν χρόνον
     ἀναστράφητε
18   εἰδότες ὅτι
                        οὐ φθαρτοῖς, ἀργυρίῳ ἢ χρυσίῳ,
                  ἐλυτρώθητε
                        ἐκ τῆς ματαίας ὑμῶν ἀναστροφῆς πατροπαραδότου
19   ἀλλὰ τιμίῳ αἵματι
                        ὡς ἀμνοῦ ἀμώμου καὶ ἀσπίλου Χριστοῦ
20   προεγνωσμένου μὲν πρὸ καταβολῆς κόσμου,
                        φανερωθέντος δὲ ἐπ' ἐσχάτου τῶν χρόνων
                                                          δι' ὑμᾶς

21 τοὺς δι' αὐτοῦ πιστοὺς εἰς θεὸν
                  τὸν ἐγείραντα αὐτὸν ἐκ νεκρῶν
            καὶ δόξαν αὐτῷ δόντα,
                        ὥστε τὴν πίστιν ὑμῶν
                        καὶ ἐλπίδα εἶναι εἰς θεόν.

VERSE 17

καὶ εἰ πατέρα ἐπικαλεῖσθε

A first-class cond. statement (a cond. assumed to be true; see Porter 256–67). Πατέρα without the art. is qualitative, emphasizing the one who has the character of father (Wallace 244–45). The vb. ἐπικαλεῖσθε refers here not just to naming or calling something, but to invoke (i.e., in prayer, as in, e.g., LXX Ps 88:27; L. Coenen, *NIDNTT* 1.272; BDAG 373a).

τὸν ἀπροσωπολήμπτως κρίνοντα

The adv. ἀπροσωπολήμπτως is a NT *hapax* and denotes impartiality, action without ref. to rank or status (BDAG 126a; Michaels 61, observing that it derives from the Hebrew idiom "to receive the face"; see also E. Tiedtke, *NIDNTT* 1.585–87; on the form see R 297). The same idea occurs in 2:23 using δικαίως, "justly." The cognate noun προσωπολημψία occurs in Rom 2:11 and Eph 6:9 in ref. to God's impartiality, as does the cognate adj. προσωπολήμπτης in Acts 10:34. Κρίνοντα is in appos. to πατέρα (a double acc. reflecting classical usage; T 247). Eschatological judgment is in view (Dubis 30).

κατὰ τὸ ἑκάστου ἔργον

The prep. introduces the criteria for the judgment (Harris 152). Ἑκάστου is a subj. gen., i.e., the work that each person performs. Judgment by works is a uniform biblical theme (Hos 12:2; Ps 62:12; Matt 25:31ff; Rom 2:6; Rev 20:12ff), and although Peter does not develop this here, works are the criteria because they are a visible expression of the focus of faith and commitment (cf. Jas 2:12–26).

ἐν φόβῳ ἀναστράφητε

The noun φόβος occurs regularly in 1 Peter, denoting a holy fear or awe (2:18; 3:2, 16; cf. cognate vb. φοβεῖσθε in 2:17) and is best tr. "in reverence" or "in reverent fear" (NJB, NRSV, NIV). Ἀναστράφητε 2 pl. aor. pass. impv. of ἀναστρέφω, "conduct one-self" (BDAG 72d). This is the only use of this vb. in the epistle, although the cognate noun dominates (see v. 15). Another instance of an aor. impv. clearly used for a general precept (on the use of the impv. in 1 Peter, see "The Use of the Imperative in 1 Peter" in the Introduction; BDF §337[2]).

τὸν τῆς παροικίας ὑμῶν χρόνον

Τὸν χρόνον is an acc. of time denoting extent of time (see Porter 90–91), while the gen. τῆς παροικίας is partitive (Wallace 84–85). Παροικία, -ας, ἡ, "exile," "sojourn." The term refers to temporary residency without being granted full citizenship rights, i.e., an in-between legal status (see H. Bietenhard, *NIDNTT* 1.690–91; K. L. and M. A. Schmidt, *TDNT* 5.851–53; BDAG 779c; Turner, *Words* 330–31). The word is used of Israel's stay in Egypt in Acts 13:47. In Gk. inscriptions the expression τὸν τῆς παροικίας ὑμῶν χρόνον appears as a metaphor for human life (Michaels 62; see also the almost verbatim phrase in 3 *Macc* 7:19; on the gen. written *inclusio* between the head noun and the article see R 779). Elliott's insistence that this term must be understood in a purely sociological sense (Elliott 366–69), while an important corrective, goes too far. Given the eschatology of this epistle, it clearly carries eschatological overtones as well (see M. Chin, *TynBul* 42 [1991]: 96–112. Michaels 62 also has a helpful discussion. See further on 2:11).

VERSE 18

εἰδότες ὅτι οὐ φθαρτοῖς ἀργυρίῳ ἢ χρυσίῳ

Εἰδότες nom. pl. masc. of pf. act. ptc. of οἶδα. This formulation is typically used rhe-torically in the NT to provide the reason for a previous impv. (1 Cor 15:58; Eph 6:8–9; Jas 3:1; etc). Here it provides the rationale for the reverent conduct called for in v. 17, and thus the ptc. is causal in force—"for [i.e., because] you know that" (NLT, HCSB, NIV; Achtemeier 126; Dubis 31).

Φθαρτός, -ή, -όν, "subject to decay," "perishable." This adj. can have several shades of mng. (BDAG 1053d), but given that both silver and gold are not perishable metals, "perishable" can hardly be an appropriate rendering here. More accurately it is a contrast between the ephemeral and the enduring ("that don't last forever," CEV; "doomed to decay," Barclay). Peter elsewhere uses the adj. and its corresponding antonym ἄφθαρτος in this sense (1:4, 23; 3:4).

Χρυσίον, -ου, τό, "gold." Ἀργυρίῳ ἢ χρυσίῳ are dats. of material (Wallace 170). Christians were not ransomed by means of transitory items such as silver or gold. The terms are hyponyms and both are in appos. to the subst. adj. φθαρτοῖς functioning as examples of that quality.

ἐλυτρώθητε ἐκ τῆς ματαίας ὑμῶν ἀναστροφῆς πατροπαραδότου

Ἐλυτρώθητε 2 pl. aor. pass. indic. Λυτρόω, "ransom" (O. Procksch, *TDNT* 4.328–35; F. Büchsel, *TDNT* 4.340–56; Turner, *Words* 105–7). Apart from having a rich OT history used to depict God's saving acts (particularly the Exodus) and the redemption of property or slaves, this term would have been familiar to Gk. readers as it was used to denote the manumission of slaves in the market place and the redemption of prisoners of war (Elliott 369–70). This particular vb. occurs only here, in Luke 24:21, and in Titus 2:14 (BDAG 606a), but the concept of redemption is found in all strata of the NT and makes an important contribution to a multifaceted NT soteriology (Rom 3:24–25; Eph 1:7; 1 Tim 2:6; Heb 9:12, 15), probably originating from Jesus himself (Mark 10:45).

Μάταιος, -α, -ον, "worthless" ("empty," NLT, HCSB, NIV; "useless," CEV; "foolish/futile," Goodspeed, NJB, NASB, ESV; "frivolous habits of life," Weymouth). The adj. πατροπαράδοτος, -ον, "handed down from one's ancestors," does not have a distinct fem. form; the apparent pred. position is due to multiple adjs. (R 656, 777). It is in itself a neutral term (LN 33.240 classify as "communication," subdomain "teaching"), but it takes on a decidedly neg. slant here in appos. with ματαίας. In Gk. literature it was often used in a positive sense of one's family customs and heritage (BDAG 789a; Michaels 64; Prasad 212–15), but given 4:2–4 it is clear that the legacy that Peter is denouncing is Greco-Roman paganism and its associated unethical practices.

VERSE 19

ἀλλὰ τιμίῳ αἵματι ὡς ἀμνοῦ ἀμώμου καὶ ἀσπίλου Χριστοῦ

Τίμιος, -α, -ον, "precious," referring to that which is highly respected or highly valued (BDAG 1006a). Ἀμνός, -οῦ, ὁ, "lamb," in agreement with Χριστοῦ. ὡς introduces the metaphor of Christ as a spotless lamb. The instr. dat. τιμίῳ αἵματι, "by the precious blood," contrasts with ἀργυρίῳ ἢ χρυσίῳ ("by silver or gold") from the previous v. The poss. gen. Χριστοῦ is delayed until the end of the clause, possibly for emphasis, and also facilitates agreement with the ptc. προεγνωσμένου commencing v. 20.

Ἄμωμος, -ον, "blameless," refers to the absence of defect (BDAG 56a) and in the LXX is a term bound up with cultic sacrifice (Num 6:14; 19:2; Lev 1:3–5; 22:17–25). Apart from here and Heb 9:14, which also refers to the blood of Christ offered in sacrifice, the six other NT uses of this term (Eph 1:4; 5:27; Phil 2:15; Col 1:22; Jude 24; Rev 14:5) all refer to the blameless moral conduct of Christians.

Ἄσπιλος, -ον, "without stain," is used both lit. and fig. of moral perfection (BDAG 144c; Turner, *Words* 483). This word is not normally found in ceremonial contexts and is not used in the LXX. The three other NT uses (1 Tim 6:14; Jas 1:27; 2 Pet 3:14) of this word all relate to moral conduct. The two adjs. (see H. Währisch, *NIDNTT* 3.923–25) here form a hendiadys ("without defect or blemish," NRSV, HCSB; "unblemished and spotless," NASB; "without blemish or defect," NIV), with the alpha privatives and assonance used for literary effect. Although within this metaphor they refer to a sacrificial lamb, in reality they are used to stress the moral perfection of Christ (cf. 2:22 alluding to Isa 53:9).

VERSE 20

προεγνωσμένου μὲν πρὸ καταβολῆς κόσμου

The attrib. ptc. προεγνωσμένου is gen. sg. masc. of pf. pass. ptc. of προγινώσκω, "know beforehand," in agreement with Χριστοῦ. The pf. tense highlights his predetermined role in the divine will. The word can refer to merely knowing something in advance, although used of God it refers not only to prophetic foresight but to his sovereign volition or predetermined plan (P. Jacobs and H. Krienke, *NIDNTT* 1.692–93; R. Bultmann, *TDNT* 1.715–16; BDAG 866d; ZG 705; Turner, *Words* 178–79; Prasad 305).

The μέν . . . δέ cstr. is used to contrast the appearance of Christ in recent times to his election in ages past. Καταβολή, -ῆς, ἡ, "foundation" (BDAG 515a). Πρὸ καταβολῆς κόσμου is used several times in the NT (John 17:24; Eph 1:4; cf. the more common ἀπὸ καταβολῆς κόσμου in Matt 13:35; 25:34; Luke 11:50; Heb 4:3; 9:26; Rev 13:8; 17:8) as a designation for eternity past—"before the foundation of the world" (NRSV, HCSB, ESV), "long before the world began" (NLT), "before the world was created" (CEV). Κόσμου is an obj. gen.

φανερωθέντος δὲ ἐπ' ἐσχάτου τῶν χρόνων δι' ὑμᾶς

Φανερωθέντος is also in agreement with Χριστοῦ, with both pass. ptcs. προεγνωσμένου and φανερωθέντος implying the action of God. The prep. ἐπί is used with the gen. to indicate time (R 603). Ἐσχάτου τῶν χρόνων, "these last times" (NIV), "the end of the ages" (NRSV), "the end of times" (ASV), "these last days" (CEV) (cf. Heb 9:26) signifies the period after the incarnation and is equivalent to the more common term αἱ ἐσχάται ἡμέραι (Acts 2:17; 2 Tim 3:1; Heb 1:2; Jas 5:3; 2 Pet 3:3). It contrasts with ἐν καιρῷ ἐσχάτῳ, "the last time," which is used of the final day itself in 1:5.

Peter again employs the vb. φανερόω in 5:4 regarding the future revealing of Christ. Possibly pre-existence is implied here (cf. John 1:1; Phil 2:6–11; Col 1:18; Heb 1:2–3), especially given that in Jewish apocalyptic literature the Savior figure is sometimes pictured as concealed in heaven prior to his revelation (*1 Enoch* 48:6; 62:7, a work upon which Peter apparently draws in 3:18–20).

Δι' ὑμᾶς is emphatic by position, with the prep. διά here used in a sense of benefit—"for your sake" (R 583–84; ZG 705).

VERSE 21

τοὺς δι' αὐτοῦ πιστοὺς εἰς θεὸν τὸν ἐγείραντα αὐτὸν ἐκ νεκρῶν καὶ δόξαν αὐτῷ δόντα

Τοὺς πιστούς is a subst. (verbal) adj. in appos. with ὑμᾶς from the previous v. (ZG 705; see 1:4–5 for a sim. cstr.). It is debated whether the adj. should have a pass. sense of "the faithful to God," or a more active sense of "the believing/trusting ones in God." The prep. εἰς occurs nowhere else in the NT following this adj., but it is common with the vb. πιστεύω. It is preferable to understand this active sense here (so most EVV; Michaels 68; Achtemeier 132; Dubis 34), because for Peter it is the death of Jesus and his subsequent resurrection that provides the basis for faith itself (1:3; 3:18–22).

The antecedent of αὐτοῦ is Χριστοῦ from v. 19. Faith is directed to God (εἰς θεὸν) through Jesus. The art. τόν governs both ptcs. ἐγείραντα and δόντα (acc. sg. masc. of aor. act. ptc. of δίδωμι) which are in appos. to θεόν. God is the One who both raised Christ and endowed him with glory.

ὥστε τὴν πίστιν ὑμῶν καὶ ἐλπίδα εἶναι εἰς θεόν

The inf. with ὥστε can express either actual or intended result/consequence (R 1089–91; BDF §391; Selwyn 147–48), but given the opening statement in this v., which is clearly a statement of reality, it is best to cstr. this as an actual consequence (ASV, NRSV, NASB, HCSB, ESV), i.e., a consec. clause (Z §351; ZG 705). The syntax, too, is ambiguous:

1. This clause could give the consequence of τοὺς δι' αὐτοῦ πιστοὺς εἰς θεόν. In other words, the result of believing in God is that faith and hope are directed to him. However, this creates a tautology with belief-faith; or
*2. The alternative is that this clause gives the consequence of the immediately preceding clause, i.e., the consequence of God raising Jesus from the dead and giving him glory is that faith and hope are directed toward God. This is the preferred option (so Achtemeier 133).

The accs. τὴν πίστιν . . . ἐλπίδα are accs. of respect with the inf. εἶναι (R 489–90), although some have proposed that the anar. ἐλπίδα should be taken as pred., giving the rendering "so that your faith is also (may also be) hope in God" (as do Beare 108; Elliott 379, noting that the poss. pron. is placed after the first noun). But more likely the single art. is governing both nouns in a coordinate sense, making them almost synonymous (so Achtemeier 133; Davids 75; Dubis 35; cf. 1:13; 3:5, 15).

Εἰς θεόν brackets not only this v. but also vv. 17–21 (and vv. 3–21) in their entirety, thus giving the whole section a theocentric emphasis (Achtemeier 134; Michaels 70; Prasad 314). For these persecuted communities, hope lies not in the present order, but in the power of God who raised and exalted Jesus and who will soon give them glory as well (1:7, 13; 5:1, 4).

FOR FURTHER STUDY

18. Ransom/Redemption (1:18–19)

Büchsel, Friedrich. *TDNT* 4.340–56.

Dunn, James D. G. *The Theology of Paul the Apostle*. Edinburgh: T&T Clark, 1998.

Fee, Gordon D. *Pauline Christology: An Exegetical-Theological Study*. Peabody: Hendrickson, 2007.

*Gaffin, Richard B., Jr. *Resurrection and Redemption: A Study in Paul's Soteriology*. Phillipsburg: Presbyterian and Reformed, 1987.

Green, Joel B. *1 Peter*. Grand Rapids: Eerdmans, 2007.

Guthrie, Donald. *New Testament Theology*. Downers Grove: InterVarsity, 1981.

Hill, David. *Greek Words and Hebrew Meanings: Studies in the Semantics of Soteriological Terms*. Cambridge: Cambridge University Press, 2009.

Horrell, David G. *1 Peter*. London: T&T Clark, 2008.

Marshall, I. Howard. *DLNT* 1001–4.

_____. *Jesus the Saviour: Studies in New Testament Theology*. London: SPCK, 1990.

Murray, John. *ISBE* 4.61–63.

Ridderbos, Herman. *Paul: An Outline of His Theology*. Grand Rapids: Eerdmans, 1975.

19. The Christian Hope (1:13, 21)

Bauckham, Richard. "Eschatology." Pages 306–22 in *Oxford Handbook of Systematic Theology*. Edited by J. B. Webster, K. Tanner and I. R. Torrance. Oxford, New York: Oxford University Press, 2007.

Eastman, B. *DLNT* 499–501.

*Hebblethwaite, Brian. *The Christian Hope*. Hants, UK: Marshall, Morgan and Scott, 1984.

Hessel-Robinson, T. "Nurturing Hope in the Face of Ecocatastrophe: Advent, Eschatology, and the Future of Creation." *Liturgical Ministry* 19 (2010): 9–20.

Kreitzer, Larry J. *DLNT* 856–75.

Minear, Paul S. *Christian Hope and the Second Coming*. Philadelphia: Westminster, 1954.

Morse, Christopher. "The Difference Heaven Makes." *Word and World* 31 (2011): 75–83.

Pannenberg, Wolfhart. "The Task of Christian Eschatology." Pages 1–13 in *The Last Things: Biblical and Theological Perspectives on Eschatology*. Edited by C. E. Braaten and R. W. Jensen. Grand Rapids: Eerdmans, 2002.

Tongue, Denis H. *EDT* 532.

Ware, J. P. "Paul's Hope and Ours: Rediscovering Paul's Hope of the Renewed Creation." *Concordia Journal* 35 (2009): 129–139.

Witherington, Ben, III. "The Conquest of Faith and a Climax of History." Pages 432–37 in *The Epistle to the Hebrews and Christian Theology*. Edited by R. Bauckham, et al. Grand Rapids: Eerdmans, 2009.

See also For Further Study §§ 4, 6.

HOMILETICAL SUGGESTIONS

Precious Redemption through Christ (1:17–21)

1. Revere God (v. 17)
   (a) He is Father
   (b) He is the impartial judge
   (c) Conduct one's life appropriately
2. The Gift of Redemption (vv. 18–20)
   (a) The price was not mere gold or silver (v. 18)
   (b) Christ the perfect lamb (v. 19)
   (c) God's pre-ordained plan (v. 20)
3. The privilege of believers (vv. 20–21)
   (a) Christ revealed at the end of the ages (v. 20)
   (b) Faith in Christ is the avenue to God (v. 21a)
   (c) The resurrection of Christ and his subsequent glory provide the basis for faith (v. 21b)

Final Judgment (1:17)

1. Is conducted by God the impartial judge (cf. Rom 2:11) through Christ (John 5:27; 2 Cor 5:10)
2. Is on the basis of works (cf. Rom 2:6–10; 2 Cor 5:10; Rev 20:13)
3. Believers too will be judged (cf. 2 Cor 5:10)
4. The outcome of judgment is
   (a) Salvation and reward for those who belong to God through faith in Jesus (1:7–9; cf. John 5:29)
   (b) Eternal punishment for unbelievers (John 5:29; Rev 20:15)

C. THE NEW BIRTH (1:22–25)

STRUCTURE

Verses 22–25 begin with an admonition to love those in the Christian community. This mutual love is to be an example of holiness, a holiness which is now expressed in terms of ceremonial purity. Verse 23 moves into salvation imagery, utilizing new birth terminology and incorporating a citation from Isa 40:6–8.

22					Τὰς ψυχὰς ὑμῶν
	ἡγνικότες
		ἐν τῇ ὑπακοῇ τῆς ἀληθείας
			εἰς φιλαδελφίαν ἀνυπόκριτον
			ἐκ καθαρᾶς καρδίας ἀλλήλους
	<u>ἀγαπήσατε</u>
		ἐκτενῶς
23	ἀναγεγεννημένοι
		οὐκ ἐκ σπορᾶς φθαρτῆς
		ἀλλὰ			ἀφθάρτου
		διὰ λόγου ζῶντος θεοῦ καὶ μένοντος.

24	διότι πᾶσα σὰρξ ὡς χόρτος
	καὶ πᾶσα δόξα αὐτῆς ὡς ἄνθος χόρτου·
			ἐξηράνθη
		ὁ χόρτος
	καὶ τὸ ἄνθος ἐξέπεσεν·
25		τὸ δὲ ῥῆμα κυρίου μένει εἰς τὸν αἰῶνα.
	τοῦτο δὲ ἐστιν <u>τὸ ῥῆμα</u> τὸ εὐαγγελισθὲν εἰς ὑμᾶς.

VERSE 22

τὰς ψυχὰς ὑμῶν ἡγνικότες ἐν τῇ ὑπακοῇ τῆς ἀληθείας

On ψυχή, see v. 9. Ἡγνικότες nom. pl. masc. of pf. act. ptc. of ἁγνίζω, "purify" (BDAG 12c). Although there is still some considerable debate concerning the temp. value of ptcs. (see Porter 181–93; Fanning 406–19; Campbell, *Non-Indicative Verbs* 20–68), as well as the aspect of the pf. tense (see Porter 21–22; Fanning 290–305; Campbell, *Indicative Mood* 161–211), it would seem clear that here the pf. ptc. has antecedent time value relative to the main vb. ἀγαπήσατε. Nevertheless, the act of purification referred to is unclear and depends to a large extent on the interpretation of the following prep. phrase:

1. If ἐν τῇ ὑπακοῇ τῆς ἀληθείας refers to the reception of the gospel (so Elliott 383; Selwyn 149; Michaels 75; Prasad 341), then purification is bound up with God's initial act of consecration. This possibility would be supported by

the textual vars. that add πνεύματος in various forms, attempting to link this idea back to the opening salutation (1:2). But this does not adequately explain the act. voice of the ptc. ἡγνικότες ("having purified"). The textual vars. lack ms. support and are clearly secondary; or

2. It is possible that Peter intends ἐν τῇ ὑπακοῇ τῆς ἀληθείας in a more general sense of fidelity to the Christian message, yet still considers that his readers have achieved this state. Purification/holiness is thus understood in tension as both an act of God apart from human endeavor (1:2) and a lifestyle that must be actively embraced (1:15–16). This would account for the ptc. being in the act. voice but runs aground in its apparent contradiction with the command to be holy in 1:15–16, which is clearly an impv. and not a state that Peter believes has been attained.

Perhaps it is a matter of looking at the same issue from two angles. On the divine side, true consecration is an act of God through the Spirit and is not dependent on human endeavor. Yet in coming to faith, human volition has been exercised. So the ptc. ἡγνικότες presents the initial act of consecration from the perspective of the choice made by a person when embracing the gospel. In that sense it can be presented in the act. voice as a human action.

On any reckoning, the ptc. is causal in force ("because you have purified your souls . . . love one another") and the pf. tense is best understood as stative, i.e., emphasizing the current state (Jobes 123; Davids 76; Goppelt 125, makes too much of the pf. when he insists that it indicates permanence). Achtemeier (136 n. 9) believes that the ptc. cannot be causal because the ptc. ἀναγεγεννημένοι that begins the following v. is causal. But that merely begs the question as to why both ptcs. cannot have this force. Because believers have consecrated themselves, so to speak, by coming to faith in Jesus, they now have an obligation to love their fellow believers within the Christian community (NJB, NKJV, NASB).

Ὑπακοή, -ῆς, ἡ, "obedience." The dat. is instr. on any interpretation of the clause as a whole: "by obedience to the truth" (NRSV, HCSB, ESV, NIV). Τῆς ἀληθείας is an obj. gen.—obedience that is focused on the truth, rather than descriptive—a truthful obedience.

εἰς φιλαδελφίαν ἀνυπόκριτον

Φιλαδελφία, -ας, ἡ, "brotherly love." The noun (H. F. von Soden, TDNT 1.144–46; BDAG 1055c) refers to family affection and endearment and is an appropriate term for those who belong to the same household with God as Father (1:17; 2:4–10; cf. Rom 12:10; 1 Thess 4:9; Heb 13:1; 2 Pet 1:7). The cognate adj. φιλάδελφοι is used in 3:8.

The prep. εἰς is telic, indicating goal (Harris 88–90; R 594–95). The adj. ἀνυπόκριτος, -ον, "without hypocrisy" (U. Wilkens, TDNT 5.70–71) is thus "sincere," "genuine" (cf. 2:1).

ἐκ καθαρᾶς καρδίας ἀλλήλους ἀγαπήσατε ἐκτενῶς

This clause is basically a restatement of εἰς φιλαδελφίαν ἀνυπόκριτον indicating that love must not be merely a token gesture. Peter is concerned that this persecuted community pull together as a cohesive unit and love one another. It is vital for group survival in a hostile environment that internal solidarity be maintained.

There is uncertainty as to whether καθαρᾶς, "pure," should be included or omitted. The inclusion is supported by 𝔓⁷² ℵ* C Ψ Byz and a large number of minuscules, whereas A B 1852 and parts of the Latin text support the omission. There is inferior ms. support for ἀληθινῆς (ℵ² vgᵐˢˢ). Although the inclusion καθαρᾶς could be a scribal expansion, it is even more likely that it was omitted due to an error of sight. Note that both this word and the following καρδίας begin and end with the same two letters and are the same length.

The aor. impv. (ἀγαπήσατε) is again used for a general precept (see the discussion on "The Use of the Imperative in 1 Peter" in the Introduction). The adv. ἐκτενῶς can be tr. "earnestly" (HCSB; LN 25.71), "constantly" (BDAG 310b; Spicq 1.457–61; LN 68.12), "fervently" (NKJV), "deeply" (NLT, NIV). Given the tone of the following vv. with their emphasis on permanence as opposed to what is merely in passing, the rendering "constantly" is preferred (so Elliott 387; Michaels 76). The cognate adj. ἐκτενῆ is also used in 4:8 with the noun ἀγάπη.

VERSE 23

ἀναγεγεννημένοι οὐκ ἐκ σπορᾶς φθαρτῆς ἀλλὰ ἀφθάρτου

Ἀναγεγεννημένοι nom. pl. masc. of pf. pass. ptc. of ἀναγεννάω, "give new birth/ life" (BDAG 59d; F. Büchsel, *TDNT* 1.673–75; cf. ἀναγεννήσας in v. 3; see comments there). The ptc. performs a similar function to the ptc. ἡγνικότες in the previous v., although it changes the metaphor from ceremonial purification to that of birth/rebirth. It, too, is causal in force, giving an additional basis for the impv. ἀγαπήσατε, and the pf. tense is also stative. The difference is that the voice is now pass., highlighting God's action in granting rebirth.

The prep. ἐκ is used to denote orig. (R 598; BDAG 296c). The noun σπορά, -ᾶς, ἡ, can denote either seed or the act of sowing. The latter is awkward here and so the former is preferable (BDAG 939a).

Peter's fondness for the perishable/imperishable contrast continues here using the adj. φθαρτός, -ή, -όν, "perishable" (BDAG 1053d), and its alpha-privative antonym ἄφθαρτος, -ον, "imperishable" (BDAG 155d–156a). Again, the main focus of the contrast, given the quotation that follows, is between what is ephemeral and what is enduring—"his message that lives on forever" (CEV).

διὰ λόγου ζῶντος θεοῦ καὶ μένοντος

This can be taken in two ways:

*1. the prep. phrase could be epex. of ἀφθάρτου, with διά performing a similar function to ἐκ (as Achtemeier 139; Jobes 124; Dubis 38). That is, the imperishable seed is the word of God (Cassirer); or

2. διά has a (secondary) instr. sense, i.e., the imperishable seed comes through the word of God (Elliott 389; Harris 70–72).

Most EVV are ambiguous. Given that the following quotation serves to illustrate the imperishable nature of God's word, it is more likely that the word of God is the imperishable seed rather than the means by which it comes.

Both ptcs. ζῶντος and μένοντος are attrib., though they could modify λόγου, "through the living and abiding word of God," or θεοῦ, "through the word of the living and abiding God." While both options are theologically correct (God's word is enduring because God himself is living and enduring), given the following quotation which emphasizes the enduring character of God's word (cf. Heb 4:12), the former option is clearly the intended sense (EVV; *pace* Michaels 77).

VERSES 24–25a

διότι πᾶσα σὰρξ ὡς χόρτος

See v. 16. on how γέγραπται is understood. The quotation is from Isa 40:6–8 LXX. An elliptical construction with ἐστιν implied. In this and the following line ὡς is a comp. particle, "like" (cf. 1:14, 19; 2:2, 5). The word is not in the LXX text and consequently has the effect of turning a metaphor into a simile. Σάρξ looks at humanity from the perspective of mortality (Michaels 78), with πᾶσα heightening the contrast. Χόρτος, -ου, ὁ, refers to green grass in the field (BDAG 1087c).

καὶ πᾶσα δόξα αὐτῆς ὡς ἄνθος χόρτου

Ἄνθος, -ους, τό, "flower" (BDAG 80b). Ἄνθος χόρτου is lit. "flower of grass," and refers to wildflowers growing in the field ("flowers of the field," NIV).

ἐξηράνθη ὁ χόρτος, καὶ τὸ ἄνθος ἐξέπεσεν

Ἐξηράνθη 3 sg. aor. pass. indic. of ξηραίνω, "wither" (BDAG 684d). Ἐξέπεσεν 3 sg. aor. act. indic. of ἐκπίπτω, "fall off" (BDAG 308a). The two aor. tenses are gnomic, signifying universal truths (BDF §333.1; Moulton 134–35; T 73; R 836–37; Wallace 562; *pace* Moule 12). The aspect of the aor. which presents the action in summary form (Fanning 86–98) is fitting to depict this short-lived phenomenon. Pres. tense is required in English (ZG 706).

This is a vivid Palestinian image of the temporary brilliance of spring flowers in the field that are quickly scorched by the rising sun and relentless sirocco wind. Possibly a parallel is intended with pagan society (so Michaels 78) and/or the transitory nature of trials and those who inflict them (Davids 79; Achtemeier 142).

τὸ δὲ ῥῆμα κυρίου μένει εἰς τὸν αἰῶνα

Δέ is adversative. Whether κυρίου is an obj. or subj. gen. depends on its identification. In the Isaiah text θεοῦ is used (a subj. gen.), but here ambiguity exists as to whether God or Jesus is intended. Elsewhere Jesus is clearly referred to as Lord (1:3; 2:3; 3:15), and it is quite possible that the ref. to the Word of the gospel in the following line provided the impetus for Peter to substitute κυρίου with the intention of referring to Jesus Christ (Elliott 391).

With Jesus as the referent, the gen. could still be either subj. (i.e., the word that Jesus preached; so Michaels 79, believing it to be a parallel of the saying of Jesus found in the gospel tradition; Mark 13:31: "Heaven and earth will pass away, but my words will not pass away"), or obj. (the word about Jesus that was preached; so Achtemeier 141; Elliott 391). Given that "the word that was preached to you" (v. 25) is obviously the gospel, both ideas are present (plenary gen.) as the church continues to proclaim about Jesus what he himself proclaimed.

The pres. tense of μένει is supplemented and strengthened by εἰς τὸν αἰῶνα.

VERSE 25b

τοῦτο δὲ ἐστιν ῥῆμα τὸ εὐαγγελισθὲν εἰς ὑμᾶς

Ῥῆμα picks up the word from the last line of the quotation, instead of λόγος which prefaced it. Reflecting common LXX usage, here the two words function synonymously (*pace* Jobes 133). Although the distinction between them is that ῥῆμα normally refers to specific words or utterances, whereas λόγος relates to an overall message, this distinction is not always apparent in the NT (O. Betz, *NIDNTT* 3.1119–23). Λόγος is the more common term for Christian proclamation, but ῥῆμα can appear with that sense as well (Rom 10:8).

The prep. phrase εἰς ὑμᾶς occurs nowhere else in the NT following εὐαγγελίζω; normally the vb. is followed by the dat. of the person or persons to which a message is preached. Εἰς ὑμᾶς has already been used twice in this chapter (1:4, 10), and δι' ὑμᾶς appears with the same sense in v. 20, emphasizing that the grand events of salvation have been for the benefit of Peter's audience. Given that the prep. phrase concludes the section in a somewhat emphatic position, it should be rendered here not as the indir. obj. of the vb. ("preached to you"), but in line with its other uses in the chapter (so Michaels 79; Elliott 392; Achtemeier 142; see also Harris 88–90). This would give the tr. "this is the word of the gospel that has been proclaimed for your sake" (*pace* EVV), thus capturing the sense of εὐαγγελίζω while still allowing the prep. phrase to retain its final position in the sentence.

These beleaguered communities are therefore encouraged in the midst of trials that God's word, which has declared new birth for all who believe, is not a declaration subject to chance, decay or obsolescence, but an enduring promise without qualification.

FOR FURTHER STUDY

20. Community Ethics (1:22)

Brawley, Robert, ed. *Character Ethics and the New Testament.* Louisville: Westminster John Knox, 2007.

*Burridge, Richard A. *Imitating Jesus: An Inclusive Approach to New Testament Ethics.* Grand Rapids: Eerdmans, 2007.

Hays, Richard B. *The Moral Vision of the New Testament.* San Francisco: HarperCollins, 1996.

Matera, Frank J. *New Testament Ethics: The Legacies of Jesus and Paul.* Louisville: Westminster John Knox, 1996.

Meeks, Wayne A. *The Origins of Christian Morality: The First Two Centuries.* New Haven, CT: Yale University Press, 1993.

Pregeant, Russell. *Knowing Truth, Doing Good: Engaging New Testament Ethics.* Minneapolis: Fortress, 2008.

Schrage, Wolfgang. *The Ethics of the New Testament.* Philadelphia: Fortress, 1988.

Verhey, Allen. *The Great Reversal: Ethics in the New Testament.* Grand Rapids: Eerdmans, 1984.

————. *DLNT* 347–53.

See also For Further Study §§ 17, 22.

21. New Birth (1:23–25)

Bromiley, Geoffrey W. *ISBE* 4:.67–71.

Büchsel, Friedrich. *TDNT* 1.673–75.

Burkhardt, Helmut. *The Biblical Doctrine of Regeneration.* Downers Grove: InterVarsity, 1978.

Dunn, James D. G. *The Theology of Paul the Apostle.* Edinburgh: T&T Clark, 1998.

Fee, Gordon D. *Pauline Christology: An Exegetical-Theological Study.* Peabody, MA: Hendrickson, 2007.

Goldsworthy, Graeme. *NDBT* 720–23.

Packer, James I. *EDT* 924–26.

Porsch, Felix. *EDNT* 1.76–77.

Ridderbos, Herman. *Paul: An Outline of His Theology.* Grand Rapids: Eerdmans, 1975.

Ringwald, A. *NIDNTT* 1.176–80.

Robinson, J. B. *IDB* 4.24–29.

*Toon, Peter. *Born Again: A Biblical and Theological Study of Regeneration.* Grand Rapids: Baker, 1987.

Wilkins, Michael J. *DLNT* 792–95.

HOMILETICAL SUGGESTIONS

The New Birth (1:22–25)

1. New birth has its outworking in Christian community ethics (v. 22)
2. New birth is effected through God's word (v. 23)
3. God's word is eternal in contrast to the ephemeral nature of humanity (vv. 24–25a)
4. God's word is the gospel proclaimed (v. 25b)

Faith, Hope, and Love (1:13–25)

1. Faith
   (a) is in God
   (b) is through Jesus (1:21)

2. Hope
    (a) results from a changed lifestyle (1:13a, 23)
    (b) is in God (1:21), but must be oriented toward the future return of Jesus
        (1:13b)
3. Love
    (a) must also result from a change of lifestyle (1:22)
    (b) is tied to obedience (1:22)
    (c) is demonstrated in sincere responses to others in the Christian community
        (1:22)

Living in the Shadow of the End (1:13–21)

1. Jesus will one day be revealed to all (cf. Phil 2:10–11)
2. Christians must have a future-oriented hope (1:13)
3. The end must impact the present in terms of individual and corporate ethical
   responsibility (1:13–15, 22)

D. MATURE CHRISTIAN LIVING (2:1–3)

STRUCTURE

The opening ptc. ἀποθέμενοι introduces a call to holiness expressed in neg. terms of the vices to be purged from a believer's life. Verse 2 contains the main impv. ἐπιποθήσατε utilizing the metaphor of physical nourishment to convey the need for spiritual growth.

1   ἀποθέμενοι οὖν πᾶσαν κακίαν
            καὶ πάντα δόλον
            καὶ ὑποκρίσεις
            καὶ φθόνους
            καὶ πάσας καταλαλιάς
2   ὡς ἀρτιγέννητα βρέφη
              τὸ λογικὸν ἄδολον γάλα
  ἐπιποθήσατε
    ἵνα
          ἐν αὐτῷ
        αὐξηθῆτε
          εἰς σωτηρίαν
3   εἰ ἐγεύσασθε
        ὅτι χρηστὸς ὁ κύριος.

VERSE 1

ἀποθέμενοι οὖν πᾶσαν κακίαν καὶ πάντα δόλον καὶ ὑποκρίσεις καὶ φθόνους καὶ πάσας καταλαλιάς

Οὖν makes this ethical appeal a clear consequence of the new birth spoken of at the end of ch. 1. Ἀποθέμενοι is nom. pl. masc. of aor. mid. ptc. of ἀποτίθημι, "throw off." The ptc. is dependent on the impv. ἐπιποθήσατε in the following v. and thus has derived impv. character (see discussion on "Imperatival Participles in 1 Peter" in the Introduction). It also clearly denotes action prior to the main impv. as evil must be discarded in order for growth to occur. The vb. is commonly used for undressing and is part of Peter's fondness for clothing metaphors (1:13; 4:1; 5:5). The fig. use of the term for purging of sin ("rid yourselves," Weymouth, NRSV, HCSB, NIV; "putting aside," NASB) is common in the NT and appears to be idiomatic (BDAG 124a; H. Weigelt, *NIDNTT* 1.314–16; Jobes 131; Goppelt 128; see Rom 13:12; Eph 4:22, 25; Col 3:8; Jas 1:21).

The adj. πᾶς is used with the first two and final nouns in order to cover the total magnitude of sins that such terms include (Elliott 396). It is common in NT vice lists (Gal 5:19–21; Eph 4:31; Col 3:8; Jas 1:21). Both the nouns κακία, -ας, ἡ (BDAG 500b) and δόλος, -ου, ὁ (BDAG 256c) are rather general in character, with the first denoting wickedness in general (ZG 706) and the second focusing on deceit or treachery. Δόλος is used later in the letter parallel with both ἁμαρτία (2:22) and κακός (3:10).

Ὑπόκρισις, -εως, ἡ, "hypocrisy," "pretense," contrasts with ἀνυπόκριτον in 1:22. The pl. (also with the following noun) fulfills the same function as the adj. πᾶς (*Pluralis Poeticus* used for abstract subjects; T 27–28; R 408; Michaels 86). Φθόνος, -ου, ὁ, "envy," was often used in secular Gk. of begrudging others' possessions or their good fortune (LSJ 1930b; BDAG 1054d).

The verbal form (καταλαλέω) of the noun καταλαλιά, -ᾶς, ἡ, "slander" (BDAG 519d), is used in 2:12; 3:16 for what the recipients are receiving from others. Thus they must not repay in kind, with Christ functioning as the model (2:21–25).

VERSE 2

ὡς ἀρτιγέννητα βρέφη

Ὡς introduces a metaphor of sorts, though there is a sense in which believers are children in that they call God "Father" and have received new birth (1:3, 17, 23). The adj. ἀρτιγέννητος, -ον, "newborn" (BDAG 136b; F. Büchsel, *TDNT* 1.672), picks up the cognate vb. ἀναγεννάω from 1:23 (cf. 1:3). Βρέφος, -ους, το, "baby," "infant" (BDAG 183d–184a), applies to Christians no matter what their level of maturity; therefore, the metaphor of milk is not used pejoratively of immaturity as it is in 1 Cor 3:1–3 and Heb 5:12.

τὸ λογικὸν ἄδολον γάλα ἐπιποθήσατε

The rendering of the adj. λογικός, -ή, -όν (on the form see MH 378) is invariably determined by what one understands the noun γάλα, γάλακτος, τό, "milk" (see Turner, *Words* 289–90) to represent. Lit. the adj. means "that which pertains to a word." It also appears in Rom 12:1 with apparently the same sense as here, where it is variously rendered "spiritual" (NIV, NRSV, NJB), "worship offered by mind and heart" (NEB), or "reasonable" (KJV, Weymouth).

On the basis of etymology, λογικὸν ἄδολον γάλα is often taken to refer to the word of God (as reflected in NKJV, NASB) and rendered as "spiritual" (Goodspeed, NRSV, CEV, NIV, G. Kittell, *TDNT* 4.142–43; Turner, *Words* 497; ZG 706; Davids 83; Elliott 401; Achtemeier 147). Some take this in the sense of spiritual nourishment (so Goppelt 131 n. 470), whereas others argue that it does not imply spiritual as opposed to physical but rather metaphorical as opposed to literal. In other words, it indicates the presence of a metaphor (BDAG 598b; Michaels 87; for a discussion of this word in 1 Pet 2:2, incl. various translations, see D. G. McCartney, "Logikos in 1 Peter 2:2," *ZNW* 82 [1991]: 128–32).

While the immediately preceding context does speak of the word, it does so in the sense of providing regeneration. Here the focus is on growth in the Christian life. The word of God clearly does provide both, but that begs the question as to whether this is Peter's primary intention here, particularly given that this epistle is written at a time before "the gospel of Jesus Christ (was) fully and formally inscripturated in the NT" (Jobes 137).

Λογικός was a favorite expression of the Stoic philosophers, signifying that which was reasonable or rational, in the sense of being true to perceived reality (the λόγος). Jobes proposes a similar sense here (also LN 73.5). Peter is exhorting his readers first to eliminate sin, which is incongruent with their professed faith and new life, and second to long for that which is entirely reasonable, i.e., compatible, with such faith and life. An appropriate rendering would be "long for the proper uncontaminated milk." The "milk" would thus be a rather broad metaphor that is "the sustaining life of God given in mercy to his children" (Michaels 88–89; cf. Jobes 137). Christians are therefore to pursue what is appropriate and proper. Their focus must move away from the destructive vices mentioned in v. 1, and focus solely on that which provides nourishment and growth. This includes the word of the gospel but is wider than it. In fact, given the following verse where the nourishment metaphor continues, an extremely good case can be made that the milk is Christ himself (so Jobes 139–40).

Ἄδολος, -ον, "without contamination," "pure" (often used of farm products (LSJ 24b; BDAG 21c), provides a word play with δόλος in the previous v. For those who regard the milk as the word of God, "uncontaminated" primarily refers to pure doctrine (e.g., Achtemeier 147). On the interpretation offered above it refers to an absence of the sins described in v. 1.

Ἐπιποθήσατε 2 pl. aor. act. impv. of ἐπιποθέω, "desire" (BDAG 377c; H. Schönweiss, *NIDNTT* 1.456–58). The compound vb. is intensive (R 563–65), expressing an earnest desire, with the aor. impv. used characteristically by Peter for a general precept (see discussion on "The Use of the Imperative in 1 Peter" in the Introduction).

ἵνα ἐν αὐτῷ αὐξηθῆτε εἰς σωτηρίαν

Αὐξηθῆτε 2 pl. aor. pass. subjunc. of αὐξάνω, "grow" (intrans.), "cause to grow" (trans.). The ἵνα clause expresses the purpose of longing for this proper milk, with the dat. ἐν αὐτῷ instr., "by it" (Z §119). The prep. εἰς in εἰς σωτηρίαν is telic (goal; see Harris 88–90; R 594–95). Peter can express salvation as a goal because it is primarily future and bound up with the final revelation of Jesus (1:5, 7, 13; 4:13; cf. Rom 5:10–11; 13:11; Heb 9:28). See further on 1:9.

VERSE 3

εἰ ἐγεύσασθε ὅτι χρηστὸς ὁ κύριος

The particle εἰ is not so much cond. "if" as causal "since" (BDAG 278a; Elliott 402; Goppelt 132 n. 50), for Peter is convinced that believers have experienced the goodness of the Lord. The ambiguity of εἰ has provided the impetus for the stronger term εἴπερ, since, in some mss. Εἴπερ is read by ℵ² C P Ψ 1739 *Byz*. However, εἰ is more strongly attested by 𝔓⁷² ℵ* A B and is the more difficult rdg.

Ἐγεύσασθε (2 pl. aor. mid. indic. of γεύομαι, "taste") continues the theme of nourishment/food, with the word often used in the NT as a graphic metaphor for experience (Mark 9:1; Heb 2:9; 6:4; BDAG 195c).

An obvious word play links χρηστός and Χριστός. The two words would have been pronounced almost identically, and this may have given rise to the variant rdg. where Χριστός is read by 𝔓⁷² K L 049 and some minuscules, thus making a theological statement rather than a more subtle play on words (R 192). The allusion to Ps 34:8 (33:9 LXX; also used in 3:10, 12) makes the rdg. in the text (א A B C Ψ 1739 *Byz*) almost certain, as does the continuation of the metaphor of nourishment (so Michaels 82). In the Psalm text κύριος is God, but elsewhere Peter uses κύριος of Jesus (1:3, 25; 3:15), and the following v. clearly indicates that he is the focus here.

Χρηστός, -ή, -όν can be "kind" (NLT; cf. Eph 4:32; Luke 6:35; Rom 2:4) or "good" (NRSV, CEV, HCSB) with no difference in sense here (BDAG 1090a; Spicq 3.511–16; ZG 706). Ὅτι is used after vbs. of sense perception to introduce the content of that perception (R 1034–35; BDAG 731d; Z §416).

FOR FURTHER STUDY

22. Christian Maturity/Spiritual Growth (2:1–3)

Barth, Karl. *The Christian Life*. Grand Rapids: Eerdmans, 1981.
Callen, Barry L. *Authentic Spirituality*. Grand Rapids: Baker, 2001.
*Chan, Simon. *Spiritual Theology: A Systematic Study of the Christian Life*. Downers Grove: InterVarsity, 1998.
Collins, Gary R. *The Soul Search*. Nashville: Thomas Nelson, 1998.
Esler, Philip F. *New Testament Theology: Communion and Community*. Minneapolis: Fortress, 2005.
Inrig, Gary. *A Call to Excellence*. Wheaton, IL: Victor, 1986.
Klein, William W. *DPL* 699–701.
MacArthur, John. *Keys to Spiritual Growth: Unlock the Door to Spiritual Maturity*. Grand Rapids: Fleming H. Revell, 1991.
Meye, Robert P. *DPL* 906–16.
Oppenwall, Nola J. *ISBE* 3.764–65.
Packer, James I. and Loren Wilkinson, eds. *Alive to God: Studies in Spirituality*. Downers Grove: InterVarsity, 1992.
Peterson, Eugene H. *Subversive Spirituality*. Grand Rapids: Eerdmans, 1997.
Powell, Samuel M. *A Theology of Christian Spirituality*. Nashville: Abingdon, 2005.
Schreiner, Thomas R. *New Testament Theology*. Grand Rapids: Baker, 2008.

See also For Further Study §§ 17, 20.

23. The Character of God (2:3)

Bartholomew, Craig G., and Michael W. Goheen. *The Drama of Scripture*. Grand Rapids: Eerdmans. 2004.
Bassler, Jouette M. *ABD* 2.1041–55.
*Bloesch, Donald G. *God the Almighty: Power, Wisdom, Holiness, Love*. Downers Grove: InterVarsity, 1995.
Carson, D. A. *The Difficult Doctrine of the Love of God*. Wheaton, IL: Crossway Books, 2000.
Erickson, Millard J. *Christian Theology*. Grand Rapids: Baker, 1985.

Guthrie, Donald, and Ralph P. Martin. *DPL* 354–69.

Helm, Paul, and Carl Trueman, eds. *The Trustworthiness of God*. Downers Grove:
    InterVarsity, 2002.

McGrath, Alister E. *Theology: The Basics*. Malden: Blackwell, 2008.

Packer, James I. *Knowing God*. Downers Grove: InterVarsity, 1993.

Schreiner, Thomas R. *New Testament Theology*. Grand Rapids: Baker, 2008.

Taylor, John V. *The Christlike God*. London: SCM, 1992.

HOMILETICAL SUGGESTIONS

Mature Christian Living (2:1–3)

1. Leaving the past behind (2:1)
2. Longing for what is compatible with the Christian life (2:2)
3. Salvation as a process (2:2; cf. Phil 2:12; Rom 13:11)
4. Experiencing the character of Jesus/God (2:3)

IV. The People of God (2:4–10)

A. CHRIST THE LIVING STONE (2:4–8)

STRUCTURE

The structure of 2:4–10 is complex due to parenthetical statements and several OT citations and allusions. The ptc. προσερχόμενοι that begins v. 4 is dependent upon the main vb. οἰκοδομεῖσθε in the following v., but the remainder of v. 4 is a parenthetical statement regarding the general rejection of God's elect stone.

4   πρὸς ὅν προσερχόμενοι <u>λίθον ζῶντα</u>
                    ὑπὸ ἀνθρώπων μὲν ἀποδεδοκιμασμένον,
                    παρὰ δὲ θεῷ ἐκλεκτὸν ἔντιμον

Verse 5 picks up the ptc. προσερχόμενοι from the previous v. The focus now shifts to believers as living stones and their priestly function.

5 καὶ αὐτοὶ   ὡς <u>λίθοι ζῶντες</u>
   <u>οἰκοδομεῖσθε</u> οἶκος <u>πνευματικὸς</u>
          εἰς ἱεράτευμα ἅγιον
          ἀνενέγκαι <u>πνευματικὰς</u> θυσίας
              εὐπροσδέκτους θεῷ
                    διὰ Ἰησοῦ Χριστοῦ.

Verse 6 introduces a citation from Isa 28:16 as a further comment on God's elect stone. Verses 7–8, after commencing with an ascription of honor for believers, then utilize Ps 118:22 and Isa 8:14 respectively to highlight the sad fate of those who reject this stone. The author concludes v. 8 with his own summary statement regarding their destiny.

6   διότι περιέχει ἐν γραφῇ·
        Ἰδοὺ τίθημι ἐν Σιὼν λίθον
                ἀκρογωνιαῖον
                ἐκλεκτὸν
                ἔντιμον
        καὶ ὁ πιστεύων ἐπ' αὐτῷ οὐ μὴ καταισχυνθῇ

7   ὑμῖν οὖν
        ἡ τιμὴ τοῖς πιστεύουσιν,
                ἀπιστοῦσιν δὲ
        λίθος ὃν ἀπεδοκίμασαν οἱ οἰκοδομοῦντες
        οὗτος ἐγενήθη εἰς κεφαλὴν γωνίας
8   καὶ
        λίθος προσκόμματος
        καὶ πέτρα σκανδάλου·

        οἳ προσκόπτουσιν
                τῷ λόγῳ ἀπειθοῦντες
                        εἰς ὃ καὶ ἐτέθησαν.

VERSE 4

πρὸς ὃν προσερχόμενοι λίθον ζῶντα

Sections of the letter are again linked with a rel. clause headed by a prep. (1:6, 8, 10; R 954). The antecedent of ὅν is ὁ κύριος (Jesus) from v. 3. Λίθον ζῶντα is in appos. to the rel. pron. ὅν, making the syntax awkward.

The ptc. προσερχόμενοι has as its subj. the 2 pl. subj. οἰκοδομεῖσθε in the following v., and given that the rest of v. 4 is a parenthetical comment on Jesus the living stone, it is probably easier to start the tr. here with the ptc. The ptc. is best understood as attendant circumstance, although whether it is impv. or indic. in force depends on how the ambiguous form οἰκοδομεῖσθε is taken. It is argued below for an indic. sense, which would give the rendering for the opening of v. 4: "As you come to him, the living stone" (ESV, NIV).

λίθος refers to a stone ready for construction and anticipates the following stone texts (J. Jeremias, *TDNT* 4.268–80; H.-G. Link, E. Tiedtke, *NIDNTT* 3.390–93). The ptc. ζῶντα (acc. sg. masc. of pres. act. ptc. of ζάω) links Jesus with the living hope (1:3) and the living word (1:23) and identifies him as risen (for use of this ptc. in the papyri, see *NewDocs* 9.36–38).

ὑπὸ ἀνθρώπων μὲν ἀποδεδοκιμασμένον

Ἀποδεδοκιμασμένον acc. sg. masc. of pf. pass. ptc. of ἀποδοκιμάζω, "reject," attrib. with λίθον ζῶντα, but in combination with the μέν . . . δέ construction (see R 1150–53), takes on concessive elements. Here the pf. highlights the state of rejection, with ἀνθρώπων being both generic and a generalization. The vb. means to reject after critical examination/testing (W. Grundmann, *TDNT* 2.255–60; H. Haarbeck, *NIDNTT* 3.808–10; BDAG 110c).

παρὰ δὲ θεῷ ἐκλεκτὸν ἔντιμον

Παρά with the dat. expresses viewpoint (BDAG 757b; ZG 706), here "in God's sight." Ἐλεκτός, -ή, -όν, "chosen." Ἔντιμος, -ον, "highly respected," "honored"

(Weymouth, CEV, NLT), or "valuable," "precious" (KJV, NJB, HCSB, NIV; BDAG 340), but considering that "honored" provides a better contrast with rejection, this is the preferred sense in this context (Elliott 411).

VERSE 5

καὶ αὐτοὶ ὡς λίθοι ζῶντες

'Ως again introduces a metaphor. Αὐτοί here is an intensive pron. (Wallace 348–49; ZG 706), "you yourselves as living stones." ζῶντες is nom. pl. masc. of pres. act. ptc. of ζάω, "live."

οἰκοδομεῖσθε οἶκος πνευματικός

Although many take οἰκοδομεῖσθε as an impv., which also gives the ptc. προσερχόμενοι in v. 4 impv. force (NEB, NRSV, TEV; BDAG 696b; Goppelt 140; Feldmeier 134), this incorrectly views Peter's statement as a call to conversion, when it is better seen as a statement of reality. As people come to faith in Jesus the living stone, they are being incorporated into God's building (NASB, HCSB, ESV, NIV; Selwyn 159; Elliott 412; Achtemeier 155; Michaels 100; Davids 87; Jobes 156–57; Dubis 47–48). The pass. implies God's action, whereas the pl. underlines the corporate nature of the building.

Οἶκος πνευματικός is problematic in the nom.:

1. Most take it as a pred. nom., which in essence makes it the dir. obj. ("a predicate amplification"; R 401) of οἰκοδομεῖσθε—"you are being built into a spiritual house" (Weymouth, NRSV, NLT, NIV; Michaels 100; Goppelt 134, Dubis 48 picking up the double acc. category from Wallace 186). This, however, would be a unique cstr. to give that sense, esp. given that the nom. would then perform essentially the same function as the following prep. phrase with εἰς; or

*2. More likely, it is in appos. to λίθοι ζῶντες. This would give the rendering "Even you yourselves as living stones, a spiritual house, are being built to be a holy priesthood" (Achtemeier 149, 155).

εἰς ἱεράτευμα ἅγιον

Ἱεράτευμα, -ατος, τό, "priesthood" (BDAG 469b). Εἰς regularly has telic force in this epistle (1:3, 4, 5, 7, 22; 2:7, 8, 9, 14, 21; 3:7, 9; 4:2, 7; see R 594–95; Harris 88–90)—the purpose of the spiritual house is to be a holy priesthood (see βασίλειον ἱεράτευμα in v. 9 below).

ἀνενέγκαι πνευματικὰς θυσίας

The function of a holy priesthood is to offer spiritual sacrifices: this is expressed by the inf. of purpose ἀνενέγκαι (aor. act. inf. of ἀναφέρω, "offer" (BDAG 75a; Turner, Words 10–12; on the form see R 338). Πνευματικάς indicates first that the rites are not material in the sense of animal sacrifice, and second that they pertain to life in the Spirit (J. G. D. Dunn, *NIDNTT* 3.706–7; J. Kremer, *EDNT* 3.122–23; Elliott 418, 422; Achtemeier 156; ZG 706). They include praise and thanksgiving (cf. Heb 13:15–16) but are more widely defined in terms of the author's concern for good conduct (ἀναστροφή; see 1:15; 2:12; 3:1, 2, 16).

εὐπροσδέκτους θεῷ διὰ Ἰησοῦ Χριστοῦ [This reflects the text of the forthcoming fifth edition of the UBS *Greek New Testament*. The fourth edition reads [τῷ] before θεῷ.]

Εὐπρόσδεκτος, -ον, "acceptable" (BDAG 420d–411a). Διὰ Ἰησοῦ Χριστοῦ could modify either:

1. εὐπροσδέκτους θεῷ, sacrifices are offered, and they are acceptable to God through Jesus Christ (most EVV; Dubis, 49); or
2. the inf. ἀνενέγκαι, sacrifices are offered through Jesus Christ and are acceptable to God (CEV, NLT).

The syntax probably leans toward the latter option, although in the end the difference in mng. is negligible. Both stress Jesus' role as mediator (cf. 1 Tim 2:5), underscoring the fact that he is the foundation of Christian life—the cornerstone (v. 6).

VERSE 6

διότι περιέχει ἐν γραφῇ

See on 1:16 for διότι. This is the only time in the NT that περιέχει (3 sg. pres. act. indic. of περιέχω, "stand" [intrans.; see R 800 on the effect of the prep. compound on a trans. vb.]), is used to introduce a scriptural citation. The pres. tense "it stands" has the same force as the pf. γέγραπται (BDAG 802a; MH 321; *NewDocs* 4.94). Here the citation is from Isa 28:16.

Ἰδοὺ τίθημι ἐν Σιὼν λίθον

Σιών, ἡ, "Mount Zion," "Zion." Τίθημι forms an *inclusio* with ἐτέθησαν at the end of v. 8, underscoring God's activity (Achtemeier 160 n. 142).

ἀκρογωνιαῖον ἐκλεκτὸν ἔντιμον

Ἀκρογωνιαῖος, -α, -ον, appears to be unique to Gk. and could refer to a cornerstone integral to the foundation of the building or the capstone/keystone that completes it (BDAG 39d–40a; J. Jeremias, *TDNT* 1.791–93; H. Krämer, *EDNT* 1.267–69; W. Mundle, *NIDNTT* 3.388–90; Turner, *Words* 86–88). The orig. context in Isa 28:16 explicitly mentions a foundation, and the imagery of stumbling over the stone in v. 8 suggests something in the foundation rather than higher in the structure. In addition, the ref. to the stone being κεφαλὴν γωνίας ("head of the corner") in the following v. severely weakens the case for a capstone. Nevertheless, the function the quotation performs in this context is not affected by either interpretation. The adjs. ἐκλεκτόν and ἔντιμον were used in v. 4 in anticipation of this citation (see comments there).

καὶ ὁ πιστεύων ἐπ' αὐτῷ οὐ μὴ καταισχυνθῇ

πιστεύω is followed by ἐπί (with either acc. or dat.) twelve times in the NT, with nine of those uses equivalent to the more common constr. with εἰς of believing in Jesus, and the other use taking the place of the simple dat. See Harris 235, who regards the idiom (with the acc.) as indicating metaphorical movement from past devotion to a new personal object of faith.

Καταισχυνθῇ 3 sg. aor. pass. subjunc. καταισχύνω, "disappoint," "disgrace" (BDAG 517b; H.-G. Link, *NIDNTT* 3.562–64). In the context of the shame and alienation that the readers of this epistle are experiencing, "disgrace" makes the more powerful statement. Οὐ μή expresses an emphatic neg. (see Z §444; T 96–97), "by no means" (NKJV), "never" (NLT, HCSB, NIV). To believe in Jesus may entail rejection and disgrace in the eyes of pagan society, but never in the sight of God.

VERSE 7

ὑμῖν οὖν ἡ τιμὴ τοῖς πιστεύουσιν

Τοῖς πιστεύουσιν is in appos. to ὑμῖν, "to/for you who believe." On the possibly emphatic word order see R 418; BDF §473. An elliptical cstr., where either εἰμι or ἔρχομαι (R 395–96) is supplied with the subj. ἡ τιμή: "The honor is for you who believe" (ESV). Alternatively ἡ τιμή is pred.: "There is honor for you who believe." The dat. is advantage (Achtemeier 161) or poss.

There is little warrant for translating ἡ τιμή as "precious" in ref. to Jesus the cornerstone (as do KJV, NEB, NRSV, NIV, i.e., a pred. nom. "he is precious"). Not only is this importing foreign mng. into this term, it misses the counterbalance to the end of the previous v. and the obvious socio-cultural significance where honor and shame were values integral to Greco-Roman society. Peter insists that those who trust in the cornerstone will not be put to shame but will receive "honor" (so Weymouth, NJB, HCSB, ESV; Dubis 51–52; ZG 706; NLT has "honor" but wrongly with ref. to Jesus).

ἀπιστοῦσιν δέ

Ἀπιστοῦσιν dat. pl. masc. of pres. act. ptc. of ἀπιστέω, "refuse or fail to believe" (BDAG 103b), in contrast to τοῖς πιστεύουσιν earlier in the same verse. Dat. of disadvantage or respect. The absence of the art. with this ptc. as opposed to the preceding τοῖς πιστεύουσιν may be indicating that unbelievers are not a unified group (Achtemeier 161 n. 157 citing Spicq), though this may be reading too much into the absence of the art. with ἀπιστοῦσιν.

λίθος ὃν ἀπεδοκίμασαν οἱ οἰκοδομοῦντες

Ἀπεδοκίμασαν 3 pl. aor. act. indic. of ἀποδοκιμάζω, "reject" (see v. 4). In context, οἱ οἰκοδομοῦντες are the unbelievers of the previous clause. There is some uncertainty as to whether the nominative λίθος should be read in grammatical agreement with οὗτος

($\mathfrak{P}^{72}$ $\aleph^2$ A B C*) or the accusative λίθον in agreement with the relative pronoun ὅν (ℵ* *Byz*). Neither mng. nor tr. is affected.

οὗτος ἐγενήθη εἰς κεφαλὴν γωνίας

Οὗτος may be emphatic and ironic ("this very one"). Γωνία, -ας, ἡ, "corner." Κεφαλὴν γωνίας corresponds to the more vague term ἀκρογωνιαῖον in the preceding v. It is lit. "head of the corner" and most likely refers to a stone set in the foundation of a building to ensure that it is plumbed correctly (see Elliott 429 and the note on the previous v.). Εἰς κεφαλὴν γωνίας is used in place of a pred. nom. (ZG 707).

VERSE 8

καὶ λίθος προσκόμματος καὶ πέτρα σκανδάλου

Καί links the quotation here from Isa 8:14 to that from Ps 118:22 in the previous v., continuing the thought of what the stone means for unbelievers. Πρόσκομμα, -ατος, τό, can either convey the act of stumbling or that which causes it (Turner, *Words* 298–99; G. Stählin, *TDNT* 6.745–58; J. Guhrt, *NIDNTT* 2.705–7). Here it is the former (*pace* BDAG 882a).

Σκάνδαλον, -ου, τό, that which causes stumbling (BDAG 926b–c). The two gens. προσκόμματος and σκανδάλου are gens. of product—"a stone that causes stumbling, a rock that gives offense" (so NLT, NIV; Dubis 54; for the category, see Wallace 106–7). The NT follows the LXX in using σκάνδαλον for that which hampers faithful allegiance to God (J. Guhrt, *NIDNTT* 2.707–10).

The stone passages have been used by Peter to make a powerful Christological statement and to encourage the persecuted communities to whom he writes. They also provide the basis for a fuller description of the believing community in vv. 9–10 (see Beale and Carson 1023–30).

οἳ προσκόπτουσιν τῷ λόγῳ ἀπειθοῦντες

Προσκόπτουσιν 3 pl. pres. act. indic. of προσκόπτω, "stumble." The antecedent of the rel. pron. οἵ is οἱ οἰκοδομοῦντες in v. 7. Τῷ λόγῳ is the word of the Christian gospel (cf. 1:25 and discussion there; ZG 707). The ptc. ἀπειθοῦντες (nom. pl. masc. of pres. act. ptc. of ἀπειθέω, "disobey") is causal—"they stumble because they disobey the word" (so most EVV). Ἀπειθέω takes the dat. of person or thing disobeyed (BDAG 99d) and is synonymous with ἀπιστέω in v. 7 (cf. 3:1, 30; 4:17).

εἰς ὃ καὶ ἐτέθησαν

On the telic use of εἰς see 2:5. The antecedent of the neut. rel. pron. ὅ is unclear. It could be the idea of "disobeying the word," which would be a strong statement of predestination of the wicked (Achtemeier 162–63; most EVV give this sense, though some are more ambiguous than others). But such a position is hard to reconcile with the belief of the author that the holy conduct of believers can have a positive influence in winning unbelievers for the gospel (2:12; 3:1–2; so Elliott 434). Consequently, the antecedent better relates to stumbling, in the sense that those who disobey the word are destined to stumble (Jobes 156; Michaels 107; Elliott 433–34; Cassirer: "It is those who repudiate God's message who stumble; that, indeed, is their appointed lot"). Grudem (108; also Dubis 55) misses the point in ruling out this latter interpretation on the basis that the pl. subj. of ἐτέθησαν relates to persons, not a principle. It is not the subj. of the vb. that gives this sense but the antecedent of the rel. pron. Ἐτέθησαν 3 pl. aor. pass. indic. of τίθημι, here in the sense "assign" or "appoint" (BDAG 1004a), forming an *inclusio* with v. 6.

FOR FURTHER STUDY

24. Images and Metaphors of the Church (2:5)

Beale, G. K. *A New Testament Biblical Theology: The Unfolding of the Old Testament in the New*. Grand Rapids: Baker, 2011.

Best, E. "1 Peter 2:4–10: A Reconsideration." *NovT* 11 (1969): 270–93.

Cottrell, J. "The Church: The House of God: A Sermon on Matthew 16:15–18; Ephesians 2:19–22; 1 Peter 2:1–12." Pages 7–17 in *Christ's Victorious Church*. Edited by J. Weatherly. Eugene, OR: Wipf and Stock, 2001.

Dalton, W. "The Church in 1 Peter." Pages 89–107 in *Jerusalem: Seat of Theology*. Edited by D. B. Burrell, R. Du Brul, and W. Dalton. Jerusalem: Ecumenical Institute for Theological Research, 1982.

Fung, R. Y. K. "Some Pauline Pictures of the Church." *EvQ* 53 (1981): 89–107.

Giles, K. N. *DLNT* 194–204.

Kee, H. C. *Who Are the People of God? Early Models of Community*. New Haven, CT: Yale University Press, 1995.

Kysar, R. *Stumbling in the Light: New Testament Images for a Changing Church*. St. Louis, MO: Chalice, 1999.

McCartney, D. G. *DLNT* 507–13.

Martin, R. P. *The Family and the Fellowship: New Testament Images of the Church*. Exeter: Paternoster, 1979.

*Minear, P. S., and L. E. Keck. *Images of the Church in the New Testament*. Philadelphia: James Clarke, 2007.

Osborn, R. E. "The Building Up of the Church: Reflections on a New Testament Image." *Impact* 7 (1981): 1–25.

Potter, P. "A House of Living Stones." *Ecumenical Review* 35 (1983): 350–63.

Senior, D. "Correlating Images of Church and Images of Mission in the New Testament." *Missiology* 23 (1995): 3–16.

Treux, J. "God's Spiritual House: A Study of 1 Peter 2:4–5." *Direction* 33 (2004): 185–93.

25. Christ the Living Stone/Cornerstone (2:4–8)

Best, E. "1 Peter 2:4–10: A Reconsideration." *NovT* 11 (1969): 270–93.

Caragounis, C. C. *DLNT* 1126–29.

Hobbie, P. H. "1 Peter 2:2–10." *Int* 47 (1993): 170–73.

*Howe, F. R. "Christ, the Building Stone, in Peter's Theology." *BibSac* 157 (2000): 35–43.

Jeremias, J. *TDNT* 4.268–80.

Mack, E. *ISBE* 1.784.

McKimmon, E. G. "The Living Stone and the Living Stones." *ExpTim* 122 (2011): 343–45.

Minear, P. S. "The House of Living Stones: A Study of 1 Peter 2:4–12." *Ecumenical Review* 34 (1982): 238–48.

Oss, D. A. "The Interpretation of the 'Stone' Passages by Peter and Paul: A Comparative Study." *JETS* 32 (1989): 181–200.

Treux, J. "God's Spiritual House: A Study of 1 Peter 2:4–5." *Direction* 33 (2004): 185–93.

Wagner, J. R. "Faithfulness and Fear, Stumbling and Salvation: Receptions of LXX Isaiah 8:11–18 in the New Testament." Pages 76–106 in *Word Leaps the Gaps: Essays on Scripture and Theology in Honor of Richard B. Hays*. Edited by J. R. Wagner, C. K. Rowe, and A. K. Grieb. Grand Rapids: Eerdmans, 2008.

HOMILETICAL SUGGESTIONS

Christ the Living Stone (2:4–8)

1. Christ the living stone (v. 4)
   (a) Rejected by humanity (v. 4a)
   (b) Chosen by God and precious (v. 4b)
2. Believers as living stones (v. 5)
   (a) The house is still under construction (v. 5a)
   (b) Believers as a holy priesthood offering spiritual sacrifices (v. 5b)
3. Christ the cornerstone as the foundation for life (vv. 6–8)
   (a) Belief in him brings honor (vv. 6–7a)
   (b) Unbelief and disobedience result in stumbling (vv. 7b–8)

Living Stones (2:4–8)

1. Christians take their identity from Christ the living stone. He is
   (a) God's elect
   (b) rejected by people generally
   (c) the foundation for life
2. Christians as a spiritual building
   (a) background in tabernacle/temple theology in OT
   (b) other similar NT images (1 Cor 3:16–17; Eph 2:19–21; Heb 3:1–6)
   (c) still under construction (v. 5)
   (d) a holy priesthood offering spiritual sacrifices (which in the context of this epistle is basically ethical living)

B. BELIEVERS AS THE PEOPLE OF GOD (2:9–10)

STRUCTURE

Verses 9–10 draw on several words and phrases (mainly Exod 19:5 and Hos 2:23) to highlight the privileged status and calling of God's people.

9   Ὑμεῖς δὲ γένος ἐκλεκτόν,
        βασίλειον ἱεράτευμα
        ἔθνος ἅγιον
        λαὸς εἰς περιποίησιν
            ὅπως τὰς ἀρετὰς ἐξαγγείλητε
                τοῦ ἐκ σκότους ὑμᾶς καλέσαντος
                εἰς τὸ θαυμαστὸν αὐτοῦ φῶς·

10   οἵ ποτε οὐ λαὸς
        νῦν δὲ λαὸς θεοῦ,
     οἱ οὐκ ἠλεημένοι
        νῦν δὲ ἐλεηθέντες.

VERSE 9

Ὑμεῖς δέ

The adversative δέ and the 2 pl. pers. pron. ὑμεῖς combine to create an emphatic contrast to the status and fate of the unbelievers/disobedient of the previous two vv. (*pace* Achtemeier 163). Ἔστε is implied with the following group of pred. noms. (R 395–96). The epithets are drawn from Exod 19:6 and Isa 43:20 LXX.

γένος ἐκλεκτόν

Γένος refers to those of common descent (F. Büchsel, *TDNT* 1.684–85). Ἐκλεκτόν builds on 1:1 and harks back to Jesus as the ἐκλεκτὸν λίθον in v. 6.

βασίλειον ἱεράτευμα

Βασίλειον can be taken either as a noun "kingdom/king's house" (so Selwyn 166; Elliott 435–37) or as an adj. modifying ἱεράτευμα (see v. 5) "kingly/royal priesthood" (ZG 707; Achtemeier 164–65; Michaels 108–9; Davids 91; Goppelt 149). The majority of its uses both in the LXX and in secular Greek are substantival, and Jewish tradition invariably interprets the LXX of Exod 19:6 similarly. Nevertheless, the rhythm of the immediately preceding and following epithet, with a noun and a qualifying adj., leans more toward the adj. sense here (for discussions, see J. Baehr, *NIDNTT* 3.37–38; Goppelt 149 n. 64; Elliott 435–37; Michaels 108–9, Dubis 56).

As a royal priesthood, believers are representing the King, and this priesthood is to be understood as ambassadorial, of mediating God's presence to the world, not in the sense of the priesthood of all believers (i.e. access to God) as in Hebrews.

ἔθνος ἅγιον

῎Εθνος refers to those who share a common culture (K. L. Schmidt, *TDNT* 2.364–72; N. Walter, *EDNT* 1.381–83). In Matt 21:43, Rom 10:19, and here, we see the beginning of the application of this term to the church.

For Peter, holiness is a direct consequence of being elect (1:1–2) and thus an expression of status. Nevertheless, it is also a standard of ethical conduct, grounded in the holiness of God himself (1:15–16; cf. Lev 11:44–45; 19:2; 20:7; see also 2:11–12 below).

λαὸς εἰς περιποίησιν

Λαός, in its scriptural use, refers to a group who has a common purpose or destiny (H. Bietenhard, *NIDNTT* 2.795–800), and it conveys the same thought as γένος ἐκλεκτόν. Περιποίησις, -εως, ἡ, "possession," lit. "a people for possession." Michaels (109–10) translates it as "a people destined for vindication" on the basis that περιποίησις has a future sense in 1 Thess 5:9; 2 Thess 2:14; Heb 10:39. But while the future sense is readily apparent in these NT vv., the basic mng. is still to acquire something, with a qualifying noun in the gen. supplied to clearly state what is being acquired. Without a qualifying gen. here it gives the noun a pass. sense of being acquired, i.e., by God (BDAG 804c; cf. Eph 1:14). They are God's possession because they have already been purchased with the blood of Christ (1:19).

ὅπως τὰς ἀρετὰς ἐξαγγείλητε

῞Οπως plus the subjunc. expresses the purpose of all four epithets, not just the final one. Ἐξαγγείλητε 2 pl. aor. act. subjunc. of ἐξαγγέλλω, "proclaim" (BDAG 343b). The vb. conjures up a sense of active missionary endeavour; however, in the LXX the term normally belongs in the context of public worship (Ps 9:14; 56:8; 71:15). Consequently, there is debate as to whether the focus in 1 Peter is on praise within the Christian community or declaration beyond. Michaels (110) argues for the former whereas Achtemeier (166) and Elliott (439–40) support both.

Ἀρετή, -ῆς, ἡ, "excellence," "goodness." This is the word's only NT use in the pl. (the word occurs in the sg. in Phil 4:8; 2 Pet 1:3, 5). In classical Gk. ἀρέται referred to the miracles or powerful deeds of a deity (LN 76.14). It could also refer to moral virtues and the praise of public benefactors (LN 88.11; LSJ 238b–c; Turner, *Words* 339–40; BDAG 130b; R 101; H.-G. Link and A. Ringwald, *NIDNTT* 3.925–28; Elliott 439). In the context of this epistle it encompasses all that God has done through Jesus Christ on behalf of believers.

τοῦ ἐκ σκότους ὑμᾶς καλέσαντος εἰς τὸ θαυμαστὸν αὐτοῦ φῶς

The gen. ptc. καλέσαντος is subj., i.e., the deeds performed by the One who called you out of darkness. The aor. ptc. relates to the past experience of conversion. θαυμαστός, -ή, -όν is something astonishing (BDAG 445b; W. Mundle, *NIDNTT* 2.621–26), here in a positive sense of "marvellous" (NASB, HCSB, ESV) or "wonderful" (NJB, NIV).

The darkness-light imagery is a common biblical expression for experiencing God's saving power (Isa 9:2; Matt 4:16; Acts 26:18; 2 Cor 6:14; Eph 5:8; 1 Thess 5:5).

VERSE 10

The poem in this v. draws on Hos 1:6, 9; 2:3, 25 (LXX).

οἵ ποτε οὐ λαὸς νῦν δὲ λαὸς θεοῦ

Λαός picks up and elaborates on one of the string of epithets in the previous v., λαὸς εἰς περιποίησιν, from Exod 19:6 (see above). Οἵ can be constr. in two ways:

1. As a rel. pron. that picks up ὑμεῖς from v. 9; or
2. As an art. that has acquired its accent from the enclictic ποτέ (Dubis 57).

Michaels (112) takes both instances of οἱ in this verse as arts. whereas Elliott (441) takes both as rel. prons. Equally likely, the first is a rel. pron. and the second is a def. art. making the ptcs. subst. On the neg. Οὐ with nouns see R 1163.

Νῦν δέ provides the contrast between present status and previous (ποτε) non-status. The constr. is elliptical, with ἦτε and ἔστε needing to be supplied respectively (R 395–96).

οἱ οὐκ ἠλεημένοι νῦν δὲ ἐλεηθέντες

Nom. pl. masc. of pf. pass. ptc. and aor. pass. ptc. (respectively) of ἐλεέω, "be merciful," "receive mercy" (pass.) The pf. highlights the destitute state of being without mercy (see Campbell, *Indicative Mood* 161–211; cf. Michaels 93) whereas the aor. ptc. is in keeping with the author's tendency to use the aor. tense to describe the present status or experience of believers (1:20; 2:21a, 24b; 3:6, 9; also with νῦν in 1:12; 2:25; ἄρτι in 1:6; Michaels 112). On οὐ with the ptc. see Moulton 231–32; R 1138–39; BDF §430.

This verse underscores the fact that election is unmerited and dependent upon God's prior action (1:3; cf. Eph 2:4).

FOR FURTHER STUDY

26. Believers as Priests (2:5, 9)

Best, Ernest. "1 Peter 2:4–10: A Reconsideration." *NovT* 11 (1969): 270–93.

Brockopp, Daniel C., Brian L. Helge, and David G. Truemper, eds. *Church and Ministry: Chosen Race, Royal Priesthood, Holy Nation, God's Own People*. Valparaiso, IN: Institute of Liturgical Studies, 1982.

Dalton, William J. "The Church in 1 Peter." Pages 79–91 in *Jerusalem: Seat of Theology*. Edited by D. B. Burrell, R. Du Brul, and W. Dalton. Jerusalem: Ecumenical Institute for Theological Research, 1982.

Garrett, James L., Jr. "The Priesthood of All Christians." *SwJT* 30 (1988): 3–54.

Lea, Thomas D. "The Priesthood of All Christians According to the New Testament." *SwJT* 30 (1998): 15–21.

Moulder, William J. *ISBE* 3.963–65.

Robinson, P. J. "Some Missiological Perspectives from 1 Peter 2:4–10." *Missionalia* 17 (1989): 176–87.

*Schweizer, Eduard. "The Priesthood of All Believers: 1 Peter 2:1–10." Pages 285–93 in *Worship, Theology and Ministry in the Early Church: Essays in Honor of Ralph P. Martin.* Edited by M. Wilkins. Sheffield: JSOT Press, 1992.

Walton, Steve. "Sacrifice and Priesthood in Relation to the Christian Life and Church in the New Testament." Pages 136–56 in *Sacrifice in the Bible.* Edited by R. T. Beckwith and M. J. Selman. Grand Rapids: Baker, 1995.

Steuernagel, Valdir. "An Exiled Community as a Mission Community: A Study Based on 1 Peter 2:9–10." *Evangelical Review of Theology* 10 (1986): 8–18.

27. Relationship of the Church to Israel (2:9–10)

Campbell, William S. *DLNT* 204–18.

Coenen, Lothar. *NIDNTT* 1.291–307.

Dunn, James G. D. *The Parting of the Ways between Christianity and Judaism and Their Significance for the Character of Christianity.* Philadelphia: Trinity Press International, 1991.

Elliott, John H. "The Jewish Messianic Movement: From Faction to Sect." Pages 71–91 in *Modeling Early Christianity: Social-Scientific Studies of the New Testament in Its Context.* Edited by P. F. Esler. New York: Routledge, 1994.

Kee, Howard C. *Who Are the People of God? Early Models of Community.* New Haven, CT: Yale University Press, 1995.

Meeks, Wayne A. "Breaking Away: Three New Testament Pictures of Christianity's Separation from the Jewish Communities." Pages 89–113 in *Essential Papers on Judaism and Christianity in Conflict.* Edited by J. Cohen. New York: New York University Press, 1991.

Nicklesburg, George W. E., with G. W. MacRae, eds. *Christians Among Jews and Gentiles.* Philadelphia: Fortress, 1986.

Soulen, R. Kendall. *The God of Israel and Christian Theology.* Minneapolis: Augsburg Fortress, 1996.

Swartley, William M. *Israel's Scripture Traditions and the Synoptic Gospels: Story Shaping Story.* Peabody, MA: Hendrickson, 1994.

*Tyson, J. B., ed. *Luke-Acts and the Jewish People: Eight Critical Perspectives.* Minneapolis: Augsburg, 1988.

Wilson, Stephen G. *Related Strangers: Jews and Christians 70–170 CE.* Minneapolis: Fortress, 1995.

Wright, N. T. *The New Testament and the People of God.* Minneapolis: Fortress, 1992.

See also For Further Study § 3.

HOMILETICAL SUGGESTIONS

Believers as the People of God (2:9–10)

1. Election (v. 9a)
2. Royal priesthood (v. 9a)
3. Holy (v. 9a)
4. God's possession (v. 9a)
5. Moved from darkness to light (v. 9b)
6. Proclaiming the mighty deeds of God (v. 9b)
7. Recipients of God's mercy (v. 10)

V. Obligations of the People of God (2:11–3:12)

A. LIVING AS ALIENS AND STRANGERS (2:11–12)

STRUCTURE

Παρακαλῶ goes with the complementary inf. ἀπέχεσθαι to give an exhortation ("I urge you to abstain from fleshly desires") that governs not only these introductory vv. but the entire Household Code that follows, and indeed the entire ethics of the epistle. The ὡς clause appeals to the recipients' identity as sojourners, whereas the rel. clause headed by αἵτινες stresses the destructive nature of the fleshly desires.

11 ἀγαπητοί,
   παρακαλῶ (ὑμᾶς) ὡς παροίκους καὶ παρεπιδήμους
      ἀπέχεσθαι τῶν σαρκικῶν ἐπιθυμιῶν
          αἵτινες στρατεύονται
            κατὰ τῆς ψυχῆς·

The ptc. ἔχοντες introduces the positive counterpart to the neg. exhortation in the previous v., whereas the ἵνα clause provides the purpose of this positive behavior. It will be argued below that the ptc. clause ἐκ τῶν καλῶν ἔργων ἐποπτεύοντες is dependent upon δοξάσωσιν, thus providing the basis for pagans to glorify God on the day of visitation.

12   τὴν ἀναστροφὴν ὑμῶν
      ἐν τοῖς ἔθνεσιν
  ἔχοντες κ̲α̲λ̲ή̲ν̲,
    ἵνα,   ἐν ᾧ καταλαλοῦσιν ὑμῶν ὡς κακοποιῶν
         ἐκ τῶν κ̲α̲λ̲ῶ̲ν̲ ἔργων
      ἐποπτεύοντες
      δοξάσωσιν τὸν θεὸν
        ἐν ἡμέρᾳ ἐπισκοπῆς.

VERSE 11

ἀγαπητοί, παρακαλῶ ὡς παροίκους καὶ παρεπιδήμους

Again ὡς introduces more than a simile. Believers are aliens and strangers—"the sociological expression of the eschatological nature of their existence" (Goppelt 153; cf. Dubis 60). Πάροικος, -ου, ὁ, "alien," "stranger" (BDAG 779d); see the discussion on the cognate noun παροικία in 1:17. Παρεπίδημος, -ου, ὁ, "temporary resident," "refugee," "sojourner" (BDAG 775d; W. Grundmann, *TDNT* 2.64–65; H. Bietenhard, *NIDNTT* 1.690). The term indicates temporary residency (see 1:1) and here functions as a synonym with παροίκους in a hendiadys ("temporary residents and foreigners," NLT; "sojourners and exiles," ESV; cf. LXX Gen 23:4; Ps 38:13; Eph 2:19; Heb 11:13). Both nouns are in appos. to an implied ὑμᾶς as the obj. of παρακαλῶ (BDF §407; ZG 707; Dubis 60; see R 393–394 on absent pred.).

Elliott's insistence (457–62) that the distinct nuances of the terms be brought out in tr. is unnecessary because it wrongly assumes that Peter is addressing people who had such status *prior* to conversion. More correctly Achtemeier (175 n. 35): "God took people who *were* at home and turned them into aliens and exiles . . . it is the change in status from people once at home in their culture to people now homeless in that same culture, and the issuing problems, that prompted the writing of this letter" (emphasis original).

ἀπέχεσθαι τῶν σαρκικῶν ἐπιθυμιῶν

Ἀπέχεσθαι pres. mid. inf. ἀπέχω, "receive in full"; (intrans.) "be distant" (mid. with gen., see R 517–18); "abstain from," indicating a total abstinence (BDAG 103a; H. Hanse, *TDNT* 2:828). The complementary infin. is here used with indir. discourse after a vb. of communication (παρακαλῶ; Wallace 603).

Instead of the pres. inf. (א B Ψ 049 1739 *Byz*), the pres. impv. ἀπέχεσθε is read by 𝔓[72] A C L P and some minuscules. The ms. evidence is fairly evenly weighted, but given the impvs. in the surrounding context, the inf. is probably the harder rdg. and should be preferred.

The adj. σαρκινός, -ή, -όν (BDAG 914b–c; A. C. Thiselton, *NIDNTT* 1.671–82) here refers to that which is characteristic of fallen humanity ("sinful desires," NIV; "disordered natural inclinations," NJB), not in the narrow sense of sexual sin. On ἐπιθυμία, see 1:14.

αἵτινες στρατεύονται κατὰ τῆς ψυχῆς

The rel. αἵτινες (indistinguishable from ὅς here; see Moulton 91) virtually has causal force (R 728; Achtemeier 176 n. 50), "abstain from fleshly desires because they make war against life" (sim. Weymouth).

Στρατεύονται 3 pl. pres. mid. indic. στρατεύομαι, "engage in warfare" (BDAG 947d; C. Brown, *NIDNTT* 3.958–67; O. Bauernfeind, *TDNT* 7.701–13). The image is of fallen human desire in armed conflict against true life with God (cf. Rom 7:23; Jas 4:1).

On ψυχή, see 1:9, noting particularly that it is the ψυχή that attains salvation. The rendering here, "life," avoids the misconception of a body-soul dualism and emphasizes the destructive nature of unbridled desire on the human being as a living person under God (Elliott 465; Dubis 60–61; Moule 185).

VERSE 12

τὴν ἀναστροφὴν ὑμῶν ἐν τοῖς ἔθνεσιν ἔχοντες καλήν

Ἀναστροφή, -ῆς, ἡ, "conduct" (see on 1:15, 17). Καλήν is pred. with τὴν ἀναστροφήν (R 789; Wallace 308): "keep your behavior excellent" (NASB), "keep your conduct honorable" (ESV).

Ἐν τοῖς ἔθνεσιν is an intriguing statement, given that the audience of this epistle consisted primarily of Gentiles. The point is that Peter no longer sees his Gentile readers as the pagans they once were (1:14, 18; 4:2–4) but as incorporated into the very people of God and thus part of his house (2:4–10). Paul's letter to the Ephesians includes a similar discussion (cf. Ephesians 2).

The ptc. ἔχοντες is attendant circumstance and serves as a positive counterpart to the neg. exhortation to abstain from carnal desires in the previous v. Thus, by association, it carries hortatory force (most EVV; ZG 707; Z §373; Dubis 61; Jobes 173; Elliott 465; Michaels 117; see the discussion on "Imperatival Participles in 1 Peter" in the Introduction). The present v. is an example of anacoluthon, where there is lack of agreement with (ὑμᾶς) ὡς παροίκους καὶ παρεπιδήμους to which it obviously relates (see R 439, 1134).

ἵνα ἐν ᾧ καταλαλοῦσιν ὑμῶν ὡς κακοποιῶν

Ἵνα with the subjunc. δοξάσωσιν (see below) expresses the purpose of maintaining this good conduct. Ἐν ᾧ is equivalent to the Eng. "in the situation that" (BDF §294 [4]; ZG 707; Dubis 62; Michaels 117; Elliott 467) and implies ἐν τούτῳ (R 721). Καταλαλοῦσιν 3 pl. pres. act. indic. of καταλαλέω, "slander" (W. Mundle, *NIDNTT* 3.345–46). The subj. of the vb. is the pagans of the previous clause and the vb. καταλαλέω takes the gen. of the person or thing spoken against or slandered (BDAG 519c). Κακοποιός, -οῦ, ὁ, "evildoer," "criminal" (BDAG 501a), in appos. to ὑμῶν, giving the content of the slander: "speak against you as evildoers" (ESV).

ἐκ τῶν καλῶν ἔργων ἐποπτεύοντες

Ἐκ τῶν καλῶν ἔργων is a partitive gen. (i.e., an assortment of your good works), which functions as the obj. of the ptc. (BDF §164[2]; Achtemeier 178). Ἐποπτεύοντες nom. pl. masc. of pres. act. ptc. of ἐποπτεύω, "observe" (BDAG 387d). This ptc. clause could modify either:

  *1. the subjunc. δοξάσωσιν: the pagans will glorify God because/when they observe the good deeds of his people (EVV); or
  2. καταλαλοῦσιν: the pagans slander believers when they see their good deeds.

The problem with the latter is that it leaves no basis for the pagans to glorify God at all. Note also the echo of Matt 5:16: "let your light shine before others so that when they see your good deeds they may glorify your father in heaven" (Dubis 63). The ptc. can be cstr. as either temporal ("when they see your good deeds") or causal ("because they see your good deeds").

δοξάσωσιν τὸν θεὸν ἐν ἡμέρᾳ ἐπισκοπῆς

Regarding δοξάσωσιν, see comments on the ἵνα clause above. Ἐπισκοπή, -ῆς, ἡ, refers to a visitation (BDAG 379b; L. Coenen, *NIDNTT* 1.188–92; H. W. Beyer *TDNT* 2.606–8) and has a technical sense in BGk. of a display of God's power in either a positive sense (Gen 50:24; Exod 3:16; Luke 19:44) or in a neg. sense conveying judgment (Isa 10:3; Jer 10:15; LN 34.51). Here in 1 Peter it is synonymous with the day of the revelation of Jesus (1:5, 7, 13; 4:13; Michaels 119–20; Goppelt 160) and indicates at least the possibility of the conversion of unbelievers due to the observation of good conduct of Christians. This results in them glorifying God on the day of judgment (Beale and Carson 1033) because they are now part of the company of God's people. The gen. is attrib./descriptive (R 497; Wallace 81).

This v. lends expression to the concept of mission as presence undergirding verbal proclamation in 1 Peter. Outsiders are won to God by distinctive participation of Christians in the world in conjunction with a verbal response (2:9; 3:15; see Köstenberger and O'Brien, *Salvation* 237–43).

FOR FURTHER STUDY

28. Mission in 1 Peter

Green, Joel B. *1 Peter*. Grand Rapids: Eerdmans, 2007. See pages 191–97, 279–88.
*Köstenberger, Andreas J., and Peter T. O'Brien. *Salvation to the Ends of the Earth: A Biblical Theology of Mission*. NSBT 11. Downers Grove: InterVarsity, 2001. See pages 237–43.
Robinson, P. J. "Some Missiological Perspectives from 1 Peter 2:4–10." *Missionalia* 17 (1989): 176–87.

See also For Further Study §§ 4, 14, 17, 19, 20.

HOMILETICAL SUGGESTIONS

Living as Aliens and Strangers (2:11–12)

1. Christians are an estranged people (v. 11a)
2. Appropriate conduct for an estranged people (vv. 11b–12)
   (a) Avoid sinful desires (v. 11b)
   (b) The internal war (v. 11b)
   (c) Maintain good conduct in the midst of ridicule (v. 12a)
   (d) Good conduct may win non-Christians to faith (v. 12b)

B. DUTY TO THE GOVERNING AUTHORITIES (2:13–17)

This section begins what is termed the *Household Code* or *Domestic Code*, often called by the German term *Haustafel* (pl. *Haustafeln*). This was a social code prominent in the Greco-Roman world that prescribed appropriate conduct within the household and with respect to one's duty to the city or state. The focus on the household derives from the recognition that the household was a microcosm of society, and if relationships functioned well at the household level, then this argued well for a stable and functioning society.

The *Haustafel*, or aspects of it, appear in several places in the NT (Rom 13:1; Eph 5:21–6:9; Col 3:18–4:1; Titus 3:1–2). However, both Peter and Paul provide a distinctive Christian adaptation of the code. Peter, in particular, utilizes the code to encourage and exhort his readers to a distinctive presence as God's people in the midst of a pagan, and often hostile, society.

See below For Further Study § 29.

STRUCTURE

The opening impv. ὑποτάγητε controls the entire Household Code until 3:17, but more immediately forms the basis for the injunctions of vv. 13–16. Two examples of submission to the secular authorities are given in vv. 13–14, with v. 15 utilizing a ὅτι clause to emphasize the will of God in such submission. Verse 16 is elliptical and the syntax disputed, but it is argued below that the impv. ὑποτάγητε from v. 13 controls this cstr. The section concludes in v. 17 with four short maxims again utilizing the impv., with the vb. τιμάω bracketing this final v.

13 Ὑποτάγητε πάσῃ ἀνθρωπίνῃ κτίσει διὰ τὸν κύριον,
         εἴτε βασιλεῖ ὡς ὑπερέχοντι
14   εἴτε ἡγεμόσιν ὡς δι᾽ αὐτοῦ πεμπομένοις
                   εἰς ἐκδίκησιν κακοποιῶν,
                   ἔπαινον δὲ ἀγαθοποιῶν.

15   ὅτι οὕτως ἐστὶν τὸ θέλημα τοῦ θεοῦ
                   ἀγαθοποιοῦντας φιμοῦν τὴν τῶν ἀφρόνων ἀνθρώπων ἀγνωσίαν,

16   ὡς ἐλεύθεροι
         καὶ μὴ ὡς ἐπικάλυμμα ἔχοντες τῆς κακίας τὴν ἐλευθερίαν
         ἀλλ᾽ ὡς θεοῦ δοῦλοι.

17   πάντας   τιμήσατε,
      τὴν ἀδελφότητα   ἀγαπᾶτε
      τὸν θεὸν   φοβεῖσθε,
      τὸν βασιλέα   τιμᾶτε.

VERSE 13a

Ὑποτάγητε πάσῃ ἀνθρωπίνῃ κτίσει

Ὑποτάγητε 2 pl. aor. pass. impv. of ὑποτάσσω, "submit," "subject" (BDAG 1042a; G. Delling, *TDNT* 8.39–46). This impv. governs the ptc. forms that follow in the Household Code (2:18; 3:1; see discussion on "The Imperatival Participle in 1 Peter" in the Introduction). In line with the root –τάσσω, the vb. has to do with order. In the Greco-Roman world this meant to recognize one's appropriate station in life and fulfill it accordingly (see Elliott 486–88).

Πᾶς without the art. means "every" (R 771–771). Ἀνθρώπινος, -η, -ον, relating to a person, "human" (BDAG 80d; *NewDocs* 4.86). Κτίσις, -εως, ἡ, "act of creation," "creature" (BDAG 572d–573b; W. Foerster, *TDNT* 3.1025–35; H. H. Esser, *NIDNTT* 1.378–87). In secular Gk. literature the noun κτίσις was used of a city founded by men (Strabo, *Geogr.* 12.4.8), but not for an abstract institution. In the NT it is used of God's act of creation (Rom 1:20), or what is created (Rom 8:19; 2 Cor 5:17; Heb 4:13).

The phrase πάσῃ ἀνθρωπίνῃ κτίσει is unparalleled in either BGk. or non-BGk. It is invariably tr. in either:

*1. an institutional sense: "to every human institution" (NRSV, NASB, ESV; Jobes 116). This can be further distinguished as an institution created by human beings (Weymouth; BDAG 80d; Beare 141; Selwyn 172) or an institution created by God for the benefit of humans (Best 113); or

2. a personal sense: "to every human creature" (R 772; Achtemeier 182; Michaels 124; Elliott 489; Goppelt 183).

The personal sense of "creature" forms an *inclusio* with 2:17 (note Paul's similar generic command "be subject to one another" in Eph 5:21 in introducing the Household Code) and subtly desacralizes imperial power by placing it squarely under the umbrella of the creature (Elliott 489; Goppelt 184–85). Nevertheless, the two examples that follow, the emperor and his governors, indicate that an institutional sense is to be preferred in this instance.

διὰ τὸν κύριον

This causal prep. phrase provides the ultimate rationale for subjection. It is not merely because of the demands or expectations of society, but "because of the Lord," "for the Lord's sake" (most EVV). In view of 1:3, 25; 2:3–4; 3:15 the "Lord" could be Jesus, but the focus in this section is theocentric. The expression can be understood in several ways incl.: fearing God (2:17), providing an example that has a positive effect on unbelievers (2:12), silencing foolish people (2:15), or doing what the Lord wants (CEV), but ultimately it is one important example of proper conduct in society that Peter wants his readers to realize that God highly values. If Jesus is the intended referent, then following his example may well be in mind (2:21–23).

VERSES 13b–14

εἴτε βασιλεῖ ὡς ὑπερέχοντι

The εἴτε . . . εἴτε cstr. is used to introduce two examples of those to whom subjection is due. The dat. noun βασιλεῖ and ptc. ὑπερέχοντι are in appos. to πάσῃ ἀνθρωπίνῃ κτίσει. Whether from Peter's context in Rome or that of the recipients in Asia Minor, βασιλεύς could only refer to the emperor (CEV, HCSB, ESV, NIV). Ὡς is best taken as appos., further describing the status or the role of those mentioned (Achtemeier 183 n. 49; Dubis 65; Michaels 126 takes it as causal, i.e., submit to the king because he has authority). Ὑπερέχοντι dat. sg. masc. of. pres. act. ptc. of ὑπερέχω, "surpass in extent/power/value" (BDAG 1033b). Here with βασιλεῖ it has the sense of surpassing in authority ("head of state," NLT).

εἴτε ἡγεμόσιν ὡς δι' αὐτοῦ πεμπομένοις

Ἡγεμών, -όνος, ὁ, can refer to a ruler or leader in a general sense, but in this period could relate more technically, as here, to provincial governors ("governors," most EVV) who had various official titles (BDAG 433d; F. Büchsel, *TDNT* 2.907–8; Elliott 490). Regarding ὡς, see comment on the previous phrase.

Δι' αὐτοῦ πεμπομένοις captures the sense of delegated authority from the emperor, not God (which wrongly reads the passage through the lens of Rom 13:1–7), with the prep. used of agency (BDAG 225a; Z §113; T 267).

εἰς ἐκδίκησιν κακοποιῶν

The prep. εἰς is telic (Harris 88–90), indicating the function of the office of ἡγεμών. Ἐκδίκησις, -εως, ἡ, "justice," "punishment" (BDAG 301a; U. Falkenroth, *NIDNTT* 3.92–97). The noun refers here to a legal avenging of wrong and the granting of justice. Κακοποιός, -οῦ, ὁ, "evildoer" (BDAG 501a; cf. v. 12 above). Κακοποιῶν is an obj. gen. signifying those who receive such punishment.

ἔπαινον δὲ ἀγαθοποιῶν

Ἔπαινος, -ου, ὁ, "praise," "commendation" (BDAG 357b). Ἀγαθοποιός, -οῦ, ὁ, one who does what is right or good (BDAG 3b). This positive counterpart to ἐκδίκησιν κακοποιῶν can be understood in several ways:

1. ἔπαινος refers to public acknowledgement, while the obj. gen. ἀγαθοποιῶν applies to those who engage in acts of public benefaction (Davids 100; *NewDocs* 7.233–41);
2. ἔπαινος should be taken in the sense of offering legal protection or acquittal through the court system for those who do good (Goppelt 186; Achtemeier 184; Michaels 126; Best 114); or
*3. ἔπαινος is taken in the general sense of appreciation, with ἀγαθοποιῶν relating to those who conduct themselves appropriately in society.

Against option 1, while this activity does suit the role of provincial governors, it bears little relationship to the context of Peter's readers who are neither exhorted to engage in such acts nor were probably in a position to do so (Elliott 491). Against option 2, arguably the author would have chosen other terms to convey this idea more clearly. Against option 3, this is hardly the task of provincial governors! Nevertheless, the Gk. philosophers did regard the punishment of wrong and praise of the upright as the role of the guardians of the law (see Elliott 492 for refs.). This is probably the preferred option, as Peter's statement undoubtedly performs an important rhetorical function in undergirding the encouragement to "do good"—noting that this is a key Petrine term (see the following v., also 2:12, 20; 3:6, 17; 4:19).

The author is proposing that living as a Christian does not necessarily entail disobedience toward the state (cf. Rom 13:1–7). This positive view of the governing authorities would seem to imply that the persecution and suffering depicted in this epistle do not stem from the state as such. Peter is well aware that Christians may suffer for doing what is right (3:14; 4:15–19), but additional woe should not be brought upon oneself by acting lawlessly.

VERSE 15

ὅτι οὕτως ἐστὶν τὸ θέλημα τοῦ θεοῦ

In a logical sense, ὅτι οὕτως, "because thus," is linked with the preceding (submission to the state is God's will), for submission to the state provides the immediate content for "doing good" in the clause that follows (Dubis 67, who strangely argues that ὅτι is retrospective and οὕτως is prospective). Nevertheless, it is not clear that it should be so linked grammatically. That it should be is supported by the fact that of the eleven other uses of ὅτι as a causal conj. in this epistle, ten give the reason for a prior statement (the usage in 3:9 is ambiguous, as here). In addition, οὕτως (adv. functioning as a pred. adj.; BDF §434; T 226; Dubis 67), is retrospective also in 3:5, the only other usage in 1 Peter.

However, a retrospective interpretation of ὅτι οὕτως leaves the following ptc. clause ἀγαθοποιοῦντας φιμοῦν τὴν τῶν ἀφρόνων ἀνθρώπων ἀγνωσίαν without grammatical connection. Achtemeier (179, 185), who supports a retrospective interpretation, ends up translating it with ref. to the ptc. clause. In the end, it is more satisfactory to link ὅτι οὕτως with what follows (EVV; Michaels 127; Goppelt 186 n. 37). For prospective uses of οὕτως in the NT, see BDAG 742b; BDF §434.

ἀγαθοποιοῦντας φιμοῦν τὴν τῶν ἀφρόνων ἀνθρώπων ἀγνωσίαν

Ἀγαθοποιοῦντας acc. pl. masc. of pres. act. ptc. of ἀγαθοποιέω, "do good," "do right" (BDAG 3a). Φιμοῦν pres. act. inf. φιμόω, "silence," "muzzle" (BDAG 1060b). Ἄφρων, -ον, -ονος, "foolish," "ignorant" (BDAG 159b; J. Goetzmann, NIDNTT 3.1023–26). Ἀγνωσία, -ας, ἡ, "ignorance" (BDAG 14a; E. Schütz, NIDNTT 2.406–09; R. Bultmann, TDNT 1.116–19).

The ptc. ἀγαθοποιοῦντας is instr. showing the means by which the ignorance of fool-ish people is to be silenced. Ἀγαθοποι- roots occur more times in this epistle than in the rest of the NT and form an integral part of Petrine ethics. The inf. φιμοῦν is epex. giving the content of God's will (R 1078). The implied subj. (acc. of respect) of the inf. is ὑμᾶς, thus explaining the acc. case of the ptc. (see T 148).

Note the literary effect of alliteration achieved by the series of words beginning with alpha (ἀφρόνων ἀνθρώπων ἀγνωσίαν). The noun ἀγνωσία refers to religious ignorance or lack of spiritual discernment (cf. 1 Cor 15:34), whereas the cognate noun ἄγνοια (1:14) more generally refers to a mere lack of information (BDAG 13b, 14a). It is the presence here of the adj. ἀφρόνων that confirms the ignorance as culpable.

VERSE 16

ὡς ἐλεύθεροι

Ὡς does not introduce a metaphor but states a characteristic quality (BDAG 1014d–1105a)—the reality in which believers must live. Ἐλεύθερος, -έρα, -ον, "free" (BDAG 316d–317a). The connection with the surrounding material is debated:

  *1. it qualifies the initial imperative ὑποτάγητε, "be subject," in v. 13, i.e., "be subject as free people" (Moffatt; Selwyn 173–74; Goppelt 188; Achtemeier 186; Dubis 68);
  2. it belongs with v. 15 emphasizing the manner in which "doing good" must occur (ASV, NKJV; Elliott 496);
  3. it qualifies what follows in v. 17, i.e., "as free people honor all" (Michaels 128); or
  4. it is an ellipsis, an independent statement with an implied impv. "live" (Weymouth, NRSV, NASB, HCSB, NIV; Kelly 107, 111).

In considering the options, 1 is grammatically possible, but the antecedent is quite distant. Option 2 should probably be ruled out on the basis that this v. is constructed in the nom., whereas one would expect it to be in the acc. if it were qualifying the ptc. in v. 15. Option 3 is possible, but the maxims in v. 17 have more force if read in isolation rather than having a lengthy modifying clause preceding. Option 4 is the one taken by most modern EVV, probably due to the simplicity of tr., but it does disconnect this v. from the surrounding exhortations. On the whole, options 1 or 3 are to be preferred, with a slight leaning toward 1.

καὶ μὴ ὡς ἐπικάλυμμα ἔχοντες τῆς κακίας τὴν ἐλευθερίαν

Ὡς is redundant in this clause and is probably included for symmetry with the pre-ceding and following phrases ὡς ἐλεύθεροι and ἀλλ' ὡς θεοῦ δοῦλοι (Michaels 129; R 127 notes that the usage of ὡς in this v. is "refined"). Ἐπικάλυμμα, -ατος, τό, "cover," "veil" (BDAG 373c; LSJ 636a), here used metaphorically of a "pretext" (NRSV; LN 28.56) or "excuse" (CEV, NLT) before the fact, not a cover-up (ESV, NIV) after it (Michaels 129). Elliott (496) suggests the colloquial rendering of "smokescreen." In appos. to τὴν ἐλευθερίαν.

Κακία, -ας, ἡ, "wickedness" (BDAG 500b). Τῆς κακίας is an obj. gen.—wickedness is what is excused. Ἐλευθερία, -ας, ἡ, "freedom" (BDAG 316c; Turner, *Words* 256–57). The syntax is slightly awkward. Τὴν ἐλευθερίαν is the direct obj. of the ptc. ἔχοντες which in turn carries impv. force by its dependency upon either the impv. τιμήσατε (v. 17) or ὑποτάγητε (v. 13; as argued above). See the discussion on "Imperatival Participles in 1 Peter" in the Introduction.

ἀλλ' ὡς θεοῦ δοῦλοι

Ἀλλ' ὡς is the positive counterpoint to μὴ ὡς. Δοῦλοι is best rendered here as "slaves" (HCSB, NJB, NLT, NIV) in order to highlight the paradox. The slave imagery is consistent with the idea of redemption already introduced in 1:18–19, for redemption involves the payment of a price and a transfer of ownership. Christians are thus freed to be slaves of God (cf. Gal 5:1, 13; 1 Cor 7:22; Rom 6:22), a freedom (and a slavery) that requires a choice to consistently do what is right.

VERSE 17

πάντας τιμήσατε

Τιμήσατε 2 pl. aor. act. impv. of τιμάω, "honor" (BDAG 1004d). Three factors make it necessary to explain this opening aor. impv.: (1) the following three impvs. in this v. are in the pres. tense (hence Michaels 130, insists that the pres. impvs. need explaining); (2) the other eight uses of τιμάω as an impv. in the NT all appear in the pres.; (3) the four injunctions in this v. are clearly not specific commands but general precepts for which the pres. impv. is the default tense (Fanning 325–88; see also "The Use of the Imperative in 1 Peter" in the Introduction).

The aor. is hardly ingressive denoting entry into a state or condition (so Selwyn 174, who takes it to refer to the moment of decision in the mind of the believer; for the ingressive aor., see Wallace 558–59). The gnomic aor. (see Wallace 562) is also problematic (*pace* Elliott 497), as if this is a "universally expected mode of behavior" in contrast to the other three impvs. Nor can it have the sense, over and above the following present impvs., "to begin and continue doing" (Michaels 130). The idea that the aor. impv. functions as a summary of the following three impvs. (Porter 54; McKay 80) runs aground the fact that "fearing God" is not really related to "honoring all people" (as noted by Achtemeier 187). Given that πάντας is a universal dir. obj. and picks up the opening impv. (ὑποτάγητε πάσῃ) of this section (v. 13), it is possible that the aor. impv. here was attracted to the aor. impv. there (Achtemeier 187–88).

τὴν ἀδελφότητα ἀγαπᾶτε

Ἀδελφότης, -ητος, ἡ, "brotherhood," "community of believers" (cf. 5:9; BDAG 19a; Turner, *Words* 56–57; BDF §110[1] on form), is a synonym for φιλαδελφία (1:22; cf. φιλάδελφος in 3:8) and refers to the Christian community, "family of believers" (NIV). "This collective noun depicts the believers as a surrogate kinship group whose members are committed to one another as are blood brothers and sisters" (Elliott 499). For the necessity of love toward fellow believers, see note on 1:22.

Probably in conformity with the previous aor. impv. (or possibly ἀγαπήσατε in 1:22), the aor. impv. ἀγαπήσατε is found in K L 049 *Byz*. The pres. impv. should stand as the correct rdg.

τὸν θεὸν φοβεῖσθε

Many have correctly noted that "fear" is a stronger term than "honor," with the implication that duty toward God (as slaves; v. 16) takes precedence over duty towards the emperor (Achtemeier 188). If Prov 24:21 provides the background for Peter's thought here, then the change from "fear the Lord and the king" is most instructive.

Δέ is inserted between the art. and θεόν by 𝔓⁷², thereby destroying the symmetry of the four maxims (as noted by Achtemeier 179).

τὸν βασιλέα τιμᾶτε

The final impv. forms a chiasm within this v. and an *inclusio* with 2:13. The outer points of the chiasm deal with relationships outside the believing community, whereas the inner two focus on relationships within. This v. also creates a hierarchy of relationships. All fellow human beings, foremost the emperor, are to be honored; fellow believers are to be loved; but God alone is to be feared.

FOR FURTHER STUDY

29. Household Codes (Haustafeln) (2:13–3:7)

Achtemeier 52–57.

Balch, David L. *Let Wives Be Submissive: The Domestic Code in 1 Peter*. Chico, CA: Scholars Press, 1981.

_____. "Household Codes." Pages 25–50 in *Greco-Roman Literature and the New Testament: Selected Forms and Genres*. Edited by D. E. Aune. Atlanta: Scholars Press, 1988.

Bauman-Martin, Betsy J. "Women on the Edge: New Perspectives on Women in the Petrine *Haustafel*." *JBL* 123 (2004): 253–79.

Elliott, John H. *A Home for the Homeless: A Sociological Exegesis of 1 Peter, Its Situation and Strategy*. Philadelphia: Fortress, 1981.

_____. "1 Peter, Its Situation and Strategy: A Discussion with David Balch." Pages 61–78 in *Perspectives on First Peter*. Edited by C. H. Talbert. Macon, GA: Mercer, 1986.

Hartman, Lars. "Some Unorthodox Thoughts on the 'Household-Code Form.'" Pages 219–34 in *The Social World of Formative Christianity and Judaism*. Edited by J. Neusner et al. Philadelphia: Fortress, 1988.

Hering, James P. *The Colossian and Ephesian Haustafeln in Theological Context: An Analysis of Their Origins, Relationship, and Message*. New York: Peter Lang, 2007.

Horrell, David G. "Between Conformity and Resistance: Beyond the Balch-Elliott Debate Towards a Postcolonial Reading of First Peter." Pages 111–43 in *Reading First Peter with New Eyes: Methodological Reassessments of the Letter of First Peter*. Edited by R. L. Webb and B. Bauman-Martin. London: T & T Clark, 2007.

Jeffers, James S. *Conflict at Rome: Social Order and Hierarchy in Early Christianity.*
    Minneapolis: Fortress, 1991.
Llewelyn, Stephen R. *NewDocs* 6.18–19, 48–55; 7.163–96.
Lohse, Eduard. "Parenesis and Kerygma in 1 Peter." Pages 37–59 in *Perspectives on First
    Peter.* Edited by C. H. Talbert. Macon, GA: Mercer, 1986.
Martin, Ralph P. *NIDNTT* 3.928–32.
Stambaugh, J. E., and David L. Balch. *The New Testament in Its Social Environment.*
    Philadelphia: Fortress, 1986.
Towner, Philip H. *DLNT* 513–20.

30. Christian Responsibility to the State (2:13–17)

Beckwith, Francis J. *Politics for Christians.* Downers Grove: InterVarsity, 2010.
Carson, Herbert. *Render Unto Caesar: The Christian and the State.* Eastbourne: Monarch,
    1989.
Cromartie, Michael, ed. *Caesar's Coin Revisited: Christians and the Limits of
    Government.* Grand Rapids: Eerdmans, 1996.
Kemeny, Paul C., ed. *Church, State and Public Justice: Five Views.* Downers Grove:
    InterVarsity, 2007.
Molnar, Thomas. *Twin Powers: Politics and the Sacred.* Grand Rapids: Eerdmans, 1988.
Mott, Stephen C. *A Christian Perspective on Political Thought.* Oxford: Oxford University
    Press, 1993.
Mouw, Richard J. *Politics and the Biblical Drama.* Grand Rapids: Eerdmans, 1976.
O'Donovan, Oliver. *The Desire of the Nations: Rediscovering the Roots of Political
    Theology.* Cambridge: Cambridge University Press, 1996.
Pasewark, K. A., and G. E. Paul. *The Emphatic Christian Center: Reforming Christian
    Political Debate.* Nashville: Abingdon, 1999.
Wogaman, J. Philip. *Christian Perspectives on Politics.* Revised and Expanded. Louisville:
    Westminster John Knox, 2000.
Winter, Bruce. "Seek the Welfare of the City: Social Ethics According to 1 Peter." *Them* 13
    (1988): 91–94.

HOMILETICAL SUGGESTIONS

Duty to the Governing Authorities (2:13–17)

1. Christians are to submit to the governing authorities (vv. 13–14a)
2. The role of government: punishment and commendation (v. 14b)
3. Christians must engage in appropriate behavior (vv. 15–17)
    (a) it is the will of God (v. 15)
    (b) it exposes pagan ignorance (v. 15)
    (c) Christian freedom must be used appropriately (v. 16a)
    (d) Christians are slaves of God (v. 16b)
    (e) summarizing maxims (v. 17)
        (i) honor everyone
        (ii) love the family of believers
        (iii) fear God
        (iv) honor the emperor

C. DUTY OF SLAVES: THE EXAMPLE OF CHRIST'S SUFFERING
(2:18–25)

STRUCTURE

The impv. ptc. ὑποτασσόμενοι is strictly dependent upon ὑποτάγητε in v. 13, but here introduces a new section of the Household Code dealing with the attitude of slaves to masters. The opening v. states the basic position of submission, then elaborates on this with the οὐ μόνον ("not only") and ἀλλὰ καί ("but also") phrases.

18 οἱ οἰκέται ὑποτασσόμενοι ἐν παντὶ φόβῳ τοῖς δεσπόταις,
           οὐ μόνον τοῖς ἀγαθοῖς καὶ ἐπιεικέσιν
           ἀλλὰ καὶ τοῖς σκολιοῖς.

Verses 19–21 form a chiastic arrangement, stressing that appropriate behavior under duress finds favor with God.

19 τοῦτο γὰρ χάρις,
           εἰ διὰ συνείδησιν θεοῦ ὑποφέρει τις λύπας πάσχων ἀδίκως.

20 ποῖον γὰρ κλέος
           εἰ ἁμαρτάνοντες καὶ κολαφιζόμενοι ὑπομενεῖτε;
           ἀλλ’ εἰ ἀγαθοποιοῦντες καὶ πάσχοντες ὑπομενεῖτε,
     τοῦτο χάρις παρὰ θεῷ.

Verse 21 marks the transition from the slave-master relationship to focus on the suffering of Christ as an example. Initially Christ's suffering functions as a model for slaves who are treated unjustly, but the discussion moves into broader territory and becomes soteriological in nature. Grammatically, this is accomplished by means of four rel. clauses (ὅς . . . ὅς . . . ὅς . . . οὗ). The first two clauses focus on Christ's non-retaliatory response under duress, whereas the latter two clauses concentrate on his saving work.

21 εἰς τοῦτο γὰρ ἐκλήθητε,
           ὅτι καὶ Χριστὸς ἔπαθεν ὑπὲρ ὑμῶν
                   ὑμῖν ὑπολιμπάνων ὑπογραμμόν,
                          ἵνα ἐπακολουθήσητε τοῖς ἴχνεσιν αὐτοῦ,
22 ὃς ἁμαρτίαν οὐκ ἐποίησεν
           οὐδὲ εὑρέθη δόλος ἐν τῷ στόματι αὐτοῦ,
23 ὃς λοιδορούμενος οὐκ ἀντελοιδόρει,
     πάσχων   οὐκ ἠπείλει,
                 παρεδίδου δὲ τῷ κρίνοντι δικαίως·
24 ὃς τὰς ἁμαρτίας ἡμῶν αὐτὸς ἀνήνεγκεν ἐν τῷ σώματι αὐτοῦ ἐπὶ τὸ ξύλον,
           ἵνα ταῖς ἁμαρτίαις ἀπογενόμενοι τῇ δικαιοσύνῃ ζήσωμεν,
     οὗ τῷ μώλωπι ἰάθητε.

The section concludes with contrast between the past life of believers (ἦτε γάρ, "for you were") and new circumstances (ἀλλὰ νῦν, "but now"), utilizing shepherd/sheep imagery.

25 ἦτε γὰρ ὡς πρόβατα πλανώμενοι,
    ἀλλ' ἐπεστράφητε νῦν
        ἐπὶ τὸν ποιμένα
        καὶ ἐπίσκοπον
            τῶν ψυχῶν ὑμῶν.

VERSE 18

οἱ οἰκέται ὑποτασσόμενοι ἐν παντὶ φόβῳ τοῖς δεσπόταις

Οἰκέτης, -ου, ὁ, "servant," "slave" (BDAG 694c), denotes a household servant, many of whom were well educated and held positions of responsibility in the household. Here the pl. with the art. is used as a voc., as in 3:1, 7 (Z §34; BDF §147[3]; R 264; Moule 117), as Peter characteristically addresses his readers rather than speaking indirectly of classes of people (Jobes 184–85; Goppelt 194 n. 14; Michaels 137).

Ὑποτασσόμενοι is the first of the true impv. ptcs. in 1 Peter (see the discussion on "Imperatival Participles in 1 Peter" in the Introduction), although it can be considered to come technically under the rubric of the aor. impv. ὑποτάγητε in 2:13. Slaves being subject to masters is a concrete example of universal subjection. Achtemeier (194) takes ὑποτασσόμενοι as instr. modifying the impvs. of the previous v., but those impvs. function as maxims and clearly not all of them are appropriate (i.e., loving the brotherhood) as the main vb. for this ptc. (see Jobes 200–1).

Ἐν παντὶ φόβῳ is instr. dat. of manner. Given the characteristic use of the noun φόβος in 1 Peter (see on 1:17), it is unlikely that the master is the focus (as NRSV: "with all deference"). Slaves are not to fear their masters so much as to have reverent fear for God in the way they conduct themselves before their masters (so NIV: "in reverent fear of God"). In this sense it picks up the maxim τὸν θεὸν φοβεῖσθε from v. 17 and also parallels διὰ τὸν κύριον (2:13) and συνείδησιν θεοῦ (2:19). Παντί intensifies the attitude.

Δεσπότης, -ου, ὁ, "master" (BDAG 220a; similarly, 1 Tim 6:1-2; Titus 2:9), refers to one who has total authority. Peter has chosen this word rather than κύριος as he reserves the latter term for Christ or God (Achtemeier 195; Michaels 138; Goppelt 194). The term is used with reference to God in 2 Pet 2:1; cf. Luke 2:29; Acts 4:24; 2 Tim 2:21; Jude 4; Rev 6:10.

οὐ μόνον τοῖς ἀγαθοῖς καὶ ἐπιεικέσιν ἀλλὰ καὶ τοῖς σκολιοῖς

The subst. adjs. τοῖς ἀγαθοῖς and τοῖς σκολιοῖς modify τοῖς δεσπόταις. Ἐπιεικής, -ές, "gentle," "considerate" (BDAG 371b; LSJ 632b). Σκολιός, -ά, -όν, "crooked," "twisted" (BDAG 930d; LSJ 1613b; Spicq 1.387–89), in a moral sense one who is perverse or unscrupulous (cf. Acts 2:40; Phil 2:15). In this context, where it is in contrast with "considerate," it has the sense of "harsh" (NRSV, NIV), "cruel" (CEV, NLT, HCSB), "unreasonable" (Weymouth). It is not so much the overall moral integrity of masters that is in view (*pace* Dubis 72), but their disposition toward the slave.

Καί is omitted after ἀλλά by 𝔓⁷² and several minuscules. Although the omission is the harder rdg. (ἀλλὰ καί is expected to follow οὐ μόνον), the scant ms. support makes it difficult to accept it as the orig. rdg. (for an opposing view see Michaels 133).

VERSE 19

τοῦτο γὰρ χάρις

Γάρ is a marker of clarification (BDAG 189d) of the exhortation for slaves to be submissive to even harsh masters. Τοῦτο is neut. nom. expressing abstract notion rather than grammatical agreement (R 704). It looks forward to the following cond. statement for its content, with τοῦτο γὰρ χάρις functioning as the apod. of the cond. (see further below). Χάρις is pred. (R 700). In 1 Peter, χάρις is used rather generally of what God gives, but here it has the sense of divine approval (cf. Luke 6:32–34; BDAG 1079c), a sense made more obvious by the more weakly attested variant rdg. (C Ψ several minuscules and some versions include παρὰ τῷ θεῷ, no doubt by assimilation to the end of v. 20, while a couple of minuscules include either θεῷ or θεοῦ). Χάρις parallels κλέος in the following v.

εἰ διὰ συνείδησιν θεοῦ

The prot. of this first-class condition (see on 1:17; also Porter 254–67) contains a number of grammatical issues. First, the ms. tradition is quite confused, with some mss. (C Ψ several minuscules and some versions) substituting ἀγαθήν for θεοῦ ("good conscience"), whereas 𝔓⁷² and A contain both ἀγαθήν and θεοῦ (though in varying orders). It would appear that θεοῦ was in the orig. text, as it is probably the most difficult rdg., thereby best explaining the others, and also has stronger ms. support in א Aᶜ B *Byz.*

The second issue concerns the mng. of συνείδησιν in this context and the associated force of the gen. θεοῦ. In Gk. literature συνείδησις can have the sense of either "conscience," "awareness," or "conscientiousness" (BDAG 967d–968a; MM 604d; H.-C. Hahn, *NIDNTT* 1.348–51). The expression συνείδησιν θεοῦ itself is unparalleled. While in the NT and religious literature the most common sense of συνείδησις is "conscience" (27/30 uses in the NT), the sense "awareness" or "consciousness" is apparent in 2 Cor 5:11; Heb 10:2. In addition, this latter sense is common in Josephus (*War* 4.193; *Ant.* 16.103) and attested in the papyri (*NewDocs* 3.85). "Awareness" is the appropriate sense here (ZG 708; "aware of God," NRSV; "mindful of God," ESV; "conscious of God," NIV). Up until this point, Peter has been focusing first of all on the graciousness of God in granting new birth, a living hope, redemption, and the privilege of being called his very own people, and second on God's will for appropriate conduct in pagan society. Now he is exhorting his readers to exhibit appropriate behavior based on both of these aspects. So, the focus is not so much on a godly conscience (i.e., a good conscience—with θεοῦ functioning as a descriptive gen., as NKJV, NASB), but on appropriate behavior based on an awareness of all that God has done and all that he requires. This would make θεοῦ an obj. gen. ("conscience toward God").

ὑποφέρει τις λύπας πάσχων ἀδίκως

'Υποφέρει 3 sg. pres. act. indic. of ὑποφέρω, "endure" (BDAG 1042d). This clause is part of the long prot. governed by εἰ, with τοῦτο γὰρ χάρις being the apod. (one receives divine favor when suffering unjustly because of an awareness of God). The indef. pron. τις in effect serves to widen the exhortation beyond slaves (cf. 1:6).

Λύπη, -ης, ἡ, "grief," "affliction" (BDAG 604d–605a; R. Bultmann *TDNT* 4.313–22). The noun is pl. here and points to the many and varied difficulties that Christian slaves may experience ("sorrows," NASB, ESV; "unfair treatment," NLT; "grief," HCSB). It could function as the dir. obj. of either ὑποφέρει ("enduring griefs while suffering unjustly" [Weymouth, NRSV, ESV]) or the ptc. πάσχων ("enduring while suffering griefs unjustly"). Against the latter, in its many other uses in 1 Peter πάσχω does not take a dir. obj. (Michaels 140).

Πάσχων is a temp. ptc. ("while suffering"), and this is the first use of a term that will dominate Peter's vocabulary from here (12/42 NT uses), both with respect to Christ's sufferings and those in store for believers. The adv. ἀδίκως is the key term in the cond. It is not enough to suffer; it must be suffering "unjustly" or suffering for doing right (2:12, 15; 3:13–17; 4:15–16; *NewDocs* 4.83–87) that wins divine approval.

VERSE 20

ποῖον γὰρ κλέος εἰ ἁμαρτάνοντες καὶ κολαφιζόμενοι ὑπομενεῖτε

Γάρ introduces an elaboration of v. 19, first introducing a neg. contrast, then reaffirming v. 19 using a synonymous expression. Ποῖον is qualitative (R 704) and neut. in agreement with κλέος. Κλέος, -ους, τό, "fame," "honor," "credit" (BDAG 547b; LSJ 958a), provides the sense of χάρις in v. 19. The rhetorical question ποῖον γὰρ κλέος, "for what credit," functions as the apod. of the immediately following cond. with the expected answer being, "none."

Εἰ (with fut. indic. is rare; BDF §372 [1]; T 115) introduces the prot., which consists of two temp. ptcs. (ἁμαρτάνοντες καὶ κολαφιζόμενοι) modifying the main vb. ὑπομενεῖτε. Michaels (134) suggests that the use of the pres. ptcs. followed by the fut. indic. is an alternative way of indicating antecedent action (instead of aor. ptcs. followed by a pres. indic.). However, it is not clear whether the desire to use the unfolding aspect of the pres. tense (see Fanning 98–103) or alternatively the desire to indicate that endurance persists into the future (Elliott 522) has driven the form of this cstr. The two ptcs. have a causal relationship between them ("receive a beating for doing wrong," NIV; sim. CEV, NASB; Achtemeier 197 n. 111; Goppelt 199).

Given that ἁμαρτάνοντες contrasts ἀγαθοποιοῦντες in the following clause (see comments below), the focus is probably more on sinning before God rather than doing what is wrong in the eyes of the master, although both senses could be incorporated without any difficulty (Elliott 521). Κολαφιζόμενοι nom. pl. masc. of pres. pass. ptc. of κολαφίζω, "strike with the fist" (BDAG 555c; E. M. Embry, *NIDNTT* 1.161–64), though the lit. sense is too narrow here, functions as a metaphor for suffering in general and is paralleled in the following clause by πάσχοντες. For κολαφιζόμενοι some mss. substitute the more common word κολαζόμενοι, "punish" ($\mathfrak{P}^{72}$ ℵ² P Ψ several minuscules). The text is nonetheless well represented by ℵ* A B C 33 *Byz* and should be retained as the harder rdg.

Ὑπομενεῖτε 2 pl. fut. act. indic. of ὑπομένω, "endure" (BDAG 1039b; Turner, *Words* 318–19). This vb. is a synonym for ὑποφέρει in the previous v. In both instances of the fut. indic. ὑπομενεῖτε in this v., basically the same group of mss. as in the above var. ($\mathfrak{P}^{72}$ ℵ² Ψ and a group of minuscules) read the pres. indic. ὑπομένετε. The fut. indic. is the harder rdg. as it is not as common as the pres. in cond. sentences (see BDF §372 [1]) and has superior ms. support.

ἀλλ᾽ εἰ ἀγαθοποιοῦντες καὶ πάσχοντες ὑπομενεῖτε

The positive contrast is introduced by ἀλλ᾽ εἰ which heads up another cond. statement with two temp. ptcs. (ἀγαθοποιοῦντες καὶ πάσχοντες) and the same main vb. ὑπομενεῖτε as in the previous clause. Ἀγαθοποιοῦντες nom. pl. masc. of pres. act. ptc. of ἀγαθοποιέω, "do good," "do right" (see v. 15). Conformity to the Christian ethical system, rather than doing good in the eyes of the master, is the primary focus. Again, both ptcs. are temp. and have a causal relationship between them (i.e., you suffer because you do what is right).

τοῦτο χάρις παρὰ θεῷ

See on v. 19. This functions as the apod. of the second cond. sentence and places vv. 19–20 into a chiastic pattern. Παρά here expresses viewpoint (BDAG 757b; Harris 171–72). Θεῷ highlights the fact that approval before God is the goal, not acceptance from the master.

VERSE 21

εἰς τοῦτο γὰρ ἐκλήθητε

Γάρ introduces further rationale to endure unjust suffering. Thus the immediate antecedent of τοῦτο is the second cond. statement in the previous v. regarding perseverance while suffering for doing good, but in reality it picks up the whole thought of vv. 18–20 regarding submission and endurance. Ἐκλήθητε 2 pl. aor. pass. indic. of καλέω, "call."

ὅτι καὶ Χριστὸς ἔπαθεν ὑπὲρ ὑμῶν

Ὅτι is causal and introduces the rationale for this calling. Καί is adv. "also," and is crucial to the argument. The sufferings of these Christians of Asia Minor is not a unique experience (cf. 5:9).

Ἔπαθεν ὑπὲρ ὑμῶν (also 3:18) is normally understood in the traditional creedal sense of vicarious atonement. While that is certainly possible given that Peter does speak of the atoning value of the cross in v. 24, the immediate context refers to patience in unjust suffering, with the call to follow Christ's example. It is not surprising that in place of ἔπαθεν, "suffered," 𝔓⁸¹ ℵ Ψ 1067, 1292, 2464, and some versions read ἀπέθανεν, "died." The latter rdg. is clearly secondary, being a conformity to the early Christian confessional formula of Christ dying for our sins. The text has more than ample support in 𝔓⁷² A B C *Byz* and many minuscules and versions.

There is also some confusion (not uncommon), particularly among later mss. regarding the prons. The 2 pl. ὑμῶν, ὑμῖν have superior attestation (𝔓⁷² ℵ A B C Ψ many minuscules and most versions). The Byzantine text reads ἡμῶν, ὑμῖν, whereas some minuscules have ἡμῶν, ἡμῖν. The 2 pl. prons. should be retained not only on external evidence, but also because they clearly match the 2 pl. vbs. in the v. The change to 1 pl. seems motivated by confessional concerns.

ὑμῖν ὑπολιμπάνων ὑπογραμμόν

Clear rhetorical skill conveyed by alliteration. Ὑπολιμπάνων nom. sg. masc. of pres. act. ptc. of ὑπολιμπάνω, "leave," "leave behind" (BDAG 1039a), a NT *hapax* and a rare word (LSJ 1887d). The ptc. can be cstr. as adv. of result (i.e., a consequence of his suffering), or considering the interpretation of ἔπαθεν ὑπὲρ ὑμῶν given above, could be telic indicating the purpose of his suffering (Dubis 76–77).

Ὑπογραμμός, -οῦ, ὁ, "model," "example." The word was used of a stencil that was followed in tracing and had a quite common figurative usage of a model for behavior (BDAG 1036d; Turner, *Words* 143; G. Schrenk, *TDNT* 1.772–73; F. F. Bruce, *NIDNTT* 2.291). Ὑμῖν is dat. of advantage, "for your benefit" (Dubis 76).

ἵνα ἐπακολουθήσητε τοῖς ἴχνεσιν αὐτοῦ

Ἵνα with the subjunc. expresses the purpose of the example of Christ—that of imitation. The prep. in the compound vb. ἐπακολουθήσητε is intensive (R 563–65), indicating a close following, a closeness also conveyed by the image of following "in his footsteps." *Pace* Achtemeier (199), the idea of imitation is crucial here. Yet it is not just a call to discipleship as he maintains, but of imitating Christ's response to unjust suffering. This does not mean that his circumstances must be mirrored exactly (i.e., in the sense of imitating his passion—later known by the term *imitatio Christi*); instead, his response to unjust suffering should be imitated.

Ἴχνος, -ους, τό, "footstep" (BDAG 485b; *NewDocs* 3.68). In the NT, the noun is used only in a fig. sense of "model." The dat. τοῖς ἴχνεσιν is a dat. of rule (Wallace 157–58), representing some form of standard to follow.

VERSE 22

ὃς ἁμαρτίαν οὐκ ἐποίησεν

This is the first of four rel. clauses in vv. 22–24, the antecedent being Χριστός from v. 21. The first two clauses focus on Christ's blameless character, the latter two on his saving work. The first rel. is used to introduce a quote from Isa 53:9 LXX. For earlier commentators the presence of the rel. here and in the following vv. indicated the use of an early Christian hymn or liturgical piece (see Goppelt 207–10). But more recent exegetes correctly point out that the use of the rel. is entirely in keeping with Peter's style (1:8, 12; 2:8; 3:3, 4, 6, 20–21; 4:5; 5:9; see R 954), and other supposed hymnic pieces do not contain rel. prons. (1:20; 3:18; see Elliott 543–50).

οὐδὲ εὑρέθη δόλος ἐν τῷ στόματι αὐτοῦ

Δόλος, -ου, ὁ, "deceit" (BDAG 256c). The noun looks back to 2:1 and forward to the quotation from Ps 34:12–16 in 3:10 where believers are urged to rid themselves of deceit. The implied agent of the pass. vb. is general (i.e., deceit was not found by anyone). This v. states explicitly what 1:19 states metaphorically.

VERSE 23

ὃς λοιδορούμενος οὐκ ἀντελοιδόρει πάσχων οὐκ ἠπείλει

On the rel. pron. see v. 22 above. Λοιδορούμενος nom. sg. masc. of pres. pass. ptc. of λοιδορέω, "revile," "abuse (of speech)" (BDAG 602a; H. Hanse *TDNT* 4.293–94). Ἀντελοιδόρει 3 sg. impf. act. indic. of ἀντιλοιδορέω, "return abuse" (BDAG 89d), with the ἀντι- compound indicating reciprocal action. Ἠπείλει 3 sg. impf. act. indic. of ἀπειλέω, "threaten" (BDAG 100a).

The ptcs. λοιδορούμενος and πάσχων can be cstr. as either temp., "when" (most EVV, though ESV has "although . . . when"), or concessive, "although," with the latter better capturing the contrast with the normal human tendency (Dubis 78). The unfolding aspect (Fanning 98–103) of the impf. vbs. ἀντελοιδόρει, ἠπείλει (and παρεδίδου below) may serve to depict "Jesus' consistent refusal to retaliate in kind even after repeated provocations" (Michaels 146; "never tried to get even," CEV).

παρεδίδου δὲ τῷ κρίνοντι δικαίως

Παρεδίδου 3 sg. impf. act. indic. of παραδίδωμι, "hand over," "entrust" (BDAG 761d), here "commit," "entrust" (NRSV, HCSB, ESV, NIV). The ellipsis lacks a dir. obj. and is variously supplied as "himself" (most EVV; Selwyn 179–80), "his oppressors" (Michaels 147), "the judgment" (Goppelt 212), or "his case" (NLT; ZG 708 [himself and his cause; also Barclay]; Elliott 431). "Himself" is the preferred rendering on the basis of the parallel in 4:19 ("let those who suffer in accordance with the will of God commit themselves to a faithful Creator"). On the impf. tense, see above.

Τῷ κρίνοντι δικαίως, "to him who judges justly," is obviously God (1:17; 4:5, 17), although some minuscules and Latin mss. read ἀδίκως, "unjustly," apparently seeing here a ref. to Pilate. God is consistently revealed throughout Scripture as "just" (Deut 10:17; Rom 2:2, 5, 11). The only real hope for vindication of the righteous and the exposing of evil lies in the existence of a Judge who judges impartially.

VERSE 24

ὃς τὰς ἁμαρτίας ἡμῶν αὐτὸς ἀνήνεγκεν

On the use of the rel. pron., see above on v. 22. The language here draws heavily on Isa 53:4–5, 11–12 LXX. Αὐτός is emphatic as a verbal intensifier: "he himself bore" (R 723).

Ἀνήνεγκεν 3 sg. aor. act. indic. of ἀναφέρω, "offer," "bear" (BDAG 75a; Turner, *Words* 10–12; K. Weiss, *TDNT* 9.60–61). The vb. has already been used in 2:5 of offering up spiritual sacrifices to God and in BGk. is often used in the context of cultic sacrifice (Lev 17:5; Isa 57:6; Heb 7:27; Jas 2:21). It can also be used in the physical sense of leading someone somewhere (Mark 9:2; Matt 17:1). In the LXX it translates the Heb. *sābal* in Isa 53:11, where it means to lay something upon someone in order to bear it, while in Isa 53:12 it translates *nāśā'* with the idea of taking something away. The latter mng. is, however, not the normal sense for ἀναφέρω.

Here in 1 Pet 2:24, the sense is of laying the burden of sin upon Jesus (as in Heb 9:28), whereas the mng. of leading someone somewhere is not relevant in this context. This has a secondary theological corollary of taking sin away, but this is not the primary sense of the word. So the proper rendering of the vb. here should be "bore" (NRSV, NASB, HCSB, NIV) or "carried" (Weymouth, CEV; Harris 144–45).

𝔓⁷² B and some minuscules read ὑμῶν in place of ἡμῶν. Although supported by two important mss., the weight of external evidence is against it. On the other hand, it is probably the harder rdg. as it deviates from the text of the LXX (so Achtemeier 190).

ἐν τῷ σώματι αὐτοῦ ἐπὶ τὸ ξύλον

This prep. phrase interprets the emphatic αὐτός above (Michaels 147). It was "in his body upon the tree" that "he himself bore our sins." Ξύλον, -ου, τό, "wood," "tree" (BDAG 685b; Turner, *Words* 463–64; B. Siede, *NIDNTT* 1.389–91). The noun can refer to anything made from wood and is almost a technical term in the NT for the cross of Jesus (Acts 5:30; 10:39; 13:29; Gal 3:13; so NRSV, NJB, NASB, NIV).

ἵνα ταῖς ἁμαρτίαις ἀπογενόμενοι τῇ δικαιοσύνῃ ζήσωμεν

Ἵνα plus the subjunc. ζήσωμεν expresses the purpose of Jesus bearing our sins, not expressed so much in terms of freedom from the guilt of sin, but freedom from the control of sin (Goppelt 213), resulting in the power of a transformed life (cf. Rom 6:11; 2 Cor 5:14–15).

Ἀπογενόμενοι nom. pl. masc. of aor. mid. ptc. of ἀπογίνομαι, "be done with," "have no part in," "die" (BDAG 108a; F. Büchsel, *TDNT* 1.686; *NewDocs* 2.175). In contrast with ζήσωμεν ("live") it is often rendered as "die" (most EVV, though NRSV: "free from"). The verb is normally followed by a gen. of separation, but here takes ταῖς ἁμαρτίαις as a dat. of respect (Dubis 80). The ptc. is temp., conveying preceding action, in the sense that sin must be shed before righteousness can be embraced.

Τῇ δικαιοσύνῃ should probably be cstr. as a dat. of respect in the same way as ταῖς ἁμαρτίαις with which it forms a grammatical parallel (BDF §188[2] takes as dat. of disadvantage/advantage).

οὗ τῷ μώλωπι ἰάθητε

This is the final of the four rel. clauses. Μώλωψ, -ωπος, ὁ, "bruise," "wound" (BDAG 663a). The noun is sg. and should be tr. accordingly as "wounding" (*pace* EVV). The term functions as a metonymy for the entire passion and is not merely a ref. to Christ's scourging (Elliott 536; Dubis 81). The dat. is instr. of means: "by his wounding" (ZG 708; Moule 44).

Ἰάθητε 2 pl. aor. pass. indic. of ἰάομαι, "heal" (BDAG 465a). As in Isa 53:4, physical healing is being used as a metaphor for the removal of sin. The aor. is ingressive, signifying entry into a state (Wallace 558–59; Z §250).

Under the influence of Isa 53:5 LXX, א* P 049 *Byz* add αὐτοῦ after μώλωπι. The addition could be cstr. as the more difficult rdg. as it is redundant given the rel. pron. οὗ that begins the clause (Turner, *Style* 129 cites the inclusion as an example of Sem. influence). Nevertheless, the omission is strongly supported by 𝔓⁷² 𝔓⁸¹ א꜀ A B C K Ψ and a number of minuscules.

VERSE 25

The imagery from Isaiah 53 continues, here drawing on the straying sheep image from v. 6. It is combined with sheep/shepherd imagery from Ezekiel 34.

ἦτε γὰρ ὡς πρόβατα πλανώμενοι

Γάρ introduces an explanation for why the healing just mentioned in v. 24 was necessary (Dubis 81). The masc. pl. ptc. πλανωμένοι forms an impf. periph. cstr. with ἦτε, giving the rendering "you were wandering like sheep." This rdg. is supported by a A B and several minuscules and versions. The alternative rdg. (supported by 𝔓⁷² C Ψ *Byz* and a number of minuscules), has the neut. pl. ptc. πλανωμένα (attrib.) in agreement with πρόβατα and gives the rendering "you were like wandering sheep." The textual evidence is fairly evenly weighted, but it is more likely that scribes changed the masc. to neut. under the influence of πρόβατα immediately before it (Metzger 620). Accepting the periph. impf. as the orig. rdg., ἦτε . . . πλανώμενοι captures what is characteristic of the past life (Fanning 315) and states metaphorically what 1:14 ("your previous ignorant desires") and 1:18 ("futile conduct inherited from your ancestors") state directly.

ἀλλ' ἐπεστράφητε νῦν [ἀλλ' reflects the text of the forthcoming fifth edition of the UBS *Greek New Testament*. The fourth edition reads ἀλλά.]

Ἀλλ' . . . νῦν sets up the contrast between the pagan past of the readers and their post-conversion standing. Ἐπεστράφητε 2 pl. aor. pass. indic. of ἐπιστρέφω, "turn," "return." The vb. has a technical sense in BGk. of conversion (G. Bertram, *TDNT* 7.722–29; F. Laubach, *NIDNTT* 1.354–55). The aor. together with the adv. νῦν is culminative, indicating a state reached (Wallace 559; cf. Achtemeier 204 n. 207). The pass. form of this vb. can be used in an act. sense (BDAG 382a; ZG 709), but the pass. sense can be retained (as KJV, ASV) as it parallels ἰάθητε in the previous v. and emphasizes the divine initiative in the conversion process. It should not be rendered "returned" (as do NRSV, NASB, NIV; *pace* Dubis 82), as this implies previous status with God, a status these Gentile Christians clearly did not have (2:10; cf. 1:14, 18). NLT is better: "turned."

ἐπὶ τὸν ποιμένα καὶ ἐπίσκοπον τῶν ψυχῶν ὑμῶν

'Επί here indicates movement toward a goal (BDAG 364a). Ποιμήν, -ένος, ὁ, "shepherd" (BDAG 843a; Turner, *Words* 314–15). 'Επίσκοπος, -ου, ὁ, "overseer" (BDAG 379c; Turner, *Words* 44–46, 124–27; H. W. Beyer, *TDNT* 2.608–22; L. Coenen, *NIDNTT* 1.188–92). The single art. governing the two nouns is an instance of the Granville Sharp Rule (see Wallace 279–90; R 787), whereby the two nouns both relate to the same person. Christ is "shepherd and guardian" (not God as in the OT). He is regularly depicted as shepherd in other NT writings (John 10:1–16; 21:15–17; Heb 13:20) and in 1 Pet 5:4 is designated ἀρχιποίμενος, "chief shepherd." The noun ἐπίσκοπος has a technical sense elsewhere in the NT epistles of those in church leadership responsible for oversight of local congregations (as in 5:2).

Τῶν ψυχῶν is an obj. gen. On the use of ψυχή in 1 Peter, see on 1:9 (also Moule 185).

FOR FURTHER STUDY

31. The Cross in 1 Peter (2:21–25)

*Achtemeier, Paul J. "Suffering Servant and Suffering Christ in 1 Peter." Pages 176–99 in *The Future of Christology*. Edited by A. J. Malherbe and W. A. Meeks. Minneapolis: Fortress, 1993.

Carroll, John T., and Joel B. Green. *The Death of Jesus in Early Christianity*. Peabody, MA: Hendrickson, 1995.

Hooker, Morna D. *Not Ashamed of the Gospel: New Testament Interpretations of the Death of Christ*. Grand Rapids: Eerdmans, 1995.

Matera, Francis J. *New Testament Christology*. Louisville: Westminster John Knox, 1999. See esp. pages 174–84.

Michaels lxviii–lxxiv.

Michaels, J. Ramsey. "Catholic Christologies in the Catholic Epistles." Pages 268–91 in *Contours of Christology in the New Testament*. Edited by R. N. Longenecker. Grand Rapids: Eerdmans, 2005.

Richard, Earl. "The Functional Christology of First Peter." Pages 121–39 in *Perspectives on First Peter*. Edited by C. H. Talbert. Macon, GA: Mercer, 1986.

Seifrid, Mark A. *DLNT* 278–81.

Stott, John R. W. *The Cross of Christ*. Downers Grove: InterVarsity, 1986.

Wilcox, Max. "'Upon the Tree'—Deut 21:22–23 in the New Testament." *JBL* 96 (1977): 85–99.

Taylor, Vincent. *The Atonement in the New Testament Teaching*. London: Epworth, 1958.

Tuckett, C. M. *ABD* 1.518–22.

32. The Use of Isaiah 53 in 1 Peter and the NT (2:22–24)

*Bellinger, W. H., and W. R. Farmer, eds. *Jesus and the Suffering Servant: Isaiah 53 and Christian Origins.* Harrisburg, PA: Trinity Press, 1998.

Beyer, Bryan. *Encountering the Book of Isaiah: A Historical and Theological Survey.* Grand Rapids: Baker, 2007.

Bock, Darrell L., and Mitch Glasser, eds. *The Gospel According to Isaiah 53: Encountering the Suffering Servant in Jewish and Christian Theology.* Grand Rapids: Kregel, 2012.

Chisholm, Robert B., Jr. "The Christological Fulfilment of Isaiah's Servant Songs." *BSac* 163 (2006): 387–404.

Evans, Craig A., and Stanley E. Porter, eds. *New Testament Backgrounds.* A Sheffield Reader. Sheffield: Sheffield Academic Press, 1997.

Heskett, Randall. *Messianism within the Scriptural Scroll of Isaiah.* New York: T&T Clark, 2007.

Janowski, Bernd, and Peter Stuhlmacher, eds. *The Suffering Servant: Isaiah 53 in Jewish and Christian Sources.* Grand Rapids: Eerdmans, 2004.

Kendall, R. T. *Why Jesus Died: A Meditation on Isaiah 53.* Oxford: Monarch, 2011.

Litwak, K. D. "The Use of Quotations from Isaiah 52:13–53:12 in the New Testament." *JETS* 26 (1983): 385–94.

Mitchell, C. W. *Our Suffering Savior: Exegetical Studies and Sermons for Ash Wednesday through Easter Based on Isaiah 52:13–53:12.* St. Louis, MO: Concordia, 2003.

33. Slavery in the Ancient World and the NT (2:18–21)

Barclay, J. M. G. "Paul, Philemon and the Dilemma of Christian Slave-Ownership." *NTS* 37 (1991): 161–86.

Barrow, R. H. *Slavery in the Roman Empire.* 1928. Repr. New York: Barnes and Noble, 1968.

Bartchy, S. Scott. ΜΑΛΛΟΝ ΧΡΗΣΑΙ: *First-Century Slavery and the Interpretation of 1 Corinthians 7:21.* Missoula, MT: University of Montana, 1973. Repr., Eugene, OR: Wipf & Stock, 2002.

_____. *ISBE* 4.543–46.

* _____. *ABD* 6.65–73.

_____. *DLNT* 1098–1102.

Byron, John. *Slavery Metaphors in Early Judaism and Pauline Christianity.* Tübingen: Mohr, 2003.

Coombes, I. A. H. *The Metaphor of Slavery in the Writings of the Early Church from the New Testament to the Beginning of the Fifth Century.* Sheffield: Sheffield University Press, 1998.

Elliott, John H. *A Home for the Homeless: A Sociological Exegesis of 1 Peter, Its Situation and Strategy.* Philadelphia: Fortress, 1981.

Finley, M. I., ed. *Slavery in Classical Antiquity.* 2nd ed. New York: Cambridge University Press, 1968. See esp. pages 229–36 ("Bibliographical Essay").

Fitzmyer, Joseph A. *The Letter to Philemon.* New York: Doubleday, 2000. See pages 25–33.

Harrill, J. Albert. *The Manumission of Slaves in Early Christianity.* Tübingen: Mohr, 1995.

_____. *Slaves in the New Testament: Literary, Social, and Moral Dimensions.* Minneapolis: Fortress, 2005.

Harris, Murray J. *Slave of Christ: A New Testament Metaphor for Total Devotion to Christ*. Leicester: Apollos, 1999; Downers Grove: InterVarsity, 2001.

Lyall, F. "Roman Law in the Writings of Paul: The Slave and the Freedman." *NTS* 17 (1970–71): 73–79.

_____. *Slaves, Citizens, Sons: Legal Metaphors in the Epistles*. Grand Rapids: Zondervan, 1984.

Patterson, Orlando. *Slavery and Social Death: A Comparative Study*. Cambridge, MA: Harvard University Press, 1982.

Peterson, Norman R. *Rediscovering Paul: Philemon and the Sociology of Paul's Narrative World*. Philadelphia: Fortress, 1985.

Rupprecht, A. A. "Attitudes on Slavery among the Church Fathers." Pages 261–77 in *New Dimensions in New Testament Studies*. Edited by R. N. Longenecker and M. C. Tenney. Grand Rapids: Zondervan, 1974.

Russell, K. C. *Slavery as Reality and Metaphor in the Pauline Letters*. Rome: Catholic Book Agency, 1968.

Westermann, William L. *The Slave Systems of Greek and Roman Antiquity*. Philadelphia: American Philosophical Society, 1955.

Wiedermann, Thomas. *Greek and Roman Slavery*. London: Croom Helm; Baltimore: Johns Hopkins, 1981.

See also For Further Study §§ 13, 15, 30.

HOMILETICAL SUGGESTIONS

Duty of Slaves: The Example of Christ's Suffering (2:18–25)

1. The Submission of Slaves to Masters (vv. 18–21)
   (a) Unjust treatment does not abrogate the need for submission (v. 18)
   (b) Unjust suffering finds favor with God (vv. 19–20)
   (c) Unjust suffering is part of the Christian calling (v. 21a)
   (d) The suffering of Christ as an example (v. 21b)
2. The Example of Christ (vv. 22–24)
   (a) He was blameless in character (v. 22)
   (b) He did not return abuse (v. 23a)
   (c) He committed himself to God (v. 23b)
3. The Achievement of the Cross (vv. 24–25)
   (a) Christ bore our sins (v. 24a)
   (b) We now live for righteousness, not sin (v. 24b)
   (c) Sin has been dealt with (v. 24c)
   (d) We are no longer wandering (v. 25)

D. DUTY OF WIVES AND HUSBANDS (3:1–7)

STRUCTURE

The opening ptc. ὑποτασσόμεναι ("be subject"; cf. 2:18) introduces a new section of the Household Code and controls vv. 1–7. The rationale for the submission of wives to their husbands is given by a lengthy and complex purpose (final) clause introduced by ἵνα. This clause first of all contains a cond. cstr. (v. 1), which in turn is modified by a redundant clause introduced by ἐποπτεύσαντες ("when they observe") in v. 2. The rel. clause that begins v. 3 (ὧν ἔστω, "let it not be") picks up τὴν ἐν φόβῳ ἁγνὴν ἀναστροφὴν ὑμῶν ("your reverent and pure conduct") from v. 2 and gives both a neg. and positive example of such conduct using an illustration of outer vs. inner beauty. Οὕτως γάρ ("for thus") introduces "the holy women of old" as an example of proper conduct in v. 5, with v. 6a narrowing in on Sarah. Verse 6b then specifies the relationship that believing wives have with Sarah in terms of covenant status (see the analysis below).

1   ὁμοίως αἱ γυναῖκες, ὑποτασσόμεναι τοῖς ἰδίοις ἀνδράσιν,
      ἵνα καὶ εἴ τινες ἀπειθοῦσιν τῷ λόγῳ,
           διὰ τῆς τῶν γυναικῶν ἀναστροφῆς
           ἄνευ λόγου
           κερδηθήσονται
2   ἐποπτεύσαντες τὴν ἐν φόβῳ ἁγνὴν ἀναστροφὴν ὑμῶν.

3   ὧν ἔστω οὐκ ὁ ἔξωθεν
        ἐμπλοκῆς τριχῶν
        καὶ περιθέσεως χρυσίων
        ἢ ἐνδύσεως ἱματίων κόσμος
4   ἀλλ' ὁ κρυπτὸς τῆς καρδίας ἄνθρωπος
        ἐν τῷ ἀφθάρτῳ τοῦ πρασέως καὶ ἡσυχίου πνεύματος,
               ὅ ἐστιν ἐνώπιον τοῦ θεοῦ
               πολυτελές.

5   οὕτως γάρ ποτε καὶ αἱ ἅγιαι γυναῖκες
        αἱ ἐλπίζουσαι εἰς θεὸν
           ἐκόσμουν ἑαυτὰς
           ὑποτασσόμεναι τοῖς ἰδίοις ἀνδράσιν,
6   ὡς Σάρρα ὑπήκουσεν τῷ Ἀβραὰμ
        κύριον αὐτὸν καλοῦσα,
       ἧς ἐγενήθητε τέκνα
        ἀγαθοποιοῦσαι
       καὶ μὴ φοβούμενοι μηδεμίαν πτόησιν.

By the means of οἱ ἄνδρες ὁμοίως ("likewise you husbands") the attention shifts to the obligations of believing husbands in v. 7. The v. is evenly balanced (see the analysis below) with two ptc. clauses each with an obj. followed by a phrase beginning with ὡς. A concluding art. inf. cstr. (εἰς τὸ μὴ ἐγκόπτεσθαι) stresses the purpose of the stipulated behavior.

7   οἱ ἄνδρες ὁμοίως, συνοικοῦντες
            κατὰ γνῶσιν
            ὡς ἀσθενεστέρῳ σκεύει τῷ γυναικείῳ,
            ἀπονέμοντες τιμὴν
            ὡς καὶ συγκληρονόμοις χάριτος ζωῆς
                εἰς τὸ μὴ ἐγκόπτεσθαι τὰς προσευχὰς ὑμῶν.

VERSE 1

ὁμοίως αἱ γυναῖκες

Ὁμοίως links the obedience of wives to their husbands to the obedience of slaves to their masters from the previous section (2:18–25). This does not imply that the two roles are identical, but the common element is that, according to cultural norms (see Elliott 553–59, 585–99), they both are to have a subservient role.

·   The article αἱ [included in brackets in UBS⁴; brackets removed in UBS⁵] is found in 𝔓⁷² ℵ² C Ψ *Byz* and a number of other minuscules. It is omitted by 𝔓⁸¹ ℵ* A B 81. Ms 1505 and parts of the Latin text substitute καί. It is difficult to make a decision on the basis of ms. evidence alone, but the omission may be due to the desire to highlight γυναῖκες as a voc. (Metzger 620). On the pl. noun with the art. used as a voc., see also 2:18; 3:7 (Z §34; BDF §147[3]; R 264; Moule 117).

ὑποτασσόμεναι τοῖς ἰδίοις ἀνδράσιν

As in 2:18, the ptc. ὑποτασσόμεναι falls under the general rubric of the impv. ὑποτάγητε from 2:13 and has clear impv. force (see discussion on "Imperatival Participles in 1 Peter" in the Introduction). The use of ἰδίοις confines this exhortation to the marriage relationship, thus indicating that γυναῖκες refers to wives rather than women in general.

ἵνα καὶ εἴ τινες ἀπειθοῦσιν τῷ λόγῳ

The purpose (ἵνα) of this submission is expressed by means of a first-class cond. introduced by εἴ, assuming a situation for the sake of the argument (Porter 254–67). However, καί ("even") together with the indef. pron. τινες indicates that the situation posited probably should not be cstr. as the norm (R 1026), for in Greco-Roman society a wife normally embraced the religion of her husband. Nevertheless, Peter is clearly addressing more than a hypothetical possibility (cf. 1 Cor 7:12–16).

Ἀπειθοῦσιν 3 pl. pres. act. indic. ἀπειθέω (+ dat.), "disobey," "disbelieve" (BDAG 99d). The use of this vb. could refer not only to unbelievers but to those who are actively hostile to the message of the gospel (τῷ λόγῳ; cf. 2:8; 4:17).

διὰ τῆς τῶν γυναικῶν ἀναστροφῆς ἄνευ λόγου κερδηθήσονται

This constitutes the apod. of the cond. Ἀναστροφή, -ῆς, ἡ, "conduct" (see on 1:15). The noun looks both forward and backward for its content. Submission is the fundamental element of conduct, whereas some more particular features are discussed in vv. 3–6. Τῶν γυναικῶν is a subj. gen.

Ἄνευ (+ gen), "without" (R 638). Ἄνευ λόγου provides a word play with ἀπειθοῦσιν τῷ λόγῳ—they disobey the word but can be won without a word (cf. 2:12).

Κερδηθήσονται 3 pl. fut. pass. indic. κερδαίνω, "gain," "profit," "win" (BDAG 541a; B. Siede, NIDNTT 3.136–38). The vb. comes from the sphere of commerce (LN 57.189), being taken up and used as a conversion term by the early church (Matt 18:15; 1 Cor 9:19–22). Here it means to win for the cause of the gospel. The use of the fut. indic. with ἵνα rather than a subjunc. is rare in the NT (Z §340; T 100; R 324, 984; BDF §369[2]).

VERSE 2

ἐποπτεύσαντες τὴν ἐν φόβῳ ἁγνὴν ἀναστροφὴν ὑμῶν

Ἐποπτεύσαντες nom. pl. masc. of aor. act. ptc. of ἐποπτεύω, "observe" (BDAG 387d). In this somewhat redundant clause, the ptc. can be cstr. as either temp. ("when," HCSB, ESV, NIV), causal ("because," CEV), or instrumental ("by," NLT), with much the same overall sense. In contrast to 2:12 where the pres. ptc. of this vb. is used, the aor. may here be placing things in a temp. sequence: observation followed by conversion (Michaels 158; Achtemeier 210). Although 𝔓⁷² ℵ 1505 and several other mss. have the pres. ptc. ἐποπτεύοντες, the aor. ptc. has wider support in ℵᶜ A B C P Ψ 33 Byz. The pres. ptc. may be a conformity to 2:12.

For Peter's characteristic use of ἐν φόβῳ, see on 2:18. As there, this refers to an attitude directed toward God (1:17; 2:17) rather than the husband. This is made clear in v. 4 where the focus is on what is precious in God's sight, and in v. 6 by the exhortation not to be overcome by fear. Ἁγνός, -ή, -όν, "pure," "chaste" (BDAG 13d). This adj. can have connotations of sexual purity but here has a more general focus of faultless conduct (cf. 2 Cor 7:11; Phil 4:8; 1 John 3:3). For ἀναστροφή, see on 1:15.

VERSE 3

ὧν ἔστω οὐχ ὁ ἔξωθεν . . . κόσμος

The difficult syntax of vv. 3–4 consists of an extended rel. clause governed by ὧν, the antecedent of which is ὑμῶν (i.e., Christian wives) from the end of v. 2. Ἔστω οὐχ forms a neg. impv. cstr., "let it not be" (impv. is rare in a rel. clause, though see 5:9, 12; R 949) while οὐχ looks forward to ἀλλά (ἀλλ') in v. 4 to provide the contrast between inappropriate and appropriate adornment. The use of οὐ with the impv. is due to the sharp contrast made with ἀλλ' (R 947, 1161). The art. ὁ belongs with κόσμος, which here has a sense of "adornment" (BDAG 561b; Turner, Words 498–501; NewDocs 1.11) and is most likely positioned last in the clause for emphasis. Ἔξωθεν, "outside" (Barclay: "superficial"), is an adv. used adj. (BDAG 354d). For ease of trans. it is best to treat ἔξωθεν as pred. giving, "Let your adornment not be external, in the . . . ." (sim. NJB, ESV).

ἐμπλοκῆς τριχῶν καὶ περιθέσεως χρυσίων ἢ ἐνδύσεως ἱματίων

Ἐμπλοκή, -ῆς, ἡ, "braid," "braiding" (BDAG 324c). Θρίξ, τριχός, ἡ, "hair" (BDAG 459d). Περίθεσις, -εως, ἡ, "putting on," "wearing" (BDAG 801b). Χρυσίον, -ου, τό, "gold" (BDAG 1092d). Ἔνδυσις, -εως, ἡ, "putting on," "wearing" (BDAG 333c). This pred. comprises three nouns in the gen. sg. ἐμπλοκῆς, περιθέσεως, and ἐνδύσεως, which are epex. of ὁ ἔξωθεν . . . κόσμος (i.e., the outer adornment which consists in the braiding of hair), together with three pl. gen. modifiers, τριχῶν, χρυσίων, and ἱματίων, which are obj.

The final gen. combination, lit. "wearing of clothes," best rendered as "fine clothes" (HCSB, NIV), is the interpretive key to the other two pairs. Peter is not censuring these things in themselves, but insisting that they do not constitute true beauty in the sight of God.

θρίξ is pl. in the NT except when referring to one strand of hair (as in Matt 5:36; Luke 21:18; Acts 27:34). The gen. τριχῶν ("of hair") is omitted by 𝔓⁷² C Ψ and a few other mss., giving the sense that gold is part of the braiding. However, the inclusion is well supported by ℵ A B P 33, 1739, *Byz*, and the rhythm of the v. (three gen. nouns with corresponding gen. modifiers) argues strongly in favor of its retention.

VERSE 4

ἀλλ' ὁ κρυπτὸς τῆς καρδίας ἄνθρωπος

Ἀλλ' picks up οὐχ from the previous v. and provides the contrast. The entire phrase ὁ κρυπτὸς τῆς καρδίας ἄνθρωπος can be cstr. as either:

1. the subj. of an implied impv. ἔστω ("let the hidden person of the heart be [your adornment]," Dubis 88); or
2. the pred. of an implied ἔστω ὁ κόσμος ("let your adornment be the hidden person of the heart," NRSV, NASB, ESV, NIV).

Κρυπτός, -ή, -όν, "hidden," "secret" (BDAG 570d), here functions as the opposite to ἔξωθεν and thus refers to an inner quality, with ἄνθρωπος ("person") contrasting κόσμος ("adornment"). Τῆς καρδίας is best taken as an epex. gen., i.e., the heart is the inner person (ZG 709; Dubis 88) and signifies the belief of the heart being the seat of one's emotions, disposition, and allegiance (cf. 3:15; Michaels 161).

ἐν τῷ ἀφθάρτῳ τοῦ πραέως καὶ ἡσυχίου πνεύματος

Ἄφθαρτος, -ον, "imperishable" (BDAG 155d–156a). Πραΰς, πραεῖα, πραΰ, "gentle," "humble" (BDAG 861a), a prized virtue in Greek culture as well as early Christianity (Matt 5:5; Gal 5:23; Eph 4:2; Col 3:12; Titus 3:2; Elliott 566–70). Ἡσύχιος, -ον, "quiet," "peaceable" (BDAG 440d). The latter two adjs. are quite close in mng. and are often juxtaposed (cf. *1 Clem.* 13:4; *Barn.* 19:4).

The cstr. switches to the dat. for elaboration regarding this inner quality, but the precise usage is difficult to classify. Achtemeier (213) labels it a dat. of accompaniment, suggesting a rendering such as "together with" or "accompanied by." However, this obscures the fact that the dat. is epex. of ὁ κρυπτὸς τῆς καρδίας ἄνθρωπος rather than being an additional quality as such. Consequently, it is best cstr. as instr. of manner.

On the use of ἄφθαρτος in this epistle, see 1:18. Typically it refers to what is enduring as opposed to what is ephemeral ("the unfading beauty," NIV). Τοῦ πραέως καὶ ἡσυχίου πνεύματος is an epex. gen., i.e., the imperishable quality that is a humble, gentle spirit. Πνεύματος is not the Holy Spirit but one's inner disposition and is art. as it governs πραέως καὶ ἡσυχίου and distinguishes one type of disposition from another (Wallace 226).

ὅ ἐστιν ἐνώπιον τοῦ θεοῦ πολυτελές

Many commentators contend that the antecedent of the rel. pron. ὅ is most likely all of v. 4 rather than πνεύματος specifically (Michaels 162; Elliott 567). But the distinction is artificial given that the epex. πνεύματος sums up the thought and content of the v. (Dubis 88). The pred. adj. πολυτελής, -ές refers to what is expensive or of great value (BDAG 850b).

VERSE 5

οὕτως γάρ ποτε καὶ αἱ ἅγιαι γυναῖκες αἱ ἐλπίζουσαι εἰς θεὸν ἐκόσμουν ἑαυτάς

Οὕτως γάρ looks both forward (cataphoric) and backward (anaphoric), giving a concrete example of subjection to husbands, thereby linking the gentle and peaceable spirit in the previous v. to an attitude of submission from v. 1. Ποτε is an enclitic particle, adv. in nature, "formerly," "of old" (R 1147; BDAG 856d). Ποτε καὶ αἱ ἅγιαι γυναῖκες is most likely a reference to the matriarchs of Jewish religion: Sarah, Rebekah, Rachel, and Leah (Michaels 164; Achtemeier 214). The adj. ἅγιαι links them to believers of the new covenant era (2:9; Goppelt 223).

Αἱ ἐλπίζουσαι (pres. act. ptc. nom. pl. fem.) εἰς θεόν is parallel to ἐν φόβῳ in v. 2. It is because of a life orientation toward God that submission and proper conduct can occur. In this epistle, hope is almost synonymous with belief/faith and is to be characteristic of those who follow Christ (1:13, 21; 3:15; cf. 1:3).

Ἐκόσμουν 3 pl. impf. act. indic. of κοσμέω, "adorn" (BDAG 560b; J. Guhrt, *NIDNTT* 1.521–26; Spicq 2.330–35). The impf. is customary (Wallace 548), stressing habitual or characteristic behavior ("used to adorn," NRSV, NASB, NIV).

ὑποτασσόμεναι τοῖς ἰδίοις ἀνδράσιν

Ὑποτασσόμεναι is instr. of means or manner ("by," NRSV, ESV), defining adornment in terms of submissive behavior.

VERSE 6

ὡς Σάρρα ὑπήκουσεν τῷ Ἀβραάμ κύριον αὐτὸν καλοῦσα

Ὡς introduces a concrete example (BDAG 1104c) of the submission of the Jewish matriarchs to their husbands: Sarah's obedience to Abraham (on the potentially problematic use of Sarah as an example of obedience, see D. I. Sly, "1 Peter 3:6b in the Light of Philo and Josephus," *JBL* 110 [1991]: 126–29; Michaels 164–66).

Ὑπήκουσεν 3 sg. aor. act. indic. of ὑπακούω, "obey," normally in the NT with the dat. (BDAG 1028d). Καλοῦσα (nom. sg. fem. pres. act. ptc.) is adv. ptc. of manner, with αὐτόν as its dir. obj. Κύριον is in appos. to αὐτόν.

ἧς ἐγενήθητε τέκνα

The antecedent of the rel. ἧς is Sarah. The aorist ἐγενήθητε is ingressive, depicting the entry into a state or condition (Wallace 558–59) and relates to the time of conversion. The question here is whether becoming Sarah's children is an ethical (so Achtemeier 216) or theological statement, and a resolution is important as it impinges on the interpretation of the two ptcs., ἀγαθοποιοῦσαι and μὴ φοβούμεναι, that follow. On the one hand, "children of" may be meant in the Sem. sense of one who imitates a quality. Taken this way, the focus is ethical. However, this flies in the face of the traditional use of Sarah/Abraham as parents of the chosen people (see Isa 51:2, 4; Josephus, *War* 5.379). The designation "children of Abraham" is certainly more common as a label of covenant status (Ps 105:6; Luke 13:16), and that it embodies a feeling of (supposed) covenantal security is evident not only in later Jewish writings (*b. 'Erub.* 19a; *b. Sabb.* 33b; *Gen. Rab.* 48.8; *Exod. Rab.* 19.4) but also in early Christian literature (Matt 1:73; 3:8–9; Justin, *Dial.* 140). The classic Christian expression of Sarah as the mother of Christian believers comes from Paul who, in a rather complex allegory, argues that all who are free from the law have become children of the promise with Sarah as their mother (Gal 4:21–31). In later rabbinic literature, Sarah is viewed as the (nursing) mother of all Gentile proselytes (*Pesiq. Rab.* 18a; *Tanh.* 32a, 54b). Given this, it is difficult to see how ἧς ἐγενήθητε τέκνα indicates anything other than membership of the people of God, i.e., a covenant designation.

ἀγαθοποιοῦσαι καὶ μὴ φοβούμεναι μηδεμίαν πτόησιν

Ἀγαθοποιοῦσαι nom. pl. fem. of pres. act. ptc. of ἀγαθοποιέω (see on 2:15). Φοβούμεναι nom. pl. fem. of pres. mid. ptc. of φοβέω. Given that ἧς ἐγενήθητε τέκνα is a covenant designation (see above), it is erroneous to treat these two ptcs. as cond., as do some commentators (Goppelt 224; cf. Z §257; Fanning 270; Wallace 633) and many EVV (NRSV, NASB, ESV, NIV; Moffatt takes the ptcs. as modifying αἱ ἅγιαι γυναῖκες αἱ ἐλπίζουσαι εἰς θεὸν ἐκόσμουν ἑαυτάς, with the ref. to Sarah and her children being a parenthesis, but this is unlikely). Achtemeier (216) argues against the cond. sense but then opts for instr. ("by") or attendant circumstances ("when"). But this still makes being children of Sarah a consequence of doing good and not being afraid, when clearly covenant status is a gift of God's grace through faith (1:1, 18–21; 2:9–10).

Rather, as a result of covenant status, a certain lifestyle is demanded. Consequently, the ptcs. should be cstr. as result (see Wallace 637–39). Elliott (573) follows this line, arguing that the ptcs. "describe the present conduct and confidence consequent upon becoming Sarah's spiritual children through conversion." He then opts for an indic. sense, rendering the phrase as "you became her children now doing what is right and not fearing any terror." This is an attractive proposal as it avoids any sense of becoming Sarah's children through merit, but the tr. is unwieldy. A better option is to allow the resultative force to work out as an impv. (Michaels 166–67): "you have become Sarah's children, so do good and do not fear any intimidation." This not only allows the impv. to grow out of the indic. (as it does elsewhere in 1 Peter), but the ptcs. then align with other pres. ptcs. that are used in the Household Code as impvs. (2:18; 3:1, 7). See further Greg W. Forbes, "Children of Sarah: Interpreting 1 Peter 3:6b," *BBR* 15 (2005): 105–9.

Μηδεμίαν πτόησιν is the dir. obj. of μὴ φοβούμεναι (cognate acc., see R 479), with the repetition of μή . . . μηδεμίαν an emphatic neg. (Porter 283) ("do not fear any intimidation at all"). Πτόησις, -εως, ἡ, is either the act of intimidation/causing fear or the experience of so being (BDAG 895b; LN 25.265). Either suits the context here, where the specific focus would be on believing wives not fearing the intimidation of unbelieving husbands (possibly drawing upon Prov 3:25 LXX, noting that Prov 3:34 is quoted in 5:5 [cf. 4:8, 17]). A similar, though more generally oriented, exhortation appears in 3:14.

VERSE 7

οἱ ἄνδρες ὁμοίως

This use of the art. with the nom. has voc. force (cf. 2:18; 3:7 [Z §34; BDF §147[3]; R 264; Moule 117]). Ὁμοίως is used differently here than in 3:1 where it was linking in a rather loose sense the subjection of wives to husbands and the subjection of slaves to masters. Here it is reciprocal, shifting attention from the wife to the husband, although the reciprocal duty is not defined as "submission."

συνοικοῦντες κατὰ γνῶσιν ὡς ἀσθενεστέρῳ σκεύει τῷ γυναικείῳ

Συνοικοῦντες nom. pl. masc. of pres. act. ptc. of συνοικέω, "live with" (BDAG 973d). The ptc. is impv. (Michaels 167; BDF §468[2]; Fanning 387; Wallace 651), fulfilling the role of the main vb. in this v. (see discussion on "Imperatival Participles in 1 Peter" in the Introduction). Σκεῦος, -ους, τό, "object," "vessel" (C. Maurer, *TDNT* 7.358–67; BDAG 927c). In its fig. uses, the noun can mean:

1. a person as an instr. or agent (Acts 9:5);
2. the human body as a vessel of the Spirit (*Barn.* 7:3);
3. the human body (2 Cor 4:7); or
4. a man's wife (possibly 1 Thess 4:4; also rabbinic Judaism).

The third sense applies here, and together with ἀσθενεστέρῳ (comp. of ἀσθενής, ές, "weak," "sick") indicates inferior physical strength (see Elliott 576–78 for references in non-BGk. regarding the physical inferiority of women; *NewDocs* 4.131–33 for petitions that appeal to the frailty of women).

Γυναικεῖος, -α, -ον, "female," subst.: "woman," "wife" (BDAG 208d; *NewDocs* 3.26), is the obj. of συνοικοῦντες (dat. due to συν- compound). Some take the adj. to refer to any female members of the household (as Achtemeier 217; Jobes 207), but the immediate context makes it plain that wives are in view (Elliott 475).

Κατὰ γνῶσιν is lit. "according to knowledge," but the content of this knowledge is unclear, and together with what follows, can be cstr. in several ways:

*1. γνῶσιν is rendered "knowledge," or "recognition" (Weymouth), with ὡς being a marker of content (BDAG 1105c), so that ἀσθενεστέρῳ σκεύει gives the content of this knowledge, knowledge related to the wife. This gives "Live with your wife with the recognition that they are physically inferior" (sim. Weymouth, NASB);

2. γνῶσιν is rendered "consideration," and the entire phrase ὡς ἀσθενεστέρῳ σκεύει τῷ γυναικείῳ is taken as the first of two reasons for ἀπονέμοντες τιμήν ("showing [them] honor") which follows. This gives: "Live with your wives with consideration, showing them honor as ("because" if ὡς is causal, so Elliott 576) physically inferior and as joint heirs" (sim. ASV, NRSV, NKJV, CEV, ESV, NIV). Under this rendering, "consideration" could relate to the wife or to a knowledge of God's requirements (Achtemeier 218), but more likely the former.

Option 1 is preferable, due not only to word order (as under 2 ἀσθενεστέρῳ σκεύει is removed from τῷ γυναικείῳ), but also the obvious parallelism between the two phrases consisting of ptc. and dir. obj. followed by a phrase beginning with ὡς (Elliott 578; Dubis 94).

ἀπονέμοντες τιμὴν ὡς καὶ συγκληρονόμοις χάριτος ζωῆς

Ἀπονέμοντες nom. pl. masc. of. pres. act. ptc. of ἀπονέμω, "assign," "accord," "show" (BDAG 118b; *NewDocs* 1.62). The ptc. does carry impv. force, but as it is dependent upon the initial ptc. συνοικοῦντες, it is primarily a ptc. of manner—showing of respect/honor must characterize the way in which the husband must live with his wife (Achtemeier 217 n. 167; Elliott 579).

Here ὡς can either be cstr. as (1) a marker introducing the perspective from which someone is viewed (BDAG 1104d), or (2) causal, showing the reason why respect must be shown (BDAG 1105a).

Συγκληρονόμος, -ον, "jointly inheriting," subst.: "co-heir" (BDAG 952b; *NewDocs* 1.135). This demonstrates that a believing wife is in view. Although it would be normal for a wife to adopt her husband's religion, we have already seen in the above section that this is not always a given. Jobes (208) in fact tr. καί as "even" and takes this as an instruction to treat a non-believing wife as if she were a co-heir. However, against

Jobes, there is no indication in this section that anyone other than believing wives are in view.

Instead of the dat. ptc. συγκληρονόμοις read by 𝔓⁷²⁸¹ ℵ² B 33, 69, 323, 1241, 1739, the nom. pl. ptc. συγκληρονόμοι is read by A C P Ψ *Byz*. There is no difference in mng., but the dat. ptc. focuses on the wife as joint heir (the adj. has no unique fem. form), picking up the dat. τῷ γυναικείῳ, whereas the nom. ptc. focuses on the husband in line with the other noms. in this v. Metzger (620–21) believes that scribes may have felt uncomfortable with the abrupt switch from the dat. sg. to the dat. pl. and thus amended the text to the nom. The dat. should be retained on the basis of slightly superior ms. support and also the preceding parallel clause with ὡς plus dat. (Michaels 155).

Χάριτος is an obj. gen., whereas ζωῆς can be variously cstr. as epex. (grace which is/consists in life, Weymouth, NRSV, NIV; ZG 709; most commentators), descriptive (living grace), or destination (grace that leads to life). ℵ A C² and some other mss. read ποικίλης χάριτος ζωῆς ("manifold grace of life"), possibly by assimilation to 4:10, whereas 𝔓⁷² has χάριτος ζωῆς αἰωνίου ("grace of eternal life"). The shorter rdg. in the text should be retained on the basis of 𝔓⁸¹ᵛⁱᵈ B C* P Ψ 33, 1739 *Byz*.

εἰς τὸ μὴ ἐγκόπτεσθαι τὰς προσευχὰς ὑμῶν

Ἐγκόπτεσθαι pres. pass. inf. of ἐγκόπτω, "hinder," "thwart" (BDAG 274b; C. H. Peisker, *NIDNTT* 2.220–21). The art. inf. cstr. εἰς τὸ μὴ ἐγκόπτεσθαι indicates purpose (R 1071–72), modifying both the preceding ptc. clauses (Dubis 96). It is unclear, however, whether prayers are hindered because of a neglect of prayer in a nonfunctioning marriage (so Cassirer: "so that your prayers may not suffer interruption") or because God chooses to ignore them. Given the quotation from Psalm 34 which follows in v. 12, regarding God's ear being open to the righteous, the latter is probably the primary sense. Τὰς προσευχάς is acc. of respect with the inf. The pl. ὑμῶν (subj. gen.) could refer to the husband and wife (Michaels 171; Goppelt 228; Elliott 581) or to husbands collectively (Achtemeier 218; Davids 123 n. 20).

FOR FURTHER STUDY

34. Marriage and Family in the NT (3:1–7)

Balch, David, and Carolyn Osiek, eds. *Early Christian Families in Context*. Grand Rapids: Eerdmans, 2003.

Balla, Peter. *The Child-Parent Relationship in the New Testament and Its Environment*. Tübingen: Mohr, 2003.

Bower, Robert K., and Gary L. Knapp, *ISBE* 3.261–66.

Burke, Trevor. *Family Matters*. Edinburgh: Clark, 2004.

Campbell, Ken, ed. *Marriage and Family in the Biblical World*. Wheaton, IL: InterVarsity, 2003.

Isaacs, Nathan, and Ella D. Isaacs, *ISBE* 4.75–78.

NewDocs 1.36.

Osiek, Carolyn, and David Balch. *Families in the New Testament World*. Philadelphia: Westminster John Knox, 1997.

HOMILETICAL SUGGESTIONS

Duty of Wives and Husbands (3:1–7)

1. Submission of wives to husbands (vv. 1–6)
    (a) To win unbelieving husbands to the faith (vv. 1b–2)
    (b) Proper adornment (vv. 3–4)
        (i) Not in externals (v. 3)
        (ii) In a gentle and humble spirit (v. 4)
    (c) The example of the Jewish matriarchs (vv. 5–6)
2. Husbands must be considerate to their wives (v. 7)
    (a) They are physically inferior
    (b) They are joint heirs of grace that leads to life
    (c) So that prayers may not be hindered

The Status of Women in Marriage (3:1–7)

1. Women are not inferior to men
    (a) Co-heirs of God's grace (3:7)
    (b) Both man and woman created in the image of God
    (c) Physical inferiority is the point of 3:7
2. Submission motif in the NT
    (a) A wife should expect her husband to love her sacrificially (Eph 5:25)
    (b) A husband is required to honor his wife so that his prayers may not be hindered (1 Pet 3:7)
    (c) The wife and husband are equal in value (Gal 3:28) and co-heirs (1 Pet 3:7)

E. UNITY AND LOVE (3:8–12)

STRUCTURE

The section commences with five pred. adjs., which outline the appropriate attitudes and characteristics for Christian behavior. Verse 9a shifts to the neg. μὴ ἀποδιδόντες, "do not repay," to forbid retaliatory responses, then contrasts this undesirable attitude with τοὐναντίον δέ, "but rather." The ὅτι clause in v. 9b summarizes what comes prior with the ἵνα clause being consec. (see the analysis, below). Verses 10–12 consist of a citation from Ps 34:13–17 LXX (Eng. 34:12–16), further illustrating the qualities that God desires in his people.

8 Τὸ δὲ τέλος πάντες   ὁμόφρονες,
                          συμπαθεῖς,
                          φιλάδελφοι,
                          εὔσπλαγχνοι,
                          ταπεινόφρονες,
9   μὴ ἀποδιδόντες κακὸν ἀντὶ κακοῦ
                          ἢ λοιδορίαν ἀντὶ λοιδορίας,
                  τοὐναντίον δὲ εὐλογοῦντες
                          ὅτι εἰς τοῦτο ἐκλήθητε
                          ἵνα εὐλογίαν κληρονομήσητε.

10 ὁ γὰρ θέλων ζωὴν ἀγαπᾶν
            καὶ ἰδεῖν ἡμέρας ἀγαθὰς
                  παυσάτω τὴν γλῶσσαν ἀπὸ κακοῦ
                  καὶ χείλη τοῦ μὴ λαλῆσαι δόλον,
11   ἐκκλινάτω δὲ ἀπὸ κακοῦ
                  καὶ ποιησάτω ἀγαθόν,
                  ζητησάτω εἰρήνην
                  καὶ διωξάτω αὐτήν·
12   ὅτι ὀφθαλμοὶ κυρίου ἐπὶ δικαίους
                  καὶ ὦτα αὐτοῦ εἰς δέησιν αὐτῶν,
                  πρόσωπον δὲ κυρίου ἐπὶ ποιοῦντας κακά.

VERSE 8

τὸ δὲ τέλος πάντες ὁμόφρονες, συμπαθεῖς, φιλάδελφοι, εὔσπλαγχνοι, ταπεινόφρονες

Τὸ δὲ τέλος, "finally" (Z §74; Moule 34) is an adv. acc. (R 487), akin to the more common Pauline τὸ λοιπόν (Michaels 176; Achtemeier 222). It more likely indicates the final part of the *Haustafel* rather than the end of the letter as such (Dubis 97; Achtemeier 222). Πάντες (also with an impv. in 5:5b) indicates that Peter is now addressing all in the Christian community. The cstr. is elliptical with an implied impv.

(BDF §98) ἔστε (Moulton 180; R 945) or γίνεσθε ("be") or impv. ptc. ὄντες (Achtemeier 222 [although he maintains that the ptc. is instr. rather than impv.]; Selwyn 188; see the discussion on "Imperatival Participles in 1 Peter" in the Introduction).

Ὁμόφρων, -ον, "likeminded," "harmonious" (BDAG 709d). The idea is of a unity of purpose ("agree among yourselves," NJB; LN 30.21) rather than complete uniformity in thought. The adj. itself is a NT *hapax*, though the thought is common in the Pauline literature (Rom 12:16; 15:5; 1 Cor 1:10; Phil 2:2; 4:2). Συμπαθής, -ές, "sympathetic," "understanding" (BDAG 958c) is also a NT *hapax*, though the cognate vb. is used in Heb 10:34 in the same sense. The term was used in non-BGk. regarding the sharing of a variety of emotions and feelings (LSJ 1680b; *NewDocs* 2.58–60; Michaels 176).

Elliott's (603) proposed chiastic arrangement is persuasive, with the outer adjs. emphasizing an attitude of mind, the middle two adjs. focusing on compassion, with φιλάδελφοι (φιλάδελφος, -ον, "having mutual affection" [BDAG 1055d; *NewDocs* 1.117–18; 3.87]) being the central term. This is not surprising given Peter's emphasis throughout the letter on social cohesion—see the cognates in 1:22; 2:17.

Εὔσπλαγχνος, -ον, "tenderhearted," "compassionate" (BDAG 413c; Turner, *Words* 78–79), is derived from σπλάγχνα, "intestines," which were considered the seat of the emotions. With ταπεινόφρων, -ον, -ονος, "humble" (BDAG 989d–990a; Spicq 3.369–71; Turner, *Words* 216–18), we see a shift in the LXX and NT from a neg. sense in secular Gk. literature bound up with shame and lack of honor (e.g., Plutarch, *Mor.* 336e; 475e) to a more positive virtue of humility ("self-effacing," NJB).

In place of ταπεινόφρονες, which is strongly supported by 𝔓⁷² ℵ A B C Ψ and many other mss., P 049 *Byz* read φιλόφρονες, "hospitable/friendly," whereas L together with some other mss. and early Latin texts read both adjs. The text should be retained on the basis of overwhelming ms. evidence.

VERSE 9

μὴ ἀποδιδόντες κακὸν ἀντὶ κακοῦ ἢ λοιδορίαν ἀντὶ λοιδορίας

The ptc. ἀποδιδόντες, "repay," is used impv. (see the discussion on "Imperatival Participles in 1 Peter" in the Introduction) and together with μή forms the neg. counterpart to the positive exhortations of the previous v. Λοιδορία, -ας, ἡ, "abuse," "insult" (BDAG 602a). The language of non-retaliation recalls the example of Christ in 2:23, with the prep. ἀντί indicating reciprocal action (R 573). It appears that the focus has shifted primarily from attitudes toward those within the Christian community to appropriate response to aggressive outsiders (so most commentators, e.g., Elliott 606; Michaels 177–78). The correspondence of Peter's language here with Rom 12:17; 1 Thess 5:15 is best explained by a common early Christian parenetic tradition, drawing on the teaching and actions of Jesus (Matt 5:43–44; Luke 6:27–28).

τοὐναντίον δὲ εὐλογοῦντες

Τοὐναντίον is a contraction of τὸ ἐναντίον (ZG 710; R 208) and together with δέ is a strong adversative, "on the contrary" (HCSB, NIV), contrasting the undesirable behavior of retaliation. Εὐλογοῦντες, "bless," is also an impv. ptc. (Fanning 386; Z §373; see the discussion on "Imperatival Participles in 1 Peter" in the Introduction) and more likely refers to invoking the grace of God rather than the more general secular usage of speaking well of someone (Achtemeier 224; Elliott 608; Dubis 99). Either way, it forms a distinct contrast with the customary expectation for "an immediate and crafty verbal riposte" (Elliott 607).

ὅτι εἰς τοῦτο ἐκλήθητε ἵνα εὐλογίαν κληρονομήσητε

2 pl. aor. act. subj. of κληρονομέω, "inherit" (BDAG 547d). Εὐλογία, -ας, ἡ, "blessing" (BDAG 408d). The referent for ὅτι εἰς τοῦτο ἐκλήθητε is unclear, and the entire expression ὅτι εἰς τοῦτο ἐκλήθητε ἵνα εὐλογίαν κληρονομήσητε can be taken in three ways:

1. ὅτι εἰς τοῦτο ἐκλήθητε looks backward to εὐλογοῦντες for its referent, i.e., believers are called not to retaliate but to bless. The ἵνα clause is then taken as final, expressing purpose (NJB, NIV; see BDAG 475c);
*2. ὅτι εἰς τοῦτο ἐκλήθητε looks backward, with the ἵνα clause taken as consecutive, expressing result (NLT; see BDAG 477a); or
3. ὅτι εἰς τοῦτο ἐκλήθητε looks forward, making the ἵνα clause epex. of the calling, giving its content, i.e. "you were called to inherit a blessing" (Weymouth, NASB; Kelly 137; Goppelt 234; Davids 126–27; see BDAG 476b).

The other two uses of εἰς τοῦτο in this epistle do not provide much help, clearly pointing backward in 2:21 and forward in 4:6. Nevertheless, both 2:21–24, which focuses on the example of Christ in not returning abuse, and the following citation from Ps 34:12–16, which focuses likewise on abstaining from evil, point strongly to a backward-looking focus for ὅτι εἰς τοῦτο ἐκλήθητε, as does the obvious εὐλογοῦντες . . . εὐλογίαν correspondence (so ZG 710; Elliott 609; Achtemeier 224; Michaels 178–79; Jobes 219; Dubis 99). Taken this way, the ἵνα clause is more likely to indicate consequence than purpose; otherwise, quite out of character in this epistle, inheriting a blessing becomes somewhat conditional on one's ethical response rather than based on the actions of God in Jesus Christ (1:3; so Achtemeier 224). Thus, followers of Jesus are called to imitate his example of non-retaliation in response to verbal abuse, with the corollary that a blessing awaits. The language of inheritance recalls 1:4 and 3:7.

VERSE 10

ὁ γὰρ θέλων ζωὴν ἀγαπᾶν καὶ ἰδεῖν ἡμέρας ἀγαθάς

The quotation from Ps 33:13–17 LXX (ET 34:12–16) is introduced simply by γάρ. Although the vocabulary is basically the same as the extant LXX text, the citation evidences a number of syntactical changes (for a complete list of differences compared to the LXX text, see Achtemeier 225).

The subst. ptc. ὁ θέλων is used with the complimentary infs. ἀγαπᾶν and ἰδεῖν (aor. act. inf. of ὁράω). Together, the whole clause forms the subj. of the following 3 sg.

impv. παυσάτω (the LXX has 2 sg.). It would be an overstatement to insist that Peter has shifted a this-worldly hope to the eschatological future (*pace* Michaels 180; Elliott 612; Dubis 100). Rather, "life" and "good days" are experienced via new birth and are part of the living hope that the Christian experiences in the present ("If you want to enjoy life and see many happy days," NLT, sim. Weymouth; "Do you really love life? Do you want to be happy?" CEV). Thus while this verse certainly has an eschatological dimension, present experience is not excluded (so Goppelt 236; Jobes 224; Davids 128; Achtemeier 226).

παυσάτω τὴν γλῶσσαν ἀπὸ κακοῦ καὶ χείλη τοῦ μὴ λαλῆσαι δόλον

Παυσάτω 3 sg. aor. act. impv. of παύω, "stop," "cease" (BDAG 790a). Δόλος, -ου, ὁ, "deceit," "treachery" (BDAG 256c). The gen. of separation ἀπὸ κακοῦ is paralleled by the neg. of the art. infin. τοῦ μὴ λαλῆσαι, as in the LXX text. In this case, μή used with the inf. after a verb expressing a neg. concept is redundant (R 1171; BDAG 645a). For the gen. art. with the inf., see MH 449–50; Wallace 234–35; BDF §400; R 1066–68.

VERSE 11

ἐκκλινάτω δὲ ἀπὸ κακοῦ καὶ ποιησάτω ἀγαθόν

The text of the LXX is followed verbatim apart from the substitution of the 3 sg. for the 2 sg. impvs., and the addition of δέ. Ἐκκλινάτω 3 sg. aor. act. impv. of ἐκκλίνω, "turn away" (BDAG 304d), followed once more by the gen. of separation ἀπὸ κακοῦ. On vbs. compounded with one prep. and followed by a different prep. see R 561; Moule 92.

ζητησάτω εἰρήνην καὶ διωξάτω αὐτήν

Ζητησάτω 3 sg. aor. act. imp. of ζητέω. Διωξάτω 3 sg. aor. act. imp. of διώκω. Whereas the previous line in the citation contained a neg. idea ("turn away") followed by a positive ("do"), here the impvs. ("seek" and "pursue") are synonyms.

The sentiments of vv. 10–11 virtually encapsulate the ethics of the epistle, with the emphasis on avoiding evil, particularly sinful speech, and doing good. Specifically, doing good involves both neg. and positive action. It necessitates the avoidance of sins of the tongue (cf. Jas 1:26; 3:1–12), which in this epistle would include retaliation with either abuse or threats of judgment or the like. It also requires a commitment to peace, a virtue that is dominant in NT ethics (Matt 5:9; 2 Cor 13:11; Gal 5:22; 1 Thess 5:13).

VERSE 12

ὅτι ὀφθαλμοὶ κυρίου ἐπὶ δικαίους καὶ ὦτα αὐτοῦ εἰς δέησιν αὐτῶν

Ὅτι is causal and not in the LXX text. Its inclusion here defines the "righteous" as those who do good and pursue peace, and the incentive for so doing is painted in terms of both divine favor and retribution. Thus, as in 2:19, behavior is motivated by a very real consciousness of God's character and actions.

An elliptical cstr. where ὀφθαλμοὶ κυρίου is the subj. of an implied εἰσίν, and ὦτα αὐτοῦ the subj. of an implied vb. such as ἀνοιγοῦσιν, "open" (NRSV, NLT, HCSB, ESV; "attentive," NIV). Ἐπί relates to direction or goal (BDAG 364a), similarly εἰς (BDAG 290a; Dubis 103). Δέησις, -εως, ἡ, "prayer" (BDAG 213d; Turner, *Words* 342).

πρόσωπον δὲ κυρίου ἐπὶ ποιοῦντας κακά

Note the two different senses of the prep. ἐπί in this v. In the opening clause it has a positive sense of "upon," whereas in this clause a neg. sense of "against," in line with Sem. idiom (BDAG 366a; Moule 49; Michaels 181). Πρόσωπον κυρίου is the subj. of an implied ἔστιν.

The final line of Ps 33:17 LXX, τοῦ ἐξολεθρεῦσαι ἐκ γῆς τὸ μνημόσυνον αὐτῶν, "to eliminate their memory from the earth," is omitted, probably because the final line of the citation given in the Petrine text functions not only as a statement directed against unbelievers (and thus an encouragement for those who are persecuted by them), but also as a warning for those who err within the Christian community (Goppelt 237; Achtemeier 227 n. 89).

FOR FURTHER STUDY

See For Further Study §§ 17, 20, 23.

HOMILETICAL SUGGESTIONS

Unity and Love (3:8–12)
1. Five desirable qualities (v. 8)
2. Do not retaliate but bless (v. 9)
   (a) part of the Christian calling
   (b) will result in inheriting a blessing
3. Supporting citation (Ps 34:13–17 LXX) (vv. 10–12)
   (a) turn from evil and do good (vv. 10–11)
   (b) the favor and disfavor of God (v. 12)

VI. Suffering for the Cause of Righteousness (3:13–22)

A. SUFFERING UNJUSTLY (3:13–17)

STRUCTURE

The section opens with two cond. sentences; the first (v. 13) is framed as a rhetorical question, while the second (v. 14a) is concessionary with εἰ καί ("even if"). Vv. 14b–15a offer a contrast between fear and intimidation and revering Christ as Lord. V. 15b stresses the need to explain the Christian hope when questioned about it, whereas v. 16a insists (with the use of ἀλλά) that this is to be done with the appropriate motive and attitude. The ἵνα clause that concludes v. 16 indicates the purpose of such a response to unbelievers. The section concludes with a comp. statement (κρεῖττον . . . ἤ), with a parenthetical cond. (εἰ), on the familiar theme of suffering for proper behavior rather than suffering for doing evil.

13 καὶ τίς ὁ κακώσων ὑμᾶς,
        ἐὰν τοῦ ἀγαθοῦ ζηλωταὶ γένησθε;
14 ἀλλ' εἰ καὶ πάσχοιτε διὰ δικαιοσύνην, μακάριοι.

   τὸν δὲ <u>φόβον</u> αὐτῶν <u>μὴ φοβηθῆτε</u>
               <u>μηδὲ ταραχθῆτε</u>,
15 κύριον δὲ τὸν Χριστὸν <u>ἁγιάσατε</u> ἐν ταῖς καρδίαις ὑμῶν,
               ἕτοιμοι ἀεὶ πρὸς ἀπολογίαν παντὶ τῷ αἰτοῦντι ὑμᾶς
                                    λόγον
                             περὶ τῆς ἐν ὑμῖν
                                 ἐλπίδος,
16
                        ἀλλὰ μετὰ πραΰτητος καὶ <u>φόβου</u>,
                        συνείδησιν ἔχοντες ἀγαθήν,
  ἵνα ἐν ᾧ καταλαλεῖσθε
        καταισχυνθῶσιν οἱ ἐπηρεάζοντες ὑμῶν τὴν ἀγαθὴν ἐν Χριστῷ ἀναστροφήν.

17　κρεῖττον γὰρ ἀγαθοποιοῦντας, εἰ θέλοι τὸ θέλημα τοῦ θεοῦ, πάσχειν ἢ
　　　　　　　　　　　　　　　　　　　　　　　　κακοποιοῦντας.

VERSE 13

καὶ τίς ὁ κακώσων ὑμᾶς ἐὰν τοῦ ἀγαθοῦ ζηλωταὶ γένησθε

Following on from the Scripture citation, καί is used to introduce an abrupt question expressing wonder (BDAG 495b). The apod. is first and is framed as a rhetorical question, with the expected answer "no one." Κακώσων nom. sg. masc. of fut. act. ptc. of κακόω, "harm," "mistreat" (BDAG 502a). One of only thirteen uses of the fut. ptc. in the NT (see R 877–78, 1118–19; BDF §351). Here the ptc. expresses subsequent time ("will harm you," NRSV; "going to harm you," NIV) to the prot. (Wallace 614).

Ζηλωτής, -οῦ, ὁ, "enthusiast," "zealot" (BDAG 427d; H.-C. Hahn, *NIDNTT* 3.1166–68; A. Stumpff, *TDNT* 2.882–88). Here a pred. nom. with γένησθε (subjunc. with ἐάν) indicating one who is zealous ("eager," NRSV, CEV, NIV) for a cause (Titus 2:14; 1 Cor 14:12; Acts 22:3; Gal 1:14; LN 25.77), namely "the good." The subst. adj. τοῦ ἀγαθοῦ is an obj. gen. signifying what is zealously pursued. The "good" has already been defined in 2:11–3:12 and will now be developed further.

Some mss. (K L P 69 *Byz* vg^ms) read μιμηταί, "imitators," rather than ζηλωταί, "zealots," which is probably a deliberate attempt to soften a term that came to have quite neg. connotations after the Jewish War of AD 66–70 (Achtemeier 228; Michaels 183). The ms. tradition is also quite confused regarding γένησθε (supported by ℵ^c A C P 33, 1739 *Byz*). Alternative readings are as follows: Ψ substitutes ἔστε, B has the opt. γένοισθε (which together with its reading of εἰ forms a fourth class cond. in line with εἰ πάσχοιτε in the following v.), while 𝔓^72 ℵ* and a few other mss. have the aor. impv. γένεσθε. The latter is certainly the most difficult rdg. as it does not fit with ἐάν, but in the end γένησθε should be retained due to its diversity of ms. support.

Elsewhere in this epistle it is clear that the author does expect Christians to suffer at least verbal abuse for doing what is right (1:6; 2:12, 19–21; 3:9,17; 4:12–16). There are two possibilities for understanding the cond. here:

*1. the intention is rhetorical or proverbial, designed as a further incentive to appropriate conduct (2:14; cf. Ps 91:7–12; in various forms Goppelt 240; Davids 130; Jobes 226–27). This positive affirmation is then mitigated somewhat in the following v. by a further cond. statement; or
2. Alternatively, "harm" is to be taken in an absolute sense of a robbing of one's status before God, including eschatological blessings (cf. Matt 10:28–31; so Achtemeier 229–30; Elliott 620). Thus the possibility of physical suffering is not denied and, in fact, is taken up in the following v.

In its other NT uses, κακόω never refers to eschatological harm. Furthermore, the clearest sense of ἀλλ᾽ εἰ καί in the following v. is concessive ("but even if"), thus placing πάσχοιτε (a vb. which clearly relates to physical suffering in this epistle) and κακώσων in parallel (Dubis 106). Option 1 is to be preferred.

VERSE 14

ἀλλ' εἰ καὶ πάσχοιτε διὰ δικαιοσύνην μακάριοι

Given the interpretation offered for the previous v., the rare fourth-class cond. (Porter 263–64; Z §323–24; McKay 174; Turner, *Insights* 169–70; Wallace 699–700; R 1021–21; BDF §385[2]) using εἰ plus the opt. πάσχοιτε (2 pl. pres. act. opt. πάσχω) qualifies a proverbial type statement in light of the actual situation of the readers rather than presenting a present perspective in contrast to the eschatological future.

It has already been seen that suffering for doing good (here "for the sake of righteousness") is more than a hypothetical possibility; it is, in fact, part of the Christian calling (2:21). So rather than indicate a remote possibility (*pace* Wallace 484, 700), the use of the rare opt. mood serves a rhetorical function, encouraging the recipients to do good (Michaels 186; sim. Goppelt 241, "He emphasizes the openness of the situation in order to protect the church from fatalistic resignation and to encourage it toward a positive form of conduct"; Achtemeier 231 believes that the opt. is used to express a "sporadic reality").

Ἀλλ' εἰ καί presents a strong contrast with the apod. (*NewDocs* 6.69). The apod. is elliptical (R 1023), with the need to supply ἔστε with the pred. nom. μακάριοι (as per א C and a few other mss.). There is some divergence among EVV as to whether a present "are" (NRSV, NASB, HCSB, NIV) or future "will be" (NLT, CEV, ESV) is required, but the close parallel with 4:14 suggests the former (Dubis 107–8). The saying has affinities with Matt 5:10, and the idea of receiving a blessing recalls v. 9 (cf. 1:7).

τὸν δὲ φόβον αὐτῶν μὴ φοβηθῆτε μηδὲ ταραχθῆτε

Μηδὲ ταραχθῆτε is omitted by 𝔓⁷² B L, probably by homoioteleuton, but is retained by א A C P Ψ 33, 1739 and the majority text in line with Isa 8:12b LXX. Ταραχθῆτε 2 pl. aor. pass. subj. of ταράσσω, "shake," "agitate," "trouble" (BDAG 990d; H. Müller, *NIDNTT* 3.709–10; Spicq 3.372–76; MM 625d). The cognate acc. (Moule 32; R 477–78; BDF §153[1]) τὸν φόβον αὐτῶν is ambiguous. It is lit. "do not fear the fear of them," which could be:

1. an exhortation "not to fear what they fear" (NRSV, HCSB). This is the sense of the MT and the LXX with the sg. αὐτοῦ (antecedent is λαός, *pace* Michaels 186–87 who maintains it is the king of Assyria) of the LXX referring to the people's fear of the Syrio-Ephramite alliance; or
2. an emphatic way of saying "do not fear them" ("do not fear their intimidation," NASB, sim. NIV).

Αὐτῶν is an example of *constructio ad sensum*, where the antecedent of the pron. must be understood from the larger narrative (BDF §282[3]). In the discussion above, αὐτῶν is a subj. gen. in option 1; in option 2 it is obj. (though the rendering in NASB, NIV makes it subj. in a different sense). Most favor option 2 at least partly on the basis of the change from the singular αὐτοῦ of the LXX to the plural αὐτῶν (ZG 710; Moule 40; T 212; Michaels 186–87; Achtemeier 232; Davids 130–31; Jobes 229; Elliott 624–25).

However, this grammatical change in itself does not resolve the ambiguity (e.g., Dubis 108 favors a subj. gen. in the sense of unbelievers fearing "the suffering and shame that Christians experience"). Rather, the obj. gen. is more likely due to contextual factors; the personal worries or fears of those who malign God's people are simply not in view in this epistle, whereas there are warnings against being intimidated by unbelievers themselves (3:6; 4:2–4, 13 [implicitly]).

VERSE 15

κύριον δὲ τὸν Χριστὸν ἁγιάσατε ἐν ταῖς καρδίαις ὑμῶν

Δέ is adversative, contrasting v. 14b. Under external threat believers are not to fear others, but to acknowledge the authority of Christ. The language of LXX Isa continues; the present passage echoes 8:13a, with Peter substituting Χριστόν for αὐτόν (although in line with the LXX, the majority text reads θεόν. However, Χριστόν not only has early and reliable support [𝔓⁷² ℵ A B C Ψ etc.]; it is more in keeping with Peter's usual reference to Christ as κύριος [1:3; 2:3]), and adding ἐν ταῖς καρδίαις ὑμῶν.

Κύριον δὲ τὸν Χριστόν can be taken in two ways:

1. κύριον is a complement with τὸν Χριστόν in a double acc. relationship giving, "Christ/Messiah as Lord" (ASV, NRSV, NASB, HCSB, NIV; ZG 710; Selwyn 192; Achtemeier 232); or
2. κύριον is the dir. obj. of ἁγιάσατε, with τὸν Χριστόν in appos. giving, "the Lord Christ" (NJB, [NKJV: "God"]; Michaels 187), or "Christ the Lord" (ESV).

Although Dubis contends that the LXX preserves the appos. structure of the MT, the LXX κύριον αὐτὸν ἁγιάσατε is itself ambiguous and can be taken as: "sanctify the Lord himself" (Michaels 187), "sanctify him as Lord," or "sanctify him, the Lord" (Dubis 110, although he seems to indicate that the appos. works the other way around: "sanctify the Lord, him"). In the end, it is difficult to decide between the options, and in any event the mng. is largely unaffected.

Ἁγιάσατε 2 pl. aor. act. impv. of ἁγιάζω, "sanctify," "make holy" (BDAG 9d; Turner, Words 83–85). Here the vb. has a declarative sense; i.e., it is acknowledging Christ as holy and according him his proper place rather than making him holy ("proclaim," NJB; "reverence," RSV; "revere," NIV; "honor," CEV; Michaels 187; Achtemeier 232 n. 50). The aor. impv. should be taken in a programmatic sense (see the discussion on "The Use of the Imperative in 1 Peter" in the Introduction).

Ἐν ταῖς καρδίαις ὑμῶν is locat. of sphere and metaphorical for "of your life" (CEV, NLT). Rather than indicate only a state of mind (i.e., the heart as the seat of the emotions), it is likely that the prep. phrase specifies an approach to life. The inner acknowledgment of Christ's authority in the life of the Christian must be paralleled by a readiness to live and witness externally to the hope that this brings.

ἕτοιμοι ἀεὶ πρὸς ἀπολογίαν παντὶ τῷ αἰτοῦντι ὑμᾶς λόγον περὶ τῆς ἐν ὑμῖν ἐλπίδος

῞Ετοιμος, -η, -ον, "ready" (BDAG 401a). ῞Ετοιμοι carries a sense of eschatological urgency given its uses in eschatological contexts elsewhere in this epistle (1:5; 4:5; Michaels 188). Ἀεί, "always" (adv.). The prep. πρός conveys purpose (BDAG 874c; Wallace 380–82), whereas the prep. phrase πρὸς ἀπολογίαν gives ἕτοιμοι its content.

The elliptical phrase ἕτοιμοι ἀεὶ πρὸς ἀπολογίαν is clearly related to κύριον δὲ τὸν Χριστὸν ἁγιάσατε ἐν ταῖς καρδίαις ὑμῶν, although the manner of this relationship is unclear:

*1. it could be impv. due to the link with ἁγιάσατε, thus an impv. form of εἰμί (ἔστε) needs to be supplied: "always be ready" (NRSV, CEV, HCSB, NIV; Elliott 626); or

2. it can be cstr. as instr. of means, with the ptc. ὄντες supplied: "by always being ready" (Achtemeier 233 n. 54; sim. ASV, NASB, ESV).

On either interpretation ἕτοιμοι is pred., but even if we adopt option 2 there is still derived impv. force (see the discussion on "Imperatival Participles in 1 Peter" in the Introduction).

Ἀπολογία, -ας, ἡ, "defense" (BDAG 117a; U. Kellermann, *EDNT* 1.137). The noun is a legal term used of a formal defense in a courtroom setting (Acts 22:1; 25:16; 2 Tim 4:16). This does not imply that the recipients of this letter were being formerly indicted for their faith (*pace* Beare 164), as the term can also relate to a less formal response in the face of criticism or request (1 Cor 9:3; 2 Cor 7:11). The use of ἀεί together with παντί supports this less formal setting (Davids 131; Elliott 627), although Michaels (188) puts it well in stating, "Peter sees his readers as being 'on trial' everyday as they live for Christ in a pagan society."

Ὑμᾶς and λόγον form a double acc. (see R 482; Wallace 181–89 lists it as "debated") for the subst. ptc. τῷ αἰτοῦντι. Most modern EVV render ὑμᾶς as the dir. obj. and use the prep "for" (HCSB, ESV), or the inf. "to give" (NASB, NIV) with λόγον ("to every-one who asks you for/to give a reason"), although NRSV cstr. λόγον as the dir. obj. and renders ὑμᾶς as "from you," giving "to anyone who demands from you an accounting."

Here λόγον (see BDAG 601b) refers to a "reason" (NKJV, HCSB, ESV), "answer" (CEV, NIV), or "account" (NRSV, NASB). Τῆς ἐλπίδος recalls the "living hope" (1:3), which is grounded in God (1:21). Ἐν ὑμῖν could be rendered "among you" in order to stress the corporate dimension of the Christian hope (as do Achtemeier 233–34; Michaels 189). Nevertheless, the hope is not only corporate; it is also the possession of each individual Christian by means of the new birth (1:3, 23).

VERSE 16

ἀλλὰ μετὰ πραΰτητος καὶ φόβου

Ἀλλά has a weakened adversative sense, introducing a qualification (BDF §448[6]) to the injunction of the previous v. regarding giving a defense of the faith. This is another ellipsis, functioning impv. ("do it," NRSV; "do this," HCSB, NIV). Πραΰτης, -ητος, ἡ, "gentleness," "courtesy" (BDAG 861a; cf. the cognate adj. in 3:4), which most likely refers to an attitude toward the questioner rather than toward God. On the use of φόβος in 1 Peter, see 1:17. Again the focus is on reverent fear of God (NRSV, NASB), notwithstanding the many EVV that take it as a parallel attitude to πραΰτητος directed to the questioner ("respect," NJB, ESV, NIV; ZG 710).

συνείδησιν ἔχοντες ἀγαθήν

In contrast to 2:19 (see the discussion there) where συνείδησιν has the sense of mental awareness (i.e., consciousness), here it has the more common NT sense of "conscience." It thereby helps explain the sense of φόβου in the previous clause as an orientation toward God (Achtemeier 236; Elliott 630).

The ptc. ἔχοντες could be attendant circumstance, and thus carry impv. force due to its link with the implied impv. of the previous v. and clause (ESV, NIV). Achtemeier (235) agrees that it is attendant circumstance, but wrongly denies its impv. force. As Wallace (640) states, the attendant circumstance ptc. "'piggy-backs' on the mood of the main vb." A number of EVV take it as a direct impv. (NRSV, CEV, NLT, NASB; also ZG 710; Elliott 629).

However, it is better cstr. as a ptc. of result; i.e., "do it with gentleness and reverence and so maintain a good conscience," although even in this sense the impv. quality is not totally abolished. On the ptc. of result, see Wallace 637–39, who argues that a pres. ptc. following a main vb. should be cstr. as a ptc. of result rather than attendant circumstance (which normally precedes the main vb.). See also the discussion on "Imperatival Participles in 1 Peter" in the Introduction.

ἵνα ἐν ᾧ καταλαλεῖσθε καταισχυνθῶσιν οἱ ἐπηρεάζοντες ὑμῶν τὴν ἀγαθὴν ἐν Χριστῷ ἀναστροφήν

Καταλαλεῖσθε 2 pl. pres. pass. indic. of καταλαλέω, "slander," "abuse" (BDAG 519c; W. Mundle, NIDNTT 3.345–46). Καταισχυνθῶσιν 3 pl. aor. pass. subjunc. of καταισχύνω, "shame," "disgrace" (BDAG 517b; H.-G. Link, NIDNTT 3.562–64). Ἐπηρεάζοντες nom. pl. masc. of pres. act. ptc. of ἐπηρεάζω, "mistreat," "malign" (BDAG 362d), used only here and Luke 6:28 in the NT, although Peter has elsewhere spoken of insulting language using the synonyms λοιδορέω/λοιδορία (2:23; 3:9), ὀνειδίζω (4:14), and καταλαλέω/καταλαλία (2:1, 12). Rather than the pres. ptc. indicating continuous disparaging (Elliott 631), it has iterative force indicating repeated action. Ἀναστροφή, -ῆς, ἡ, "conduct" (see on 1:15, 17).

A number of important mss. (א A C P 33, 81, 945) read καταλαλοῦσιν ὑμῶν ὡς κακοποιῶν, while several other minuscules and the majority text follow suit except for the subjunc. form καταλαλῶσιν. The text is supported by 𝔓⁷² B Ψ 614, 630, 1175, 1241, 1505, 1611, 1739, 1852, 1881, 2138, 2298. Despite the diversified support for the longer reading, it has been clearly influenced by 2:12 and possibly motivated by the extremely rare use of the pass. form of καταλαλέω. The shorter rdg. should be retained.

Ἵνα with the subjunc. καταισχυνθῶσιν expresses the purpose of a gentle defense of the Christian hope in terms of shaming those who are hostile to the believer. The vb. is positioned first in the clause for emphasis (Turner, *Style* 125). Compare with 2:12 where the stated purpose of proper conduct is the (apparent) conversion of the unbeliever and 2:15 where it is a silencing of their ignorance. It is unclear here whether the shame should be understood as a preview to conversion in the present (Dubis 113–14), or eschatological in focus related to the day of visitation mentioned in 2:12. In any event, it contrasts the ultimate fortunes of the faithful who will never be put to shame (2:6–7).

Ἐν ᾧ is equivalent to the Eng. "in the situation that" (NASB; cf. 2:12; BDF §294 [4]; ZG 707; Dubis 113; Michaels 117; Elliott 467) and implies ἐν τούτῳ (R 721). Its antecedent is conceptual rather than grammatical (Wallace 342–43). Ὑμῶν τὴν ἀγαθὴν ἐν Χριστῷ ἀναστροφήν is the dir. obj of οἱ ἐπηρεάζοντες. The dat. ἐν Χριστῷ is common in the Pauline letters, but Paul's developed mystical sense should not be understood here. It should probably be taken as a locat. of sphere and serves to define good conduct not in cultural terms but with regard to one's relationship to Christ ("because you belong to Christ," NLT; Achtemeier 236 n. 101; Davids 133). Ὑμῶν is a subj. gen. On ἀναστροφή see 1:15, 17.

VERSE 17

κρεῖττον γὰρ ἀγαθοποιοῦντας . . . πάσχειν ἢ κακοποιοῦντας

Ἀγαθοποιοῦντας acc. pl. masc. of pres. act. ptc. of ἀγαθοποιέω, "do good," "do right" (BDAG 3a). Κακοποιοῦντας acc. pl. masc. of pres. act. ptc. of κακοποιέω, "do wrong," "do evil" (BDAG 501a). The comp. adj. κρείττων, -ον, -ονος (also κρείσσων, -ον, -ονος; see R 217–18 on the interchange of consonants), "better" (BDAG 566a), is pred. with an implied ἔστιν, and neut. with the inf. (see Wallace 588–89). The inf. πάσχειν is subst., functioning as the subj. of the implied ἔστιν ("to suffer . . . is better"), and is implied with κακοποιοῦντας. The ptcs. ἀγαθοποιοῦντας and κακοποιοῦντας are both causal ("it is better to suffer because you do good than because you do evil").

The form of this saying is a "better-proverb" or *Tobspruch*, found in the Synoptic tradition (Mark 9:43, 45, 47; Matt 18:8–9) and the wider NT (1 Cor 7:9; 2 Pet 2:21). The eschatological focus of the Synoptic passages, together with the unlikelihood, given such passages as 4:2–4, that "doing evil" (from a Christian point of view only) would be the occasion for suffering in a pagan society, leads Michaels (191–92) to relate πάσχειν κακοποιοῦντας to the suffering that unbelievers experience at the final judgment (i.e., the v. presents a contrast between suffering now for doing good and suffering eternally for doing evil). Nevertheless, most commentators understand the maxim to be a repetition of the thought of 2:20 and an anticipation of 4:15 in warning Christians against violations of the secular law, such as murder, theft, etc. (Davids 133–34; Elliott 36). In this sense, it reflects a truism endorsed by secular moral philosophers (see Plato, *Gorg.* 474b; 474c; 508c; Cicero, *Tusc.* 5.56). However, in 1 Peter it rises above a cultural truism by virtue of the fact that it is directly linked to the purposes of God (Achtemeier 238).

εἰ θέλοι τὸ θέλημα τοῦ θεοῦ

Θέλοι 3 sg. pres. act. opt. of θέλω. The point of the opt. mood is not to indicate that suffering is only a remote possibility; instead, it forms part of the rhetorical strategy of this section, forming an *inclusio* with 3:14 (see there on the use of the opt. in a cond. cstr.). The alliteration (θ . . . θ . . . θ) contributes to the rhetorical effect at a literary level.

The placement of this clause between the "doing good" and "doing evil" alternatives is significant, as is the recognition that πάσχειν is not the subj. of θέλοι but of an implied ἔστιν (see above). Elliott (635) sums it up well: "The qualification, *if this should be God's will*, refers to suffering *for doing what is right* and not simply suffering per se. The point is not that God wills suffering but that *God wills doing what is right* rather than doing what is wrong . . . even if and when this results in suffering" (emphasis original). This v. thus forms part of a consistent ethical strand that runs throughout the entire epistle (2:21–24; 3:14; 4:14–16). Christians can be encouraged that innocent suffering is not outside of God's control (cf. 1:6; 4:19).

FOR FURTHER STUDY

See For Further Study §§ 13, 19.

HOMILETICAL SUGGESTIONS

Suffering Unjustly (3:13–17)

1. Suffering for doing what is right (vv. 13–14)
   (a) Is less likely (v. 13)
   (b) Brings a blessing (v. 14a)
   (c) Do not fear those who instigate it (v. 14b)
2. Giving an accounting of the Christian hope (vv. 15–16)
   (a) Revere Christ as Lord (v. 15a)
   (b) Explaining the Christian Hope (vv. 15b–16)
       (i) to all who ask
       (ii) with the appropriate attitude
       (iii) shaming those who insult
3. Appropriate Suffering (v. 17)
   (a) Suffering for doing good may be the will of God
   (b) Suffering for doing wrong is inappropriate

B. THE SUFFERING AND VINDICATION OF CHRIST (3:18–22)

STRUCTURE

This is undoubtedly one of the most difficult passages in the NT exegetically, theologically, and structurally. From the structure given below it is evident that to some extent the complexities exist because of several parenthetical statements that disrupt the main argument. The passage begins and ends with a focus on Christ, and it appears that the main purpose of the section is to depict the transition from his suffering to exaltation.

V. 18 commences with Christ's suffering, but, via a μέν . . . δέ cstr. at the end of the v., the focus shifts from death to life. By means of the rel. ἐν ᾧ, v. 19 picks up the final word (πνεύματι) from v. 18 (see argument below) and embarks on a parenthesis to depict what happened "in the Spirit." V. 20 in turn picks up on πνεύμασιν, "spirits," from v. 19 and discloses something of their identity. The reference to the ark provides another transition midway through v. 20 (by means of the rel. εἰς ἥν) to mention the salvation of Noah and his family.

V. 21 commences with the rel. ὅ, picking up "water" from the conclusion of v. 20 and making a statement about Christian baptism. The instr. δι' ἀναστάσεως Ἰησοῦ Χριστοῦ, "through the resurrection of Jesus Christ," provides the connection back to the main thread of the argument. V. 22 utilizes the rel. ὅς linking back to Christ to depict the final stage of his journey: his exaltation at the right hand of God.

18 ὅτι καὶ Χριστὸς ἅπαξ περὶ ἁμαρτιῶν ἔπαθεν,
　　　　δίκαιος ὑπὲρ ἀδίκων,
　　　　　　　ἵνα ὑμᾶς προσαγάγῃ τῷ θεῷ
　　　　　　　　　θανατωθεὶς μὲν σαρκὶ
　　　　　　　　　ζωοποιηθεὶς δὲ πνεύματι·

19 ἐν ᾧ καὶ τοῖς ἐν φυλακῇ πνεύμασιν πορευθεὶς ἐκήρυξεν
20　　　　　　　　　　ἀπειθήσασίν ποτε
　　　　　　　　　　　　ὅτε ἀπεξεδέχετο ἡ τοῦ θεοῦ μακροθυμία
　　　　　　　　　　　　ἐν ἡμέραις Νῶε
　　　　　　　　　　　　κατασκευαζομένης κιβωτοῦ

εἰς ἣν ὀλίγοι, τοῦτ' ἔστιν ὀκτὼ ψυχαί, διεσώθησαν δι' ὕδατος

21 ὃ καὶ ὑμᾶς ἀντίτυπον νῦν σῴζει βάπτισμα,
　　　　　　　οὐ σαρκὸς ἀπόθεσις ῥύπου
　　　　　　　ἀλλὰ συνειδήσεως ἀγαθῆς ἐπερώτημα εἰς θεόν
　　　　　　　　　δι' ἀναστάσεως Ἰησοῦ Χριστοῦ

22 ὅς ἐστιν ἐν δεξιᾷ τοῦ θεοῦ
　　　πορευθεὶς εἰς οὐρανὸν
　　　ὑποταγέντων αὐτῷ ἀγγέλων καὶ ἐξουσιῶν καὶ δυνάμεων.

VERSE 18

ὅτι καὶ Χριστὸς ἅπαξ περὶ ἁμαρτιῶν ἔπαθεν

The text is extremely confused here. Many mss. read ἀπέθανεν, "died" (also NJB, CEV, NASB) instead of ἔπαθεν, "suffered," some of which add ὑπὲρ ὑμῶν, "on your behalf," ($\mathfrak{P}^{72}$ A Ψ 1241, 1292, 1505, 1611, 1735), others add ὑπὲρ ἡμῶν, "on our behalf" (א C^{2vid} and a number of minuscules). L 81, 2464 read ἔπαθεν and add ὑπὲρ ἡμῶν. The rdg. in the text περὶ ἁμαρτιῶν ἔπαθεν, "suffered for sins," is supported by B P and the majority text. In evaluating the ms. data, the longer readings should be rejected as confessional expansions. Furthermore, it is more likely that a scribe would change ἔπαθεν to ἀπέθανεν than vice versa, thus conforming to the traditional creedal formula that Christ died for our sins (see also the var. rdg. in 2:21). Finally, while it is clear that Christ's suffering includes his death, the term "suffering" is more appropriate in the immediate context. In conclusion, περὶ ἁμαρτιῶν ἔπαθεν should be retained as it best explains the rise of the alternative rdgs. See further Metzger 622–23.

The use of the causal conj. ὅτι shows that the section division is somewhat artificial, although it is valid due to an overall change in subject matter. As in 2:21, ὅτι καὶ Χριστός introduces the suffering of Christ as an example for suffering believers; i.e., καί is "also," and so provides the rationale for vv. 13–17 (this is debated among commentators—see further Achtemeier 243–44; Elliott 639). Here, however, it is not his patient endurance that is in view, but suffering as a path to glory. Consequently, the point of 3:18–22 is not that believers imitate Christ's suffering; instead, it assures them that Christ has overcome death and reigns victorious over the forces of evil. The way of suffering leads to glory and divine vindication. By implication, followers of Christ will tread the same path, confident that he can lead them on a path he has trod himself (Achtemeier 243–46; Elliott 638).

The temp. adv. ἅπαξ, "once," "once for all time" (BDAG 97b; Spicq 1.139–42) is prominent in the epistle to the Hebrews in connection with Christ's sacrificial death, but it is not given theological elaboration here in 1 Peter. Rather, the point is that suffering is finished. Περὶ ἁμαρτιῶν is not further clarified here, although this expression is utilized in the LXX and the NT to refer to atonement for sin (BDAG 798a; Harris 182–83). Περί in this sense is interchangeable with ὑπέρ (cf. Heb 10:12 with 10:26; BDF §229[1]; ZG 711).

δίκαιος ὑπὲρ ἀδίκων

Christ as δίκαιος (in appos. to Χριστός) may be influenced by LXX Isa 53:11 and is elsewhere highlighted by the citation from Isa 53:4, 12 in 2:22 and is depicted metaphorically using cultic language in 1:19. This serves to reinforce the concept of innocent suffering so crucial for the author, esp. given the obvious link to δικαίους ("the righteous") in 3:12 and δικαιοσύνην ("righteousness") in 3:14 (Davids 135; Goppelt 251). The identity of the ἀδίκων, "unrighteous," is not stated explicitly, but clearly Peter understands it to be his readers (see 1:14, 18; 4:2–4; and the fact that they need to be lead to God).

Most EVV trans. δίκαιος ὑπὲρ ἀδίκων as "the righteous (just) for the unrighteous (unjust)," but this tends to obscure the fact that Christ is in the "righteous" category all by himself. "Unrighteous" refers to everyone else. It could be rendered "the righteous one for the unrighteous many" (Achtemeier 239; sim. Weymouth), but this gives the impression of a title ("Righteous One," as in Acts 3:14; 7:52; 22:14), which does not appear to be the case here. A better alternative is to retain the anar. Gk.—"a righteous man for unrighteous people," in order to highlight the qualitative aspect (Dubis 116; sim. Michaels 194, 202; Barclay: "He, the good, died for us, the bad").

ἵνα ὑμᾶς προσαγάγῃ τῷ θεῷ

The purpose clause with ἵνα explains Christ's suffering not in terms of an example as in 2:21, but as leading his followers to God (cf. Heb 2:10). This implies previous alienation from God, elsewhere explained as a life of decadence (1:14, 18; 4:2–4) and pictured using the wandering sheep metaphor (2:25). The leading is a process that culminates with the reception of glory and honor at the final revelation of Jesus (Michaels 203).

Προσαγάγῃ 3 sg. aor. act. subjunc. of προσάγω, "bring to," "lead to" (BDAG 875d). The 2 pl. pron. ὑμᾶς is read by 𝔓⁷² B Ψ P *Byz* and a number of other minuscules. The 1 pl. ἡμᾶς is read by ℵ² A C K L and several other minuscules, while A omits the pron. entirely. Ὑμᾶς should be retained on the basis of the consistent 2 pl. address in the preceding context and the likelihood that scribes strove to make the text more inclusive (particularly given the important doctrinal statement).

θανατωθεὶς μὲν σαρκὶ ζωοποιηθεὶς δὲ πνεύματι

Θανατωθεὶς nom. sg. masc. of. aor. pass. ptc. of θανατόω, "put to death" (BDAG 443d). Ζωοποιηθεὶς nom. sg. masc. of. aor. pass. ptc. of ζωοποιέω, "make alive" (BDAG 431d; Turner, *Words* 361). Both ptcs. are dependent upon προσαγάγῃ, with the emphasis falling on ζωοποιηθείς (Achtemeier 249; Elliott 644; Michaels 205). In terms of their relationship to προσαγάγῃ, they stand in either a causal (i.e., he leads to God because he was put to death and was made alive) or an instr. relationship (i.e., he leads to God by means of his death and resurrection [Dubis 117 favors the latter]). Many EVV obscure this connection by beginning a new sentence (Weymouth, NJB, NRSV, NIV; CEV has "when").

Given that the μέν . . . δέ cstr. provides a contrast (𝔓⁷² omits μέν, as do A*ᵛⁱᵈ Ψ 1285, and adds ἐν prior to πνεύματι. The μέν . . . δέ cstr. should be retained on the basis of early and diversified ms. support [a Aᶜ B C P 33, 1739 *Byz*]), θανατωθεὶς is also concessive with respect to ζωοποιηθείς, i.e., "although put to death . . . . he was made alive" (as noted by Michaels 205; Jobes 240). The μέν . . . δέ cstr. clearly provides a symmetry to the clause and consequently the dats. σαρκί and πνεύματι should likely be cstr. in the same way (Dalton 141; Elliott 645; Jobes 240). Not all are in agreement: Wallace (343) contends that this passage may reflect a hymnic fragment and thus we should allow "poetic license," whereas Dubis (118) appeals to the sim. ambiguous cstr. in 1 Tim 3:16. This approach is reflected in the trans. "in the flesh . . . by the Spirit" (NKJV). If the dats. are cstr. in the same way, this tends to rule out instr. force, because although "made alive by the Spirit" is suitable, "put to death by the flesh" would be a strange euphemism for the human participants in the crucifixion (*pace* Achtemeier 250).

Consequently, the dats. are best taken as locs. of sphere (Kelly 151; Best 151; Goppelt 246; R 523) or dats. of respect/ref. (Elliott 645; Michaels 204; ZG 711), with the same sense. Christ was put to death in the realm of the flesh but made alive in the realm of the Spirit. This does not imply a dualism between the material and immaterial, which is a Gk. philosophical notion quite foreign to biblical thought, but a contrast between the weakness of human nature (σάρξ is used in this sense in 1:24; 4:1, 2, 6) and the power of the life to come. In other words, Christ has moved from an earthly existence into the realm of resurrection life, the latter indicated by the frequent use of ζωοποιέω in the NT of the resurrection (John 5:21; Rom 4:17; 8:11; 1 Cor 15:52; cf. συζωοποιέω in Eph 2:5; Col 2:13). Consequently, it is virtually a consensus among modern commentators that this is not a reference to an intermediate state (e.g., Dalton 135–42; Davids 137; Michaels 205; Goppelt 253–54).

It is unclear whether "Spirit" should be capitalized or not. Having rejected the instr. sense for πνεύματι and opted for a locat. of sphere (i.e., mode/realm of existence), the parallel with σαρκί probably favors a lower case "spirit" (Michaels 204; ASV, NJB, NRSV, NASB, ESV). Nevertheless, the spiritual realm is inseparably bound up with the Spirit of God, so capitalization is not misleading.

VERSE 19

ἐν ᾧ καὶ τοῖς ἐν φυλακῇ πνεύμασιν πορευθεὶς ἐκήρυξεν

Here the exegetical problems begin in earnest. As grammatical factors are interwoven with other exegetical and theological concerns, we will first summarize the major interpretive issues and approaches, showing how grammatical factors weigh upon each of them. We will then be in a position to offer some conclusions based on the grammatical analysis.

The first of several difficult grammatical issues concerns the antecedent and sense of ἐν ᾧ (sim. 1:6; 2:12; 3:16; 4:4; Wallace 343; Moule 131). The likely options are as follows:

*1. πνεύματι, with ἐν as locat. giving the sense that Christ preached to the spirits in prison in the spiritual realm (Dalton 144–45; Michaels 206; Weymouth, NRSV, NASB, HCSB, ESV);

2. πνεύματι, with ἐν as instr. giving the sense that Christ preached to the spirits by the Spirit (Achtemeier 252; NKJV);

3. the whole of v. 18, giving "in the process of which he went" (Selwyn 197; Davids 138. *Pace* Selwyn 197, the fact that there is no other instance in the NT of a dat. of ref. acting as the antecedent for a rel. pron. does not appear to be decisive in ruling out that option here);

4. ἐν ᾧ is a rel. temp. conj., "at which time" (Jobes 243; sim. NIV); or

5. ἐν ᾧ is a circumstantial conj., "in this connection" (Elliott 652; Goppelt 255–56).

The most natural sense is to take ἐν ᾧ with πνεύματι (ZG 711; Turner, *Insights* 171; Dubis 119), and, given the interpretation of πνεύματι offered above, option 1 is preferred. Nevertheless, on any of the above understandings, it clearly relates to an event that occurred post-resurrection (see above on v. 18) and leaves little room for any theory of what happened between Christ's death and resurrection (Achtemeier 252).

The function of καί is also disputed. The strength of regarding ἐν ᾧ as instr. (which also depends on πνεύματι in v. 18d being instr.—a position against which I have argued) is that καί can logically be rendered "also," i.e., the Spirit is responsible for the resurrection and the activity of v. 19 (Achtemeier 252). Without this sense the conj. appears to be redundant because there is no activity of Christ mentioned in v. 18d—the vbs. are pass. Michaels (206) suggests a translation "even," but this appears to imply that Christ preached to someone else as well, a point not sustained by the context. In the end, καί should be rendered "also," but understood as a further stage in the heavenly journey (put to death—made alive—ascended to the heavens with a proclamation to the spirits in the process), rather than something additional that Christ himself performed (so Dubis 119).

The second interpretive crux concerns the identity of τοῖς ἐν φυλακῇ πνεύμασιν. They are variously understood as:

1. the wicked who perished in the flood. Christ preached to them at a time contemporaneous with the resurrection event (Beare 172; Goppelt 259; Barclay);
2. the wicked who perished in the flood. Christ preached to them in his preexistent state through Noah while they were alive; this view claims wider contextual support from 1:11, where Peter mentions the spirit of Christ inspiring the OT prophets. They are now "in prison" from the author's perspective (Feinberg 303–336; Grudem 157–61, 203–39; cf. NASB), or in prison metaphorically with respect to sin (Kelly 153);
3. the dead prior to Christ (Green 118–38); or
→ *4. fallen angels. This builds on a Jewish exegetical tradition (see Elliott 653, 693–705) which understood the "sons of God" in Gen 6:2 to be fallen angels who cohabited with human women (so most modern commentators: e.g., Dalton 145–49; Elliott 651–62; Achtemeier 252–62; Davids 139–41; sim. Michaels 207–11).

There are two grammatical issues that impinge on the resolution of the identity of τοῖς ἐν φυλακῇ πνεύμασιν. The first is whether the pl. πνεύματα is capable of referring to human beings without being so qualified. The noun only appears in the pl. related to human beings in Heb 12:23 and there is explained with a qualifying gen. δικαίων (i.e., "spirits of the just"). It is also so qualified in its uses with respect to humans in *I Enoch* (20.6; 22.3; etc.), particularly in those sections that parallel this passage in 1 Peter (as noted by Jobes 259). In its NT uses, πνεύματα usually refers to spiritual beings (e.g., Heb 1:14; Rev 3:1; 5:6), often evil (e.g., Matt 8:16; 12:45; Luke 10:20; 1 Tim 4:1; Rev 16:14). Furthermore, in the current passage Peter uses ψυχή of human beings (3:20). The second grammatical issue is also lexical and concerns φυλακῇ. Nowhere in the NT is this term used of the abode of the human dead, but it is clearly used of the location of Satan or the demons (Rev 18:2; 20:7; cf. 2 Pet 2:4; see Achtemeier 256). Option 4 also has in its favor a number of striking parallels with *1 Enoch*, where proclamation is made to these fallen angels (variously designated as "watchers" or "angels") who are now bound in chains, in some form of prison, also with reference to the time of Noah (*1 Enoch* 12–16; 18:14; 21:10; 69:28; see further Dalton 165–76; Elliott 653–62, 697–705).

A third interpretive issue concerns the meaning and timing of ἐκήρυξεν. Is this a proclamation of victory and subjugation or of forgiveness/release (i.e. the gospel)? EVV are fairly evenly divided between "proclaimed, made proclamation" (NRSV, NASB, HCSB, ESV, NIV) and "preached" (ASV, NJB, CEV), with "preached" more likely to imply the gospel as its content. While in the NT κηρύσσω is normally used for the proclaiming of the gospel, it does have the general, less technical meaning of proclaiming news in general (e.g., Luke 12:3; Rom 2:21; Rev 5:2; see the excursus in Achtemeier 262). Also pertinent is that in 1 Peter, the good news of salvation is conveyed by εὐαγγελίζω (1:12, 25; 4:6); this is the only use of κηρύσσω in the epistle. This would make a proclamation of the gospel less likely here. Finally, note that Enoch is commanded to go (πορεύομαι) and rebuke the fallen angels (though κηρύσσω is not used; *1 Enoch* 12:4–6; 13:1; 14:3–7; 16:3).

As to the timing of Christ's proclamation, the Gk. syntax clearly favors the proclamation while they were in prison, with attempts to make it otherwise quite forced. V. 20 indicates that they "disobeyed long ago" (ποτέ), not that the proclamation was long ago (so Michaels 211; see further below). Based on the understanding of v. 18 above, there is also no contextual warrant for understanding this proclamation to be made between Christ's death and resurrection.

The proclamation of Christ to the spirits in prison thus relates to an event post-resurrection, not in his preexistent state; i.e. it was made while they were in prison. The spirits are most likely spiritual beings, and the language depends on a fallen angel tradition in Jewish thought, with some clear and striking parallels to *1 Enoch*. Approaches that regard the spirits as the souls of humans often suffer from the tendency to read this passage (wrongly) in conjunction with 1 Pet 4:6 (as does Goppelt 259; see on 4:6). The proclamation was not one of forgiveness but of an announcement of victory and hence further subjugation. This accords with other NT references regarding the defeat of Satan and evil powers at the cross/resurrection (Eph 1:20–22; Col 2:15; Heb 2:14) and more particularly the final statement of authority in the current section (3:22). In this connection, it needs to be borne in mind that the controlling idea of vv. 18–22 is that of vindication and entry into heaven, not a descent into hell. Furthermore, a descent into hell cannot be substantiated by the vb. πορευθείς. In v. 22 the same ptc. is used of Christ's entry into heaven (as in Acts 1:10–11; cf. John 14:2–3, 28; 16:28), and indeed the whole section seems to be depicting a heavenly journey rather than a descent to anywhere (Elliott 653–54. Achtemeier [257] notes that other NT passages that depict a descent of some sort use καταβαίνω [Rom 10:7;

Eph 4:9–10]). For a helpful discussion of the development of the doctrine of Christ's descent into hell and its relationship to 1 Pet 3:19, see Elliott 706–10.

All this has direct pastoral concern for the original recipients in two senses. First, they can be assured that the evil forces that seek to ensnare them (5:8–9), probably through their connection to the harassment by unbelievers, have no ultimate power (Achtemeier 261; Elliott 661). Second, the imprisonment of the disobedient spirits functions as a further incentive to be obedient and do good, maintaining a separate lifestyle from the disobedient pagans (Elliott 659). Thus, the interpretation offered here not only has more likelihood exegetically; it also has more cogent explanatory power in terms of its pastoral purpose.

VERSE 20

ἀπειθήσασίν ποτε ὅτε ἀπεξεδέχετο ἡ τοῦ θεοῦ μακροθυμία ἐν ἡμέραις Νῶε

Ἀπειθήσασίν dat. pl. masc. of aor. act. ptc. of ἀπειθέω, "disobey" (BDAG 99d). Ποτέ is "long ago" (3:5; NJB, NLT, NIV) or "formerly" (2:10; NRSV, NKJV, ESV), here the former, and is given its content by the ὅτε clause. Ἀπεξεδέχετο 3 sg. impf. mid. indic. of ἀπεκδέχομαι, "wait eagerly," "wait patiently" (BDAG 100d; Turner, *Words* 490). The latter rendering is preferable in this context, as the former may give the mistaken impression that God was eagerly looking forward to the flood (Michaels 212). Most EVV render as "God waited patiently" (NRSV, NJB, NLT, HCSB, NIV; cf. NASB: "The patience of God kept waiting"). The vb. reinforces the nom. μακροθυμία (μακροθυμία, -ας, ἡ, "patience" [BDAG 612d; Turner, *Words* 315–18]). The period referred to is between the sin of the sons of God (Gen 6:1–4) and the flood (Gen 7:11), which tradition placed at 120 years based on Gen 6:3. Νῶε, ὁ, "Noah."

Most commentators and EVV take the ptc. ἀπειθήσασίν as attrib. with τοῖς πνεύμασιν, "the spirits who disobeyed" (Weymouth, NRSV, NKJV, NASB, NIV; Elliott 658; Michaels 211). In this case, the art. is omitted by ellipsis (T 153; Dubis 122). Alternatively, it is adv./anar. following the def. subst. (so Achtemeier 262; Grudem 233–36). Given that it is adv., it could then be cstr. as either temp., "after they disobeyed," or causal, "because they disobeyed" (ESV). Both adv. senses of the ptc. do not align well with the view of the pre-existent Christ preaching to living human beings through Noah (see above on v. 19).

Although elsewhere the vb. ἀπειθέω is used of unbelievers (2:8; 3:1; 4:17), this does not lend support to the view that "the spirits in prison" are the souls of departed humans. The counterarguments are too strong for this. Nevertheless, the intention may be to imply that there is a direct link between disobedient spirits and the slanderous behavior of pagan neighbors who abuse believers (Michaels 211).

κατασκευαζομένης κιβωτοῦ

Κατασκευαζομένης gen. sg. fem. of pres. pass. ptc. of κατασκευάζω, "build," "prepare" (BDAG 526d). Κιβωτός, -ου, ἡ, "ark" (BDAG 544b). The gen. abs. focuses the patience of God on the time taken to construct the ark (Gen 6:5–7:11).

εἰς ἣν ὀλίγοι, τοῦτ' ἔστιν ὀκτὼ ψυχαί, διεσώθησαν δι' ὕδατος

Εἰς is here equivalent to ἐν in a locat. sense (cf. 5:12; BDF §205; Moule 68; T 254; Harris 84–88). The antecedent of εἰς ἥν is the fem. noun κιβωτοῦ. Ὀλίγοι is masc. (the fem. form ὀλίγαι is read by C P Ψ 0285, 1739, Byz vgᵐˢˢ, probably in an attempt to agree with the fem. noun ψυχαί that follows shortly), used here generically of people, and together with τοῦτ' ἔστιν ὀκτὼ ψυχαί, which defines it more precisely (an epex. appos. [R 399]), is the subj. of διεσώθησαν. It is possible that ὀλίγοι is meant to encourage the readers considering that they too are a persecuted minority destined for salvation (Achtemeier 265). The noun ψυχή is used five times in this epistle, always in connection with salvation (1:9, 22; 2:25; 4:19) and never in the sense of a contrast to the physical (see further on 1:9). Διεσώθησαν 3 pl. aor. pass. indic. of διασῴζω, "rescue," "bring safely through" (BDAG 237b).

There is debate concerning what is meant by being saved δι' ὕδατος, "through water." The prep. διά could be instr. (BDAG 224c), "saved by water" (KJV; ZG 711; Moule 56; Best 147; Porter 150 regards it as instr. of secondary agency), or local (BDAG 223d), "brought safely through the water" (Weymouth, CEV, NASB, ESV; Achtemeier 266; Elliott 667; Dubis 123. Selwyn 202–3 opts for both senses). The latter suits the flood story, but it would appear that in view of the following v. Peter means the former. There it has as its point of correspondence δι' ἀναστάσεως Ἰησοῦ Χριστοῦ, which is clearly instr., thus supporting the instr. force here. Michaels (213; also Jobes 252) opts for an instr. sense, pointing out that, in a sense, the flood waters brought them safely through the flood by supporting the ark. Ingeniously, Achtemeier (265–66) suggests that Noah and his family were saved from the wickedness of their human contemporaries (rather than the flood) through the water. Although this proposal would suit an instrumental sense for διά, Achtemeier actually opts for a local sense. For repetition of prep. after compound vb., see Moule 91; R 560.

VERSE 21

ὃ καὶ ὑμᾶς ἀντίτυπον νῦν σῴζει βάπτισμα

The rel. pron. ὅ is omitted by 𝔓⁷² ℵ* 436, 1067, 1409, probably due to the awkwardness of the syntax. A few minuscules read the dat. rel. ᾧ. The neut. nom. ὅ should be retained on the basis of strong and diversified support from ℵ² A B C Ψ Byz and most minuscules and versions. C L 614, 630, 1241, 1505, and the majority text read ἡμᾶς instead of ὑμᾶς, which is more strongly supported by 𝔓⁷² ℵ A B P Ψ 049, 0285, 69, 81, 945, 1739 and a number of other minuscules together with the Vulg. 2 pl. prons. also feature more prominently in the surrounding context.

Ἀντίτυπος, -ον, "corresponding to," subst.: "antitype," "replica" (BDAG 90d; Turner, Words 168–70; H. Müller, NIDNTT 3.903–06; L. Goppelt, TDNT 8.246–59). Βάπτισμα, -ατος, τό, "baptism" (BDAG 165c; Turner, Words 37–41). The temp. adv. νῦν moves the discussion from the time of Noah to that of Peter's contemporaries, with καὶ ὑμᾶς ("also you") possibly occupying an emphatic position (Elliott 669), serving to underscore that it is the readers who are Peter's main concern. The basic sense is relatively clear, but the syntax is quite awkward with problems once more centering on the antecedent of the rel. pron. ὅ and whether ἀντίτυπον should be treated as an adj. or a pred. noun. There also seems to be some confusion over the adj. mng., stemming from a dual usage in CGk. of "corresponding to," or "opposed to" (Turner, *Words* 168). Thus BDAG lists as "corresponding to" (90d–91a), whereas some commentators render as "antitypical" (e.g., Reicke 145).

The noun τύπος is used in Gk. literature to depict a correspondence in an event or item. It can refer to either the original or the copy (cf. Acts 7:43 with 7:44; see *NewDocs* 4.42; Spicq 3.384–87; H. Müller, *NIDNTT* 3.903–6), as can ἀντίτυπος, the latter appearing only here in the NT where it refers to the corresponding event. The correspondence is clearly between Christian baptism and the waters of the flood (*pace* Selwyn 203, who suggests the correspondence lies between Christians and Noah). In fact, Elliott correctly points out that the typology goes beyond salvation through water but parallels "a few were saved through water" with "you baptism now saves through the resurrection of Jesus Christ" (Elliott 669).

With respect to the syntax, the main options are as follows:

1. the antecedent of the rel. ὅ is the previous word ὕδατος, with ἀντίτυπον in appos. to ὑμᾶς. Thus, the contrast is between ὀλίγοι ("a few") and believers (Selwyn 203–4; Dubis 125), giving "which, also you as an antitype, baptism now saves;"

2. the antecedent of the rel. ὅ is the previous word ὕδατος, or the preceding statement "saved through water" as a whole (R 714), with ἀντίτυπον as a pred. noun ("antitype") to βάπτισμα (so Goppelt 247: "were delivered through the water; as antitype to this, baptism now also delivers you");

*3. same antecedent as option 1, with ἀντίτυπον taken adj., "corresponding to" (so Elliott 640, 671: "saved through water. Corresponding to this, baptism now saves you too" [he opts for the poorly attested var. ᾧ in order to give this sense]; Michaels 213: "This water—or baptism, which corresponds to it—now saves you as well");

4. the rel. pron. is the subj. of σώζει, with both ἀντίτυπον and βάπτισμα in appos. to the rel. This gives a rather clumsy "saved through water, which also now saves you as baptism, its antitype" (Achtemeier 240, 266); or

5. the (proleptic) antecedent of the rel. is βάπτισμα, with ἀντίτυπον as its pred. Thus "saved through water, which antitypical baptism now saves you" (Reicke 145).

Option 3, or its sense, is favored by most EVV (NJB, NRSV, NASB, HCSB, ESV), although renderings vary slightly.

The interpretation offered here is also consistent with a wider NT soteriology in which regeneration is a work of the Spirit and a divine initiative, and not mechanically tied to the rite of baptism (see further the discussion below under ῥύπου).

οὐ σαρκὸς ἀπόθεσις ῥύπου

Ἀπόθεσις, -εως, ἡ, "removal" (BDAG 110d). The οὐ . . . ἀλλά cstr. is a parenthesis
that qualifies σῴζει βάπτισμα, with both sides of the equation having interpretive difficulties. Ῥύπος, -ου, ὁ, "dirt" (BDAG 908b; Spicq 3.225–26), is an obj. gen. (Wallace
119) signifying what is removed. The term has a metaphorical sense of soiled behavior, hence "filth" (ASV, NKJV, HCSB), "wickedness" (as in LXX Job 11:15; Isa 4:4).
Σαρκός can either be cstr. as a gen. of separation ("the removal of dirt from the flesh,"
NASB; sim. NRSV, ESV; Wallace 108), or, if trans. with respect to the metaphor, a
poss. gen. ("putting away of the filth of the flesh;" ASV, NKJV, HCSB).

Οὐ σαρκὸς ἀπόθεσις ῥύπου is in appos. to βάπτισμα and is obviously a statement
about what baptism is not, but it has been understood in two quite different ways:

1. ῥύπου has its lit. sense, with σάρξ referring to the human body. The statement is an insistence that baptism is far more than a purification rite. It is not
   about ritual purity that was so important to Judaism and some other religious
   groups in the Greco-Roman world. In other words, it is not about outward
   cleansing but an inner purity (Goppelt 268; Elliott 678–79). A more radical
   version of this approach sees here a contrast with the Jewish rite of circumci-
   sion (Dalton 199–206, followed by Kelly 161–62; Achtemeier 269). But this
   epistle is nowhere else concerned with Christian-Jewish relations, and the
   approach is appropriately refuted by Michaels (215); or

*2. The statement is an insistence that that baptism does not function as a
   mechanical rite of spiritual cleansing. Ῥύπου is here taken in its metaphorical
   sense, with σάρξ used in its classic NT sense of the sinful nature. The entire
   phrase thus refers to the purging of sin. A similar expression having this
   meaning occurs in Jas 1:21 with the cognate noun ῥυπαρία and the cognate
   vb. ἀποθέμενοι, a vb. already used in 1 Pet 2:1 of getting rid of inappropriate
   behavior. Consequently, the purpose here is to emphasize that baptism does
   not function as an automatic rite of forgiveness/spiritual cleansing; it must be
   accompanied by some form of response to God (so Jobes 254–55; Michaels
   214–16). This response is delineated in the following phrase.

Option 2 is to be preferred, for it harmonizes well with the author's repeated insistence
on doing good as a response to God's gracious action (1:15–16; 2:12; 3:6, 13–14,
16–17).

ἀλλὰ συνειδήσεως ἀγαθῆς ἐπερώτημα εἰς θεόν

Ἀλλά correlates with οὐ to complete the contrast. Baptism is not an automatic rite,
but must be accompanied by a heartfelt response to God. Again, ambiguity exists over
key terms, in particular the precise sense of ἐπερώτημα, -ατος, τό, "appeal," and the
force of the gen. συνειδήσεως with its modifier ἀγαθῆς. The noun ἐπερώτημα is a NT
hapax. Its verbal root means "request"/"appeal" (LN 33.162), but the noun has an
attested sense in the papyri of "pledge" (LSJ 618d; H. Greeven, *TDNT* 2.688–89;
Spicq 2.32–33; e.g., see the marriage contracts in *POxy.* 6.905; 10.1273). So, the term

could be indicating either something requested or something given. The problem is compounded by the gen. συνειδήσεως, which could be either subj. or obj. This gives four possible meanings:

1. συνειδήσεως is a subj. gen. and ἐπερώτημα means "pledge." This yields, "but a pledge to God (i.e., some form of commitment) from a good conscience" (Selwyn 205; Davids 145);

2. συνειδήσεως is a subj. gen. and ἐπερώτημα means "appeal." This results in, "but an appeal to God (i.e., for something such as grace or forgiveness) from a good conscience" (Michaels, 195, 216–17; Cassirer);

*3. συνειδήσεως is an obj. gen. and ἐπερώτημα means "pledge." This gives, "but a pledge to God to maintain a good conscience" (Dubis 127; Jobes 255; Elliott 681; Dalton 206–10; Achtemeier 271–72; NJB, HCSB, NIV); or

4. συνειδήσεως is an obj. gen. and ἐπερώτημα means "appeal." This issues in, "but an appeal to God for a good conscience (i.e., a right attitude)" (Goppelt 271; Feldmeier 208; NRSV, NASB, ESV).

In baptism, the candidate was required to give a confession of faith in Jesus Christ in response to questions posed (Achtemeier 271). This aligns more with the idea of a pledge made to God rather than an appeal to him (Elliott 680, notes the resemblance to pledges taken by initiates to the Qumran community [1QS 5.8–10; CD 15.6–11; 16.1–5]). In addition, if the pledge is made from a good conscience this presumes some existing regenerative work. But Peter's point is that salvation is mediated via the baptismal rite, not that it existed prior to this. Also supporting option 3 is the corresponding obj. gen. ῥύπου (Dubis 126; ZG 712). This option is the one most favored by modern commentators.

δι' ἀναστάσεως Ἰησοῦ Χριστοῦ

The prep. phrase could modify the immediately preceding phrase, i.e., the pledge to God is offered or made possible through the resurrection of Jesus Christ, but more likely it modifies σῴζει (Dubis 127; ZG 712; Goppelt 267 n. 83) and hence the entire v. It forms a counterpart to Noah's family being saved δι' ὕδατος. Christians are now saved by means of (διά is instr.) the resurrection of Jesus Christ.

Peter has already spoken of the resurrection bringing new birth (1:3); now the resurrection is pictured as the objective basis for operation of the baptismal rite. This serves to emphasize that even though baptism must be accompanied by a human response, salvation is not our initiative but God's. It is ultimately the resurrection of Jesus that makes the new possible (cf. Rom 6:4–11; Eph 2:6; Col 2:12).

VERSE 22

ὅς ἐστιν ἐν δεξιᾷ τοῦ θεοῦ

The rel. pron. ὅς picks up Ἰησοῦ Χριστοῦ, thus resuming the Christological focus. The three sections of this v. all draw on traditional and creedal material. Ἐν δεξιᾷ θεοῦ is a locat. of place and is a common NT picture of the ascended Christ, with the right hand being the position of honor (Acts 2:33; Rom 8:34; Col 3:1; Heb 10:12; etc., drawing on Ps 110:1).

πορευθεὶς εἰς οὐρανόν

The temp. ptc. πορευθείς, logically preceding sitting at the right hand of God, resumes the thought of a heavenly journey. This is the controlling idea of the section, picking up what was left aside in v. 19 (see comments there).

ὑποταγέντων αὐτῷ ἀγγέλων καὶ ἐξουσιῶν καὶ δυνάμεων

Ὑποταγέντων gen. pl. masc. of aor. pass. ptc. of ὑποτάσσω, "subject." The gen. abs. gives a final statement of victory and authority and rounds off the entire section. We should read this in light of v. 19 and the proclamation of victory made to the spirits in prison (Achtemeier 273; see comments there). Ὑποταγέντων is best taken as a ptc. of result, showing the consequences of Christ's ascension in victory and his status at the right hand of God (Achtemeier 240, takes it as temp. with the rendering, "who, having gone into heaven after angels and authorities and powers were made subordinate to him, is at the right hand of God." This links the subjection back to the time of proclamation of victory in v. 19; sim. NASB) The pass. implies the action of God (Weymouth, NRSV, NKJV, ESV).

Little distinction can be drawn between ἀγγέλων, ἐξουσιῶν, and δυνάμεων ("angels, authorities, and powers"). Similar terms are often linked in the NT and appear to denote the entire ranks of the spirit world (Rom 8:38–39; 1 Cor 15:24–27; Eph 1:21; 3:10; 6:12; Col 1:16; 2:10, 15). The point is to emphasize Christ's complete and universal authority. On the connection between the spiritual powers and unbelievers in their attacks on Christians, see the conclusion to 3:19 (also Elliott 688–89). Goppelt (273) notes that the reference to the spiritual powers "has only an indirect role in the parenesis." Yet it has a role nonetheless.

FOR FURTHER STUDY

35. Christ's Proclamation to the Spirits in Prison (3:18–22)

Dubis, Mark. "Research on First Peter: A Survey of Scholarly Literature since 1985." *Currents in Biblical Research* 4 (2006): 199–239, esp. 220–21.

*Dalton, William J. *Christ's Proclamation to the Spirits: A Study of 1 Peter 3:18–4:6.* Second edition. Rome: Pontifical Biblical Institute, 1989.

Feinberg, John S. "1 Peter 3:18–20, Ancient Mythology, and the Intermediate State." *WTJ* 48 (1986): 303–336.

Goodspeed, E. J. "Enoch in 1 Peter 3,19." *JBL* 73 (1954): 91–92.

Grudem, Wayne A. "Christ Preaching Through Noah: 1 Peter 3:19–20 in the Light of Dominant Themes in Jewish Literature." *Trinity Journal* 7 (1986): 3–31.

Hanson, Anthony T. "Salvation Proclaimed: I. 1 Peter 3:18–22." *ExpTim* 93 (1982): 110–15.

Reicke, Bo. *The Disobedient Spirits and Christian Baptism: A Study of 1 Pet. III:19 and its Context*. Kobenhavn: Ejnar Munksgaard, 1946.

36. The Doctrine of Christ's Descent into Hell

Bagchi, David V. N. "Christ's Descent into Hell in Reformation Controversy." Pages 228–47 in *Church, the Afterlife, and the Fate of the Soul*. Edited by P. D. Clarke and T. Claydon. Woodbridge, UK: Boydell, 2009.

Bauckham, Richard. *ABD* 2.156–59

Bromiley, Geoffrey W. *ISBE* 1.926–27.

Connell, M. F. "Descensus Christi ad infernos: Christ's Descent to the Dead." *Theological Studies* 62 (2001): 262–82.

Feinberg, John S. "1 Peter 3:18–20, Ancient Mythology, and the Intermediate State." *WTJ* 48 (1986): 303–36.

Frank, Georgia. "Christ's Descent to the Underworld in Ancient Ritual and Legend." Pages 211–26 in *Apocalyptic Thought in Early Christianity*. Edited by R. J. Daly. Grand Rapids: Baker Academic, 2009.

*Grudem, Wayne A. "He Did Not Descend into Hell: A Plea for Following Scripture Instead of the Apostles' Creed." *JETS* 34 (1991): 103–13.

Harris, W. Hall, III. "The Ascent and Descent of Christ in Ephesians 4:9–10." *BSac* 151 (1994): 198–214.

Kay, J. F. "He Descended into Hell." *Word and World* 31 (2011): 17–26.

Scaer, David P. "He Did Descend into Hell: In Defense of the Apostles' Creed." *JETS* 35 (1992): 91–99.

Scharlemann, Martin. "'He Descended into Hell': An Interpretation of 1 Peter 3:18–20." *Concordia Journal* 15 (1989): 311–22.

Williams, M. D. "He Descended into Hell? An Issue of Confessional Integrity." *Presbyterion* 25 (1999): 80–90.

Wicks, Jared. "Christ's Saving Descent to the Dead: Early Witnesses from Ignatius of Antioch to Origen." *Pro Ecclesia* 17 (2008): 281–309.

HOMILETICAL SUGGESTIONS

The Suffering and Vindication of Christ (3:18–22)

1. Christ Suffered (3:18)
    (a) for sins
    (b) once for all
    (c) as a righteous man
    (d) to lead us to God
2. Christ's Proclamation to the Spirits in Prison (3:19–20)
    (a) in the spiritual realm (v. 19)
    (b) who disobeyed in the time of Noah (v. 20)
3. Christian Baptism (3:21)
    (a) corresponds to the flood
    (b) not a magical rite
    (c) effective through the resurrection of Jesus

    4. The Vindication of Christ (3:22)
       (a) has entered heaven
       (b) is at God's right hand
       (c) has authority over the spiritual powers

The Victory of Christ

    1. Over Sin (1 Pet 2:21–25; 3:18; cf. Rom 5:12–6:14)
    2. Over Death (1 Pet 3:19; cf. 1 Cor 15:54; Heb 2:14)
    3. Over Evil (1 Pet 3:19–22; cf. Col 2:15; John 12:31; 1 John 3:8)

VII. Living Appropriate
Christian Lives (4:1–11)

A. AMONG UNBELIEVERS (4:1–6)

STRUCTURE

The opening v. exhorts the readers (καὶ ὑμεῖς, "you also") to be prepared to suffer because Christ suffered (gen. abs.), with the ὅτι clause providing further rationale for this in terms of leaving sin behind. V. 2 elaborates upon πέπαυται ἁμαρτίας ("ceased from sin") using an art. inf. cstr. εἰς τὸ μηκέτι . . . βιῶσαι ("so as to live no longer") followed by a contrast between human desires and God's desire. V. 3 reinforces the need to leave the pagan lifestyle behind, cataloguing six vices that were typical of paganism. The rel. ἐν ᾧ that begins v. 4 functions as a causal conj. picking up the entire thought of v. 3 (see the analysis, below). The rel. οἵ in v. 5 picks up the subj. of ξενίζονται (i.e., the pagans) and shows their accountability before God. Mention of the "living and the dead" at the conclusion of v. 5 provides an opportunity for the author to speak of the fate of the Christian dead (see the analysis, below), with the μέν . . . δέ cstr. used to contrast the human and divine perspective on their lives.

1   Χριστοῦ οὖν <u>παθόντος σαρκὶ</u>
      καὶ ὑμεῖς τὴν αὐτὴν ἔννοιαν <u>ὁπλίσασθε,</u>
          ὅτι ὁ <u>παθὼν σαρκὶ</u> πέπαυται ἁμαρτίας

2   εἰς τὸ μηκέτι ἀνθρώπων ἐπιθυμίαις
               ἀλλὰ θελήματι θεοῦ τὸν ἐπίλοιπον ἐν <u>σαρκὶ</u> βιῶσαι <u>χρόνον.</u>

3   ἀρκετὸς γὰρ ὁ παρεληλυθὼς <u>χρόνος</u> τὸ βούλημα τῶν ἐθνῶν <u>κατειργάσθαι</u>

          πεπορευμένους ἐν ἀσελγείαις,
               ἐπιθυμίαις,
               οἰνοφλυγίαις,
               κώμοις,
               πότοις
               καὶ ἀθεμίτοις εἰδωλολατρίαις.

4   ἐν ᾧ ξενίζονται μὴ συντρεχόντων ὑμῶν
                                           εἰς τὴν αὐτὴν τῆς ἀσωτίας ἀνάχυσιν
                         βλασφημοῦντες.

5   οἳ ἀποδώσουσιν λόγον
                τῷ ἑτοίμως ἔχοντι κρῖναι ζῶντας καὶ νεκρούς.

6   εἰς τοῦτο γὰρ καὶ νεκροῖς εὐαγγελίσθη,
                       ἵνα κριθῶσι μὲν κατὰ ἀνθρώπους σαρκὶ,
                       ζῶσι   δὲ κατὰ θεὸν   πνεύματι.

VERSE 1

Χριστοῦ οὖν παθόντος σαρκί

The gen. abs. with the inferential conj. οὖν now facilitates a further lesson from the suffering of Christ, most immediately from 3:18, but also picks up the thought of *imitatio* from 2:21–24. The ptc. παθόντος is given causal force by οὖν. Σαρκί is a locat. of sphere or dat. of respect (Elliott 712) with no distinguishable difference in mng.

With varying word orders, א² A *Byz* and a number of other minuscules together with several versions add ὑπὲρ ἡμῶν, "on our behalf," after παθόντος, "having suffered." A few other minuscules read ὑπὲρ ὑμῶν, "on your behalf," whereas א* reads ἀποθανόντος ὑπὲρ ὑμῶν, "having died on your behalf." The changes all appear confessionally motivated, and the shorter rdg. should be retained on the basis of 𝔓⁷² B C Ψ 0285, 322, 323, 1243, 1739, 1881.

καὶ ὑμεῖς τὴν αὐτὴν ἔννοιαν ὁπλίσασθε

Ἔννοια, -ας, ἡ, "attitude," "intention" (BDAG 337d; G. Harder, *NIDNTT* 3.123; LN 30.5), is related to the noun νοῦς ("mind") and so is concerned with "the cognitive dimension of behavior" (Elliott 713). Ὁπλίσασθε 2 pl. aor. mid. impv. of ὁπλίζω, "equip," "arm" (BDAG 716c; LSJ 1239c; LN 77.10). The vb. is often used in a military context, and the mid. here has the sense of "arming oneself." Although the verb is a NT *hapax*, the metaphor itself is quite familiar (cf. 2:11; Rom 13:12; 2 Cor 6:7; 10:4; Eph 6:11–17; 1 Thess 5:8) and is appropriate for those living in a hostile society (Achtemeier 277; Michaels [225] correctly points out that the resolve is not to suffer, but rather to have the same attitude and response to suffering that Christ did). The aor. impv. has programmatic force here (see the discussion, "The Use of the Imperative in 1 Peter" in the Introduction). That the readers are to imitate Christ is underlined both by the emphatic καὶ ὑμεῖς ("you also") and the identical adj. αὐτήν ("same").

ὅτι ὁ παθὼν σαρκὶ πέπαυται ἁμαρτίας

First of all, the sense of the ὅτι clause is quite obscure:

*1. Ὅτι is causal ("because"), modifying the impv. ὁπλίσασθε by providing the reason why one must arm oneself (most EVV; Goppelt 280; Elliott 714; Dubis 130; Michaels 226); or

2. Ὅτι is epex. ("that"), giving content to ἔννοιαν by indicating what precisely is to be borne in mind (Moffatt, NJB; Achtemeier 278; Davids 148 n. 2).

On the one hand, the causal force already present in the opening gen. abs. may lean toward the epex. option (Achtemeier 278). On the other hand, if it is epex., then the content of the resolve must be shared by both Christ and his followers. But "ceased with sin" cannot mean the same for both parties. If it relates to some form of personal battle with sin, then Christ is ruled out on the basis of 1:18; 2:22; 3:18. If it relates to the objective defeat of sin in some way, then it can *only* relate to Christ (Goppelt 280). Thus, the causal sense is preferred.

Second, the identity of ὁ παθών is unclear:

1. It relates to Christ, thus mirroring the opening clause. Consequently, the statement acts as an elaboration of sorts on ἅπαξ ("once for all") in 3:18. It is highly unlikely that this is intended to indicate that Christ attained a sinless state after suffering, as his moral perfection has already been emphasized several times (1:18; 2:22; 3:18). So it may either be highlighting the fact that sin has been decisively dealt with in an atoning sense (2:24a; Michaels 228), or that Christ has conquered the power of sin (2:24b; Achtemeier 278); or

*2. It relates to the believer, with the clear implication that suffering has a positive ethical effect (Feldmeier 212; Elliott 715; Achtemeier 278).

At a discourse level, ὁ παθών more naturally refers to the believer (Jobes 263–64). The gen. abs. initially focuses attention on Christ, and then a shift to hortatory material follows. If the ptc. refers to Christ, then the entire ὅτι clause must be a rather awkward parenthesis, with the exhortation taken up again in v. 2.

Given that the focus of the clause is the believer, the meaning is still unclear. The idea that personal suffering itself is redemptive with respect to sin finds no place in this epistle (cf. 1:18–19; 2:21–24; 3:18) or the NT as a whole. Theologically, it could relate to the breaking of the power of sin, but this is more a Pauline thought (e.g., Rom 6:1–14, but note the different language with Paul speaking of dying with Christ in baptism as the means by which one is liberated from sin). Peter, on the other hand, tends to focus on concrete acts of sinning, rather than sin as a principle. However, the idea may be that suffering has a disciplinary function with respect to sin (Elliott 717) or more likely that suffering for one's faith provides clear indication that one is no longer living with a sinful mindset (Cassirer: "has parted company with sin;" Achtemeier 279–80; Jobes 265–66). The latter fits in nicely with vv. 2–4 and the emphasis on abandoning a pagan lifestyle, even in the face of slanderous abuse (Jobes 266).

Σαρκί is a locat. of sphere (Moule 44), or dat. of respect, in parallel with the opening clause. Πέπαυται 3 sg. pf. mid. indic. of παύω, "stop," "cease" (BDAG 790a). The perf. tense πέπαυται is consummative in the sense that it looks forward from the point of suffering. Ἁμαρτίας is gen. sg. rather than acc. pl. and is a gen. of separation with παύω

(Wallace 109; Dubis 131). In place of the gen. sg. ἁμαρτίας (𝔓⁷² ℵ* A C P 1739 *Byz*), the dat. pl. ἁμαρτίαις is read by ℵ² B Ψ and some minuscules. A couple of other mss. (049, 1881) add the prep. ἀπό prior to the gen. Although the dat. is the more difficult rdg. (as παύω normally takes the gen.), the gen. should be retained on the strength of early and diversified ms. support.

VERSE 2

εἰς τὸ μηκέτι . . . τὸν ἐπίλοιπον ἐν σαρκὶ βιῶσαι χρόνον

The prep. εἰς with the art. inf. expresses purpose (not result as NIV, or causal as NJB). Here the purpose is related to either:

1. the command to arm oneself with the same resolve as Jesus, with ὁ παθὼν σαρκὶ πέπαυται ἁμαρτίας, as a parenthetical statement (as NRSV which brackets this phrase; ZG 712; most commentators); or
2. the immediately preceding πέπαυται ἁμαρτίας, with the sense that one ceases with sin so as to live in accordance with God's will (Dubis 131).

The adv. μηκέτι modifies the inf. ("to live . . . no longer") and looks forward to ἀλλά to complete the contrast. The implied subj. (acc. of respect) of the inf. is ὑμᾶς.

Ἐπίλοιπος, -ον, "remaining" (BDAG 375b; LN 63.21). The acc. τὸν ἐπίλοιπον . . . χρόνον expresses length of time, with the dat. ἐν σαρκί having the same function as σαρκί in v. 1 (dat. of respect or locat. of sphere). Here it signifies the remainder of one's earthly existence (cf. 1:17), rather than the short period prior to the Parousia (*pace* Achtemeier 282, in agreement with Michaels 229). Βιῶσαι, aor. act. inf. of βιόω, "live," "spend one's life" (BDAG 177b; H.-G. Link, *NIDNTT* 2.374–75; LN 41.18).

ἀνθρώπων ἐπιθυμίαις ἀλλὰ θελήματι θεοῦ

This clause is inserted within the art. inf. cstr. (such extended clauses within the inf. cstr. are unusual in the NT; R 1070–71). Ἐπιθυμίαις and θελήματι are dat. of rule, which express the standard of conduct to which a person conforms (Weymouth: "governed not by human passions;" Selwyn 210; Achtemeier 280 n. 58; Wallace 157–58), rather than dat. of advantage (ESV, NIV). The divine will (expounded in 2:15, 17; 3:17, etc.), rather than human impulse, must control the lives of believers. The pl. ἐπιθυμίαις is designed to encompass the various godless activities mentioned in the following v. (cf. 1:14, 18; 2:11), although it is also listed there as one particular vice. Ἀνθρώπων is used negatively of unregenerate humanity and is a subj. gen., i.e., the desires that people have.

VERSE 3

ἀρκετὸς γὰρ ὁ παρεληλυθὼς χρόνος

Γάρ is here a subord. conj., as it introduces the reason why sinful human desires are no longer to be followed. ℵ* 630 and a considerable number of other mss. add ὑμῖν after γάρ ("for it is sufficient for you"), whereas C K L P 049, 69, 623ᶜ 2298 and a considerable number of other mss. add ἡμῖν ("for us"). The shorter reading without the dat. pron. should be retained on the basis of 𝔓⁷² ℵᶜ A B Ψ 81, 323, 614, 945, 1241, 1505, 1739 and several other mss.

Ἀρκετός, -ή, -όν, "sufficient," "adequate" (BDAG 131d). The adj. is pred. with an implied ἔστιν ("the time already past is sufficient," NASB; LN 59.45) and captures by ironic understatement (known as *litotes* or *meiosis*) what has already been stated in 1:14, 18 regarding the futile, pagan past of the readers. This ironic use of ἀρκετός, together with the pf. ptc. παρεληλυθώς (nom. sg. masc. of. pf. act. ptc. of παρέρχομαι, "pass by"; BDAG 775d, with the pf. highlighting the irrevocable nature of the past), produces renderings such as NJB: "you have spent quite long enough in the past."

τὸ βούλημα τῶν ἐθνῶν κατειργάσθαι

Βούλημα, -ατος, τό, "will" (BDAG 182a; G. Schrenk, *TDNT* 1.636–37), is used in contrast with θελήμα, for Peter uses the latter only with respect to the will of God (2:15; 3:17; 4:2, 19). Βούλημα probably has the dual sense of what the pagans wanted for themselves, as well as what they wanted others to do (Michaels 231).

Κατειργάσθαι pf. mid. inf. of κατεργάζομαι, "achieve," "accomplish" (BDAG 531b; the pf. form κατειργάσθαι is Attic [R 364]). The pf. complements the force of the preceding and the following pf. ptcs. in indicating that the past manner of life is finished (Elliott 720; Michaels 230; Dubis 133). It is also epex. (i.e., complementary inf. [R1076]) of ἀρκετός, with an implied subj. "you" (BDF §405[2]).

The subj. gen. τῶν ἐθνῶν has a certain irony, for the readers, too, are (at least predominately) Gentiles. Here the term is used pejoratively of "pagans" (NIV). The entire phrase τὸ βούλημα τῶν ἐθνῶν parallels ἀνθρώπων ἐπιθυμίαις in the previous v.

πεπορευμένους ἐν ἀσελγείαις, ἐπιθυμίαις, οἰνοφλυγίαις, κώμοις, πότοις καὶ ἀθεμίτοις εἰδωλολατρίαις

The ptc. πεπορευμένους should be cstr. as instr. of manner, with the acc. agreeing with the unexpressed acc. of respect ὑμᾶς of the inf. κατειργάσθαι. The pf. tense is used in conjunction with the previous two pfs. to consign evil to the past (Michaels 230); however, the intensive nature of its aspect (see Campbell, *Indicative Mood* 161–211) should be captured in a rendering such as "immersed in" (NASB: "having pursued a course"). In the NT, vbs. of walking are commonly used metaphorically of lifestyle (Moulton 11; Paul prefers περιπατέω).

The following six dats. are instr. of manner, with the pls. used as umbrella terms for a variety of individual vices (T 27–28: "Pluralis Poeticus for abstract subjects"; see Michaels 232 for the use of these terms in non-BGk.). Ἀσέλγεια, -ας, ἡ, refers to reckless behavior (BDAG 141d), and in the pl. is probably used of sexual immorality of various sorts ("debauchery," NIV). Ἐπιθυμία, -ας, ἡ refers to cravings in general (BDAG 372b), including sexual indulgence, but not so limited ("lusts," ASV, NKJV; "passions," NJB, NRSV).

The three nouns that follow function as virtual synonyms in this context regarding drunken festivals. Οἰνοφλυγία, -ας, ἡ, "drunkenness" (BDAG 701b). Κῶμος, -ου, ὁ can be neutral in the sense of a feast or banquet, but in the NT is used only negatively of excessive feasting ("carousing," NASB; "noisy revelry," Weymouth; cf. Rom 13:13; Gal 5:21; BDAG 580c; LN 88.287). Πότος, -ου, ὁ indicates a gathering at which wine was served, a drinking party (BDAG 857d). Here excess is implied ("drinking to excess," NJB; "wild parties," NLT).

Ἀθεμίτοις εἰδωλολατρίαις is the only noun with an adj. modifier, thus necessitating καί (BDF §460[2]). Ἀθέμιτος, -ον, "lawless" (BDAG 24a), expressing a Jewish and Christian perspective (drawing on the first commandment of the Decalogue) on idolatry that emphasizes what is already apparent in the derogatory term εἰδωλολατρία, -ας, ἡ, "image worship," "idolatry" (BDAG 280d; Turner, *Words* 229; Barclay: "idolatries which outrage common decency;" LN 88.143: "disgusting worship of idols"). The vices listed above would sometimes have been practiced in a religious setting or in social gatherings such as clubs or guilds (see Achtemeier 282; Elliott 724–25; Davids 151). This statement regarding idolatry, together with the vices mentioned above, is a key for many in determining the predominantly Gentile recipients of this letter (not all agree; see Jobes 268–69).

VERSE 4

ἐν ᾧ ξενίζονται

As in every other instance of this prep.-rel. pron. combination in 1 Peter (1:6; 2:12; 3:16, 19), the antecedent is difficult to determine (see Moule 131–32; Wallace 343). Being sg., the ref. is probably to the thought of the previous v. regarding the abandonment of a pagan lifestyle, but as this is also the sense of the following gen. abs. there is a sense in which ἐν ᾧ is anticipatory (Achtemeier 283). Either way, it functions as a causal conj. (i.e., "because of this," BDF §219[2]; Michaels 233; ESV [sim. Weymouth, NASB] is looser: "With respect to this"). Ξενίζονται 3 pl. pres. pass. indic. of ξενίζω, "astonish," "surprise" (BDAG 684a). The implied subj. is τῶν ἐθνῶν from v. 3.

μὴ συντρεχόντων ὑμῶν

Συντρεχόντων gen. pl. masc. of pres. act. ptc. of συντρέχω, "run with," "run together" (BDAG 976b). Can be cstr. as either temp., "when" (NLT, ESV; ZG 712), or causal, "because" (Dubis 135), or "that" (most EVV), an epex. usage that comes close to that proposed by Wallace as indirect discourse (see Wallace 645–46). The gen. abs. as a whole is epex. of ξενίζονται in that it shows the content of their astonishment. With considerable rhetorical skill the metaphor has shifted from walking to running, with the συν- compound expressing joint action. The unexpressed dir. obj. is αὐτοῖς.

εἰς τὴν αὐτὴν τῆς ἀσωτίας ἀνάχυσιν

Αὐτήν is an identical adj. ("same"). Ἀσωτία, -ας, ἡ, "reckless abandon," "debauchery" (BDAG 148a; Turner, *Words* 102–3), cstr. as either an obj. gen. signifying what is
in excess (Beare 181) or epex. (Dubis 135), without much conceptual distinction. It is
a summary term for all the vices mentioned in v. 3. Ἀνάχυσις, -εως, ἡ, "wide stream,"
"flood" (BDAG 75c), here used metaphorically of hedonistic excess (LN 78.26). The
entire metaphor is thus a "deliberate, almost comic, exaggeration" (Michaels 233) of
pagans running and plunging into a torrential stream of indulgence and wickedness
(NLT: "surprised when you no longer plunge into the flood of wild and destructive
things they do").

βλασφημοῦντες

It is possible to cstr. the ptc. in two ways:

*1. with what precedes (so EVV; Davids 152; Elliott 727; Dubis 136), as a ptc.
   of result, with the sense that the pagans blaspheme/slander as a result of their
   astonishment that their Christian neighbors no longer join them in this flood
   of reckless living; or

2. with what follows (so Michaels 234; Achtemeier 284), as causal, giving the
   reason why they will give an account to God.

Either option is difficult grammatically. With regard to option 1, the nom. ptc. hangs by
itself at the end of the gen. abs. and needs to be coordinated with the opening ξενίζονται
(which explains the var. rdg. [ℵ* C* 81, 323, 945, 1241, 1739] καὶ βλασφημοῦσιν, "and
they blaspheme"). But this may be a deliberate literary strategy to create rhetorical
effect. With respect to option 2, the syntax is extremely awkward having a ptc. followed by a rel. pron. For this reason option 1 is preferable.

Whether the ptc. is coordinated with v. 4 or v. 5, ambiguity still exists regarding
its unexpressed obj. Due to previous references indicating a slandering of believers
themselves (2:12, 15; 3:9, 16; 4:14), most EVV (also Davids 152; Elliott 727; ZG
713) supply "you." Against this, however, of the variety of terms used for this verbal
abuse (see on 3:16), βλασφημέω is not one of them. Consequently, it is more likely
to indicate blasphemy of God or Jesus because of the distinctive lifestyle of believers. Whether this is a direct reviling of God, or whether Peter understands attacks on
his people to constitute blasphemy of God (so Jobes 270; Michaels 234), is unclear
(NRSV: "they blaspheme").

VERSE 5

οἳ ἀποδώσουσιν λόγον

Ἀποδώσουσιν 3 pl. fut. act. indic. of ἀποδίδωμι, "give up," "render" (BDAG
109d–110a). A legal term, commonly used in the NT regarding personal accountability to God as judge (also with λόγον in Matt 12:36; Heb 13:17). Here we have an

eschatological reversal of 3:15, where now unbelievers (the antecedent is still τῶν ἐθνῶν from v. 3) will have to give an account of themselves (Elliott 729).

τῷ ἑτοίμως ἔχοντι κρῖναι ζῶντας καὶ νεκρούς

Ἑτοίμως (adv.), "readily," with ἔχω plus an inf. is a Gk. idiom indicating a readiness to do something (BDAG 401b; ZG 713; Moule 161; cf. Acts 21:13; 2 Cor 12:14; Dan 3:15 LXX). Ἑτοίμως echoes the expectation of an imminent end (4:7, 17; cf. 1:6). The inf. κρῖναι is epex., giving the content of this readiness. Although in the NT, it is often Jesus Christ who is given the role of the eschatological judge (Acts 10:42; Rom 14:9; 2 Tim 4:1), elsewhere in this epistle the judge is God the Father (1:17; 2:23), with Christ being the example *par excellence* of unjust suffering (Davids 153; Jobes 270; Elliott 730). Furthermore, Peter's uses elsewhere of the subst. ptc. in this fashion all relate to God (1:3, 15, 17, 21; 2:9, 23, etc.). Ζῶντας καὶ νεκρούς is a stereotypical NT expression for all of humanity. On paired noms. without the art., see R 793.

In an attempt to smooth out the text, and probably displaying an unawareness of the Gk. idiom (Michaels 224), some mss. (B C*vid Ψ [81], 614, 630, 1852 and others) read τῷ ἑτοίμως κρίνοντι ("to the one who judges readily"), whereas 𝔓72 945, 1241, 1739, 1881, and a few others read τῷ ἑτοίμῳ κρῖναι ("to him who is ready to judge"). However, τῷ ἑτοίμως ἔχοντι κρῖναι should be retained on the strength of ℵ A C² P *Byz* and also its inherent difficulty for those not familiar with the idiom (see above).

VERSE 6

εἰς τοῦτο γὰρ καὶ νεκροῖς εὐηγγελίσθη

Εἰς τοῦτο γὰρ looks both backward and forward. The conj. γάρ provides the link with v. 5, a link further substantiated by the words νεκρός and κρίνω. Nevertheless, εἰς τοῦτο γάρ looks forward to the ἵνα clause for its content (Selwyn 214; Michaels 238; Achtemeier 286–87). The word "reason" needs to be supplied with εἰς τοῦτο (ZG 713: "This is why"). Καί is adv. and given the interpretation offered below is more likely "also" (NJB, NKJV; Dubis 137) than "even" (most EVV). The pass. vb. εὐηγγελίσθη (only occurrence of this form of the vb. in the NT) could have Christ (Achtemeier 287; Selwyn 214) or the word (cf. 1:25b; Elliott 732) as its subj. More likely it is impersonal: "the gospel was preached" (EVV; T 291; Michaels 236).

The anar. νεκροῖς looks not at the dead as a group, but dead as a quality, i.e., to dead people (Wallace 244–45; BDF §254[2]). As to the meaning of this difficult expression there are three main options:

1. The spiritually dead. But this is not the meaning of the adj. in v. 5, and we should expect a correspondence in meaning given the clear linking of these terms (so Selwyn 214; Elliott 733). In addition, the idea of being "spiritually dead" is foreign to the thought of this epistle;
2. The dead who hear the gospel in Hades (Green 118–38; Best 156–57; Reicke 204–10), with this passage read in conjunction with 3:18–19. But we have

already ruled out this sense for the earlier passage. The language here is quite different (νεκροῖς as opposed to πνεύμασιν, εὐαγγελίσθη as opposed to ἐκήρυξεν), and there Christ clearly performs the proclamation. Furthermore, the idea that the dead receive a second chance finds no support in this epistle or the wider NT and actually hinders the repeated exhortations in this epistle to stand firm in the face of suffering (Elliott 731). Peter clearly expects a neg. outcome for some at the final judgment (4:18); or

*3. Those who heard the gospel while alive and responded but have since died ("to those who are now dead," NLT, HCSB, NIV). This is the favored option among most modern commentators (Davids 153–55; Jobes 272; Achtemeier 290; Elliott 733–34; Dalton 230–41; Dubis 137–38), not only due to the inherent difficulties in the other two proposals, but also because it aligns with the author's repeated concern to encourage his readers that divine vindication awaits those who suffer for doing good (2:18–25; 3:8–12, 13–17, 18–21; 4:12–19; 5:8–10).

ἵνα κριθῶσι μὲν κατὰ ἀνθρώπους σαρκὶ ζῶσι δὲ κατὰ θεὸν πνεύματι

This purpose clause (T 102) explains why the gospel was preached to the dead, with the μέν . . . δέ cstr. conveying a contrast similar to that of 3:18. Here μέν is concessive, which allows the emphasis to fall on the δέ clause (Selwyn 215; Achtemeier 287; Elliott 735; Z §452).

Κρίνω can mean either "judge" (EVV) or the more neg. sense of "condemn." Elsewhere in this epistle it has the former neutral sense (1:17; 2:23; 4:5), but this neutral sense is difficult to maintain here given the positive contrast intended with ζῶσι (with Achtemeier 287). The aor. tense, in combination with the concessive sense of μέν, tends to indicate that this condemnation happened prior to the time of attaining life in the Spirit. It does not, in itself, indicate that the condemnation happened prior to death (*pace* Elliott 736; Davids 154).

The sense of this clause is elusive. As in 3:18, the dats. σαρκί and πνεύματι are best taken as locat. of sphere (Achtemeier 288), presenting a contrast between physical earthly life and resurrection life. The final mng. thus rests on the force of the prep. κατά. It would be natural to assume that the prep. has the same sense in both uses (with Achtemeier 288; Elliott 737), but this alone does not solve the problem; it only restricts the options. Some EVV present the contrast as one between physical death which all experience, and life in the Spirit which God experiences (NJB, NRSV, NLT, ESV; ZG 713); however, this fails to properly appreciate the link with vv. 2–4.

Elsewhere in the NT, κατά appears with the sg. ἄνθρωπον to mean "from a human point of view" (Rom 3:5; 1 Cor 3:3; 9:8; 15:32; Gal 1:11; 3:15). The expression κατὰ θεόν is used in 5:2 (also Rom 8:27) with the sense of "what God requires." So, the most likely sense here is a comparison between human standards and God's standards (Selwyn 215; Elliott 737; Achtemeier 288; Jobes 272; Michaels 238; Dubis 138–39; see BDAG 512d). In other words, the lives of Christians who have passed from this life have been evaluated one way by their pagan neighbors, but in an entirely different manner by the divine law court. It thus constitutes yet another example of divine rever-sal (Elliott 739–40; Selwyn 338).

This neg. evaluation of believers by unbelievers more likely relates directly to the abuse and slander directed at them while they were alive, rather than the evaluation they received after they died like everyone else (so Elliott 738; *pace* Selwyn 216). This sense forms a close parallel to the thought of 2:4 ("rejected by people but in God's sight chosen and honored") and accords with the overall theological sense of the epistle whereby the righteous suffer but are ultimately vindicated by God. Its main attraction is the obvious link to vv. 2–3 and the antagonistic response given by those from whose ethical ranks followers of Jesus have since departed.

FOR FURTHER STUDY

37. Paganism in the Greco-Roman World (4:3–4)

Berchman, Robert M. "Greco-Roman Paganism: The Political Foundations of Tolerance in the Greco-Roman Period." Pages 60–98 in *Religious Tolerance in World Religions*. Edited by J. Neusner and B. D. Chilton. Philadelphia: Templeton Foundation Press, 2008.

De Villiers, P. G. R. "Interpreting the New Testament in the Light of Pagan Criticisms of Oracles and Prophecies in Greco-Roman Times." *Neot* 33 (1999): 35–57.

Kooten, G. H. van. "Christianity in the Graeco-Roman World: Socio Political, Philosophical, and Religious Interactions up to the Edict of Milan (CE 313)." Pages 3–37 in *The Routledge Companion to Early Christianity*. Edited by J. D. Bingham. London/New York: Routledge, 2010.

Lieu, Judith, John North, and Tessa Rajak, eds. *The Jews Among Pagans and Christians in the Roman Empire*. London and New York: Routledge, 1992.

Lim, Richard. "Christianization, Secularization, and the Transformation of Public Life." Pages 497–511 in *A Companion to Late Antiquity*. Edited by P. Rousseau with J. Raithel. Chichester: Wiley-Blackwell, 2009.

*MacMullen, Ramsay. *Paganism in the Roman Empire*. New Haven and London: Yale University Press, 1981.

North, John A. "Pagan Ritual and Monotheism." Pages 34–54 in *One God*. Edited by S. Mitchell and P. vanNuffelen. New York/Cambridge: Cambridge University Press, 2010.

_____. "Pagans, Polytheists and the Pendulum." Pages 125–43 in *Spread of Christianity in the First Four Centuries*. Edited by W. V. Harris. Leiden: Brill, 2005.

Sider, Robert D., ed. *Christian and the Pagan in the Roman Empire*. Washington: Catholic University of America Press, 2001.

38. Final Judgment (4:5)

Erickson, Millard J. *Christian Theology*. Grand Rapids: Baker Book House, 1985. See esp. pages 1185–1204.

Garrett, James L. *Systematic Theology: Biblical, Historical, and Evangelical*. Vol. 2. Grand Rapids: Eerdmans, 1995. See esp. pages 770–85.

Moule, Charles F. D. *Essays in New Testament Interpretation*. Cambridge: Cambridge University Press, 1982. See pages 235–49.

Hiers, Richard H. *ABD* 2.79–82.
Hoekema, Anthony A. *The Bible and the Future*. Grand Rapids: Eerdmans, 1979.
Klooster, Fred H. *ISBE* 2.1162–63.
Milne, Bruce. *The Message of Heaven and Hell*. Leicester: IVP, 2002.
Seifrid, Mark A. *DLNT* 621–25.
Toon, Peter. *Heaven and Hell: A Biblical and Theological Overview*. Nashville: Thomas Nelson, 1986.
*Travis, Stephen H. *Christ and the Judgment of God: Divine Retribution in the New Testament*. Grand Rapids: Zondervan, 1987.
Wright, Tom. *Surprised by Hope*. London: SPCK, 2007.

HOMILETICAL SUGGESTIONS

Living Appropriate Christian Lives Among Unbelievers (4:1–6)

1. Emulating the resolve of Christ (v. 1a)
2. Leaving behind a life of sin (v. 1b–3)
   (a) Preparedness to suffer as evidence (v. 1b)
   (b) Not following human desires but the will of God (v. 2)
   (c) The time is long past to follow past pagan practices (v. 3)
3. The pagan response (vv. 4–5)
   (a) Surprise (v. 4a)
   (b) Blasphemy (v. 4b)
   (c) Their accountability to God the judge (v. 5)
4. Believers who have died (v. 6)
   (a) Evaluated negatively by unbelievers
   (b) Evaluated positively by God

Security in God (4:1–6)

1. Living a godless lifestyle will:
   (a) win approval from the crowds (vv. 3–4)
   (b) come under the judgment of God (v. 5)
2. Living a godly life will:
   (a) entail a resolve to suffer if need be (v. 1)
   (b) be negatively evaluated by unbelievers (v. 6b)
   (c) win vindication from God (v. 6b)

B. AMONG BELIEVERS (4:7–11)

STRUCTURE

The opening clause ("the end of all things is near") governs the entire section. The inferential οὖν ("therefore") then introduces four directives for life in the Christian community that must ensue from this eschatological nearness. The final directive regarding service (v. 10) is illustrated by two examples in v. 11 introduced by εἴ τις ("if anyone"), followed by a ὡς clause that depicts the manner in which these are to be employed. The ἵνα clause stresses the purpose of serving this way, although the use of ἐν πᾶσιν indicates the focus is more broad. The section concludes with a doxology, with the rel. ᾧ most likely referring to God (see below).

7   πάντων δὲ τὸ τέλος ἤγγικεν.

     <u>σωφρονήσατε</u> οὖν καὶ <u>νήψατε</u> εἰς προσευχάς
8   πρὸ πάντων τὴν εἰς ἑαυτοὺς <u>ἀγάπην</u> ἐκτενῆ ἔχοντες,
     ὅτι <u>ἀγάπη</u> καλύπτει πλῆθος ἁμαρτιῶν.
9   φιλόξενοι εἰς ἀλλήλους ἄνευ γογγυσμοῦ,
10   ἕκαστος καθὼς ἔλαβεν χάρισμα εἰς ἑαυτοὺς αὐτὸ <u>διακονοῦντες</u>
     ὡς καλοὶ οἰκονόμοι ποικίλης χάριτος θεοῦ.

11   εἴ τις λαλεῖ,   ὡς λόγια θεοῦ·
                εἴ τις <u>διακονεῖ</u>, ὡς ἐξ ἰσχύος ἧς χορηγεῖ ὁ θεός,
                ἵνα ἐν πᾶσιν <u>δοξάζηται</u> ὁ <u>θεὸς</u> διὰ Ἰησοῦ Χριστοῦ,

                <u>ᾧ ἐστιν ἡ δόξα</u>
                καὶ τὸ κράτος εἰς τοὺς αἰῶνας τῶν αἰώνων, ἀμήν.

VERSE 7

πάντων δὲ τὸ τέλος ἤγγικεν

The conj. δέ provides a weak link to the preceding with a continuance of the eschatological theme. Πάντων is in the opening position and is even more encompassing than "the living and the dead" in v. 5. Τέλος has a number of meanings in the NT (see R. Schippers, *NIDNTT* 2.59–66; G. Delling, *TDNT* 8.49–57), and this range is reflected somewhat in 1 Peter. In 1:9 it has the sense of "outcome," in 3:8 it is adv. "finally," and in 4:17 "fate." Here it means "end" in the sense of the final day, elsewhere described in this epistle as the day of the revelation of Jesus Christ (1:7, 13; 4:13).

Ἤγγικεν 3 sg. pf. act. indic. of ἐγγίζω. The pf. indic. recalls the gospel tradition and the announcements of the coming kingdom (Mark 1:14–15; Matt 3:2; Luke 10:9; cf. Jas 5:8). The use of the pf. gives a heightened proximity (Campbell, *Indicative Mood* 161–211), thus an appropriate rendering would be "very near" (Weymouth: "now close at hand"), or colloq. "just around the corner" (Davids 156). *Pace* Jobes (275–76), this is not equivalent to speaking of the presence of the last days because this period of time has clearly dawned (1:20). The resurrection of Jesus has ushered in these last times and consequently brought near the final consummation of all things (i.e., the end), but that consummation, although imminent, is not yet (so Michaels 245). The present time involves a brief moment of suffering (1:6; 4:17; 5:10).

This opening statement regarding the imminence of the end controls the thought of vv. 7–11, with the ptcs. in the ensuing vv. dependent upon the aor. impvs. in v. 7. So eschatology becomes (part of) the basis for ethics (Achtemeier 294; Elliott 744).

σωφρονήσατε οὖν καὶ νήψστε εἰς προσευχάς

Σωφρονήσατε 2 pl. aor. act. impv. of σωφρονέω, "be of sound mind," "sensible" (BDAG 986d; Spicq 3.359–65; S. Wibbing, *NIDNTT* 1.501–2), having to do with an attitude of prudence; the ability to act in an appropriate manner given the circumstances, which in the Stoic and popular philosophical tradition was one of the cardinal virtues. Νήψατε 2 pl. aor. act. impv. of νήφω, "be sober" (BDAG 672c). The two aor. impvs. form a hendiadys, with the latter used in its common metaphorical sense of staying alert (cf. 1:13; *NewDocs* 2.69; O. Bauernfeind, *TDNT* 7.1097–1104; P. J. Budd, *NIDNTT* 1.514–15). Nevertheless, its literal sense forms a strong contrast with the unrestrained drinking of the pagans in v. 3 (Dubis 140). Given the eschatological context here the aor. impvs. may carry a sense of forcefulness (see further "The Use of the Imperative in 1 Peter" in the Introduction).

Εἰς is telic (Harris 88–90), representing the purpose of this vigilance in terms of prayer ("with a view to your prayers," ZG 713; "so that you may give yourselves to prayer," Weymouth), thus reflecting the concerns of 3:7, 12. This probably means vigilance in order to pray, i.e., not to be distracted by issues of suffering or by the adversary the Devil (cf. 5:8–9 where νήψατε is also employed). Προσευχάς should be linked to both impvs. (Michaels 246) and is pl. to reflect the individual acts of prayer (Goppelt 296).

As a consequence, therefore (οὖν), of the imminent end to all things, believers must be prudent and vigilant in prayer. Once more we see eschatology used as a basis for parenesis; followers of Jesus must live in the present in light of the future.

VERSE 8

πρὸ πάντων τὴν εἰς ἑαυτοὺς ἀγάπην ἐκτενῆ ἔχοντες

The inferential conj. οὖν governs not only the aor. impvs. of v. 7, but also the exhortations of vv. 8–10 (Dubis 140). The refl. pron. ἑαυτούς is here equivalent to ἀλλήλους (R 690; BDF §287), with εἰς used to mark a specific point of reference (BDAG 291a). Ἐκτενής, -ές, refers to that which perseveres, thus "constant" (NRSV; BDAG 310b; LN 68.12) rather than "fervent" (KJV, ASV, NASB; Spicq 1.457–61) or "earnestly" (ESV). The pred. adj. strictly gives the sense "keep your love for one another constant" (R 789), but for ease of trans. most EVV render as attrib. (though NASB: "keep fervent in your love for one another"). The cognate adv. ἐκτενῶς has already been utilized in 1:22. On the need for love for fellow Christians, see on 1:22; 2:17.

The ptc. ἔχοντες, together with the implied vb. with the adj. φιλόξενοι (v. 9) and the ptc. διακονοῦντες (v. 10), is strictly dependent upon the two aor. impvs. of the previous v., but as they are specifically directed toward prayer the connection is rather loose. Nevertheless, they do take on a derived impv. force (so Goppelt 297; Michaels 246; Elliott 750; see the discussion on "Imperatival Participles in 1 Peter" in the Introduction), with this force being accentuated by πρὸ πάντων, which should be taken in a logical sense, "above all" (Moule 74; R 622; Porter 171; BDF §213).

ὅτι ἀγάπη καλύπτει πλῆθος ἁμαρτιῶν

Ὅτι is causal, expressing the reason why constant love must be maintained within the Christian community. Καλύπτει 3 sg. pres. act. indic. of καλύπτω, "hide," "cover" (BDAG 505b). In place of the pres. indic. καλύπτει read by A B K Ψ 33, 81, 323, 614, 630, 441, 1505, 1739, and others, the fut. indic. καλύψει is found in 𝔓⁷² ℵ P 049 and the majority text. The ms. evidence is fairly evenly weighted, but on internal grounds it would appear best to retain the pres. indic. The fut. was possibly an attempt to align this covering of sins with the eschatological judgment mentioned in v. 5 and the end of all things in the previous v. The fut. indic. also accords with Jas 5:20. Ἁμαρτιῶν is a gen. of content (Wallace 92–94), giving the subject matter for πλῆθος.

The saying regarding love covering a multitude of sins may draw on Prov 10:12 (see Beale and Carson 1039–40), but is closer to the MT ("hatred stirs up strife, but love covers all offenses," NRSV) than the LXX (πάντας δὲ τοὺς μὴ φιλονεικοῦντας καλύπτει φιλία, "love covers all those who are not argumentative") and appears to have become a proverbial statement in the early church (Jas 5:20; *1 Clem.* 49.5; *2 Clem.* 16.4, though the refs. in Clement are probably dependent on 1 Peter). This would make the pres. tense καλύπτει gnomic, but the precise way in which sins are covered is unclear. At the outset, we should rule out any understanding that sins can be atoned for, even in part, by a human act. This finds no support elsewhere in this epistle and contradicts previous passages where Christ suffers for human sin (2:21–24; 3:18). This leaves three main possibilities:

1. The sins are the sins of the person who is loving (ZG 713), with the idea that while love is being expressed, sin is not. It is another way of saying that they are "done with sin" (2:1, 24; 4:1–2; so Michaels 247);
2. The sins are the sins of the person who is being loved, in the sense that love can keep a person from straying into sin; or
*3. "Cover" is used in the sense of "forgive" (cf. Ps 32:1), with the sense that love always forgives the other (Elliott 751). This is close to the sense of the original proverb, which is set in antithetical parallelism. If hatred stirs up strife, i.e., in the sense of making matters worse, then love covers offenses in the sense that it minimizes wrongs by refusing to take offense (with Beale and Carson 1039–40; Jobes 278–80; Achtemeier 296; Davids 158). This accords with Peter's insistence on a non-retaliatory response (2:23; 3:9).

VERSE 9

φιλόξενοι εἰς ἀλλήλους ἄνευ γογγυσμοῦ

Φιλόξενος, -ον, "hospitable" (BDAG 1058d; Spicq 3.454–57). As in 3:8, an adj. (here φιλόξενοι) is functioning as an impv., with the impv. ἐστέ, or more likely given vv. 8, 10 the ptc. ὄντες (Achtemeier 296) implied. Εἰς ἀλλήλους indicates that it is hospitality within the Christian community that is primarily in view. Ἄνευ (adv.) indicates dissociation, "without" (LN 89.120; Moule 82; R 638). Γογγυσμός, -οῦ, ὁ is an utterance made in a low tone of voice (BDAG 204c; NewDocs 4.143–44), which in a neg. sense is "grumbling" (NJB, NKJV, CEV), "murmuring" (ASV), "complaining" (NRSV, HCSB).

In the early church, individual Christians used their homes for corporate meetings (Rom 16:15; 1 Cor 16:19; Col 4:15) and also to support itinerant evangelists (3 John 5–6; Didache 11–13). The instruction here was probably meant to go beyond providing a place for official meetings and would include opportunities for mutual support and encouragement, so crucial in a hostile setting (Jobes 281).

VERSE 10

ἕκαστος καθὼς ἔλαβεν χάρισμα

This entire clause modifies the ptc. διακονοῦντες. Although not developed along Pauline lines, the assumption with ἕκαστος is that every Christian has received a gift (Rom 12:4–8; 1 Cor 12; Eph 4:10–13). Ἔλαβεν 3 sg. aor. act. indic. of λαμβάνω. The aor. ἔλαβεν is perfective. Χάρισμα, -ατος, τό, "favor," "gift" (BDAG 1081a; Turner, Words 430–31; H.–H. Esser, NIDNTT 2.115–23). Καθώς is a subord. conj., here not so much indicating extent or degree (pace BDAG 493d), as cause (BDF §453[2]; i.e., "insofar as," sim. NKJV, NASB, ESV; so Elliott 753). Peter shares Paul's term χάρισμα for the abilities given by God (cf. Rom 12:6) in order to carry out ministry within the Christian community. That they are gifts of grace is expressly stated below.

εἰς ἑαυτοὺς αὐτὸ διακονοῦντες

The prep. phrase εἰς ἑαυτούς gives a rather awkward "serving it for yourselves," with εἰς indicating purpose (Harris 88–90; NASB: "employ it in serving one another," sim. ZG 713). The refl. pron. is once more used in a reciprocal sense of "one another" (see v. 8). Αὐτό is the dir. obj. of the ptc. διακονοῦντες (διακονέω taking the acc. of the matter served), with its antecedent being χάρισμα. The ptc. διακονοῦντες is also (along with the ptc. ἔχοντες in v. 8 and the adj. φιλόξενοι in v. 9) dependent upon the aor. impvs. in v. 7 and so carries derived impv. force (see the discussion on "Imperatival Participles in 1 Peter" in the Introduction).

ὡς καλοὶ οἰκονόμοι ποικίλης χάριτος θεοῦ

The particle ὡς here indicates the manner in which something is to proceed (BDAG 1103d). The adj. καλοί is better rendered "faithful" (NIV: "faithful stewards") in this context. Οἰκονόμος, -ου, ὁ, "servant," "slave" (BDAG 698b–c). The noun refers to a trusted servant responsible for management of the household and is a fitting term given that the Christian community is depicted in this epistle as the household of God (2:4–5; 4:17; Achtemeier 298; Elliott 757; most EVV: "stewards"). Ποικίλος, -η, -ον, "diverse" (BDAG 842b). Ποικίλης χάριτος is an obj. gen. Θεοῦ could be taken as a gen. of origin/source (i.e., grace that comes from God) but is better as a subj. gen. as this highlights God as the giver of grace (Dubis 143). Peter's use of χάρις is quite diverse. It is elsewhere tied to the future revelation of Jesus (1:10, 13), yet is also linked to present suffering (2:19–20). Here it relates to gifts given to believers for mutual edification and the conducting of ministry. Consequently, the diversity of gifts indicated by ποικίλης may have a more subtle nuance (Michaels 249).

VERSE 11

εἴ τις λαλεῖ, ὡς λόγια θεοῦ

Εἴ τις is equivalent to an indef. "whoever," rather than introducing a conditional clause (BDAG 279b; Michaels 250). Λαλεῖ covers a variety of speaking gifts designed to edify the community. Ὡς λόγια θεοῦ is elliptical (see *NewDocs* 6.67–68 on the omission in an ellipsis being inferred from the previous clause), with an implied ptc. (BDF §425[4]; T 158 n. 1) such as "one who speaks" (HCSB, ESV, NIV), with an impv. such as "do it" ("do it as one who is speaking the oracles of God," NASB, sim. NRSV).

The particle ὡς indicates the manner in which something is to proceed (BDAG 1103d), with the rhetorical point being that one should treat this ministry of speaking very seriously indeed. Λόγιον, -ου, τό, "oracle," "saying" (BDAG 598b). In the NT, λόγια has a number of senses, including the Mosaic Law (Acts 7:38), the Jewish Scriptures (Rom 3:2), and God's revelation in general (Heb 5:12). The closest sense to here is found in Num 24:4, 16 LXX regarding Balaam delivering God's prophetic word (Michaels 250). Θεοῦ is a gen. of source/origin.

εἴ τις διακονεῖ, ὡς ἐξ ἰσχύος ἧς χορηγεῖ ὁ θεός

On εἴ τις, see above. Διακονεῖ picks up διακονοῦντες from the previous v. but here is more specifically related to serving gifts rather than serving by using one's gift. Again, the terminology is rather broad, but the focus is probably on practical ministries, which in Pauline terms would include such gifts as administration, leadership, and helping. Ἐξ here denotes source (LN 89.3; BDAG 296d). Ἰσχύς, -ύος, ἡ, "strength," "power" (BDAG 484b). Again, the cstr. is elliptical with an implied impv. such as "do it" (NKJV, CEV).

The rel. pron. ἧς is gen. by attraction to its antecedent ἰσχύος (see R 512; Z §16–21; Porter 251–53). Χορηγεῖ 3 sg. pres. act. indic. of χορηγέω, "supply," "provide" (BDAG

1087a; *NewDocs* 4.104). The vb. is used only twice in the NT (2 Cor 9:10), both indicating the bountiful provision of God. Elliott (760) notes that it belongs to a range of terms that refer to the generosity of benevolent patrons.

The point of ὡς ἐξ ἰσχύος ἧς χορηγεῖ ὁ θεός, rather than implying that such work can be demanding (though it may be), is to focus attention on God as the source of all that is required for successful Christian ministry. He is responsible for the gifts given to each person (v. 10), the oracles are his, and the strength to serve is his, a point accentuated in the following doxology (Michaels 251; Achtemeier 299 n. 107).

ἵνα ἐν πᾶσιν δοξάζηται ὁ θεὸς διὰ Ἰησοῦ Χριστοῦ

The ἵνα clause expresses the purpose of the exercise of spiritual gifts. However, the fact that God is to be glorified ἐν πᾶσιν ("in all things") now shifts the focus wider than the spiritual gifts themselves and prepares for the following doxology. Passages such as 2:12 and 4:16 also indicate that giving glory to God is the ultimate purpose of human life (Elliott 761). The prep. phrase διὰ Ἰησοῦ Χριστοῦ expresses intermediate agency (Wallace 433–34) and keeps Christ as the agent of God's action in focus (cf. 1:3, 11, 20–21; 2:5; 5:10).

ᾧ ἐστιν ἡ δόξα καὶ τὸ κράτος εἰς τοὺς αἰῶνας τῶν αἰώνων, ἀμήν

The dat. rel. pron. ᾧ is poss. (Dubis 145), but the antecedent is once more ambiguous. Jesus Christ is the last-mentioned name (Michaels 253, follows Selwyn 220, in taking the referent to Jesus), but God is the more likely referent, as it is to him that glory is given in the previous clause (with Achtemeier 299; Elliott 762; Goppelt 306; Davids 162). Furthermore, the entire focus in this section is theocentric, and a similar doxology in 5:11 is addressed to God.

The use of the indic. ἐστιν indicates that this ascribing of glory and power is not a wish ("be," NIV) but a fact ("belong," NJB, NRSV, NASB, HCSB, ESV). Κράτος, -ους, τό, "power," "might" (BDAG 565b). The def. arts. with δόξα and κράτος particularize the qualities (Wallace 226) and are virtually equivalent to "all glory"/"all power."

Doxologies often appear within individual NT documents (Rom 11:36; Gal 1:5; Eph 3:21; Rev 1:6; 5:13; 7:12), so the presence of the doxology here in no way designates an original ending to the epistle. Ἀμήν is a transliteration of the Heb. *'amēn* and conveys a strong affirmation of what is stated (BDAG 53c).

FOR FURTHER STUDY

39. Spiritual Gifts

Aune, David E. *Prophecy in Early Christianity and the Ancient Mediterranean World.* Grand Rapids: Eerdmans, 1983.

Carson, D. A. *Showing the Spirit.* Grand Rapids: Baker, 1987.

Conzelmann, Hans. *TDNT* 9.402–6.

Dunn, James D. G. *Jesus and the Spirit.* Philadelphia: Westminster, 1975.

Fee, Gordon D. *God's Empowering Presence: The Holy Spirit in the Letters of Paul.* Peabody, MA: Hendrickson, 1993.

———. *DPL* 339–47.

Fung, Ronald Y. K. "Ministry, Community and Spiritual Gifts." *Evangelical Quarterly* 56 (1984): 3–14.

García, Albert L. "Spiritual Gifts and the Work of the Kingdom." *Corcordia Theological Quarterly* 49 (1985): 149–60.

*Kilgallen, John J. "Reflections on Charisma(ta) in the New Testament." *Studia Missionalia* 41 (1992): 289–323.

MacGorman, Jack W. *The Gifts of the Spirit.* Nashville: Broadman, 1974.

Martin, Ralph P. *The Spirit and the Congregation.* Grand Rapids: Eerdmans, 1984.

———. *ABD* 2.1015–19.

Sullivan, Francis A. *Charisms and Charismatic Renewal.* Ann Arbor, MI: 1982.

See also For Further Study §§ 12, 20.

HOMILETICAL SUGGESTIONS

Living Appropriate Christian Lives Among Believers (4:7–11)

1. The end is near (v. 7a), the consequences of which (οὖν) are:
   (a) Be focused on prayer (v. 7b)
   (b) Show constant love for those in the Christian community (v. 8)
   (c) Show hospitality (v. 9)
   (d) Use spiritual gifts:
       (i.) to serve one another (v. 10)
   (a) speaking gifts (v. 11a)
   (b) serving gifts (v 11b)
       (ii.) to glorify God (v. 11c)
2. To God belongs all glory and power (v. 11d)

Spiritual Gifts (4:10–11)

1. Are given to each Christian as a gift of grace (cf. 1 Cor 12:4–11; Rom 12:4–8)
2. Various types of gifts (none of the listings in the various texts are exhaustive)
3. The exercise of the gifts is to:
   (a) build up the church (v. 10a; 1 Cor 12:7; 14:12)
   (b) honor God (v. 11c; 1 Cor 14:25)

VIII. Final Instructions for a Suffering People (4:12–5:14)

A. THE FIERY ORDEAL (4:12–19)

STRUCTURE

The use of ἀγαπητοί ("beloved") marks a major transition in the letter (cf. 2:11). Each of the first three vv. (vv. 12–15) begins with a statement of suffering. Verse 12 explains the purpose of this suffering as πρὸς πειρασμόν ("for testing"); v. 13 calls for a response to this suffering—χαίρετε ("rejoice"), whereas v. 14 indicates the result of the suffering—μακάριοι ("you are blessed").

Each of the three statements regarding suffering is in turn modified by a subord. clause. Verse 12 has a gen. abs. indicating that suffering is to be expected; v. 13 has a purpose clause (ἵνα) showing that a proper attitude to suffering will result in even greater rejoicing, whereas in v. 14 the ὅτι clause is causal showing the reason why believers are blessed when reviled for the name of Christ.

12 ἀγαπητοί, <u>μὴ ξενίζεσθε</u>
            τῇ ἐν ὑμῖν πυρώσει
            πρὸς πειρασμὸν
            ὑμῖν γινομένῃ
                ὡς ξένου ὑμῖν συμβαίνοντος,
13 ἀλλὰ   καθὸ κοινωνεῖτε τοῖς τοῦ <u>Χριστοῦ</u> παθήμασιν,
   <u>χαίρετε,</u>
        ἵνα καὶ   ἐν τῇ ἀποκαλύψει τῆς δόξης αὐτοῦ
        <u>χαρῆτε</u> ἀγαλλιώμενοι.

14   εἰ ὀνειδίζεσθε ἐν ὀνόματι <u>Χριστοῦ,</u>
  μακάριοι,
        ὅτι τὸ τῆς δόξης καὶ τὸ τοῦ θεοῦ πνεῦμα ἐφ᾽ ὑμᾶς ἀναπαύεται.

Verse 15 presents four examples of behavior that must not occasion suffering for believers. By means of a cond. cstr., v. 16 contrasts the above with suffering as a Christian which should not result in shame but glorifying God.

15   μὴ γάρ τις ὑμῶν <u>πασχέτω</u>
                       ὡς φονεὺς
                       ἢ κλέπτης
                       ἢ κακοποιὸς
                       ἢ ὡς ἀλλοτριεπίσκοπος·
16   εἰ δὲ   ὡς χριστιανός,
     <u>μὴ αἰσχυνέσθω,</u>
     <u>δοξαζέτω</u> δὲ τὸν θεὸν ἐν τῷ μέρει τούτῳ.

Verse 17 explains Christian suffering in terms of God's eschatological judgment (see the analysis below). Together with the following v. it provides two contrasts between the fate of believers and unbelievers. The section concludes (v. 19) with a summary statement utilizing ὥστε ("so then"), which virtually encapsulates everything the author has said concerning suffering.

17   ὅτι ὁ καιρὸς τοῦ ἄρξασθαι τὸ κρίμα ἀπὸ τοῦ οἴκου τοῦ θ̲ε̲ο̲ῦ̲·
         εἰ δὲ πρῶτον ἀφ' ἡμῶν,
     τί τὸ τέλος τῶν ἀπειθούντων τῷ τοῦ θ̲ε̲ο̲ῦ̲ εὐαγγελίῳ;
18   καὶ εἰ ὁ δίκαιος μόλις σώζεται,
     ὁ ἀσεβὴς καὶ ἁμαρτωλὸς ποῦ φανεῖται;
19   ὥστε καὶ οἱ πάσχοντες
                 κατὰ τὸ θέλημα τοῦ θ̲ε̲ο̲ῦ̲
                 πιστῷ κτίστῃ
                     παρατιθέσθωσαν τὰς ψυχὰς αὐτῶν ἐν ἀγαθοποιΐᾳ.

VERSE 12

Ἀγαπητοί, μὴ ξενίζεσθε τῇ ἐν ὑμῖν πυρώσει πρὸς πειρασμὸν ὑμῖν γινομένῃ

Ἀγαπητοί recalls 2:11, which also marks a major transition in the letter. The affectionate term has a pastoral intention as the subject of suffering is resumed (Elliott 771).

Ξενίζεσθε 2 pl. pres. pass. impv. of ξενίζω, "astonish," "surprise." An entreaty rather than a command. This vb. normally takes the dat. (here τῇ πυρώσει) of the thing causing surprise (BDAG 684a), which can be cstr. as instr. of cause (T 242; BDF §196). The word recalls 4:4, only now the situation is reversed. Unbelievers are surprised at the behavior of Christians, but Christians are not to be surprised at the behavior of unbelievers toward them (Achtemeier 305; Michaels 260; Davids 164). Previous rules regarding the neg. with the pres. impv. indicating a command to stop action in progress can no longer be sustained (see Fanning 335–40; Ken L. McKay, "Aspect in Imperatival Constructions in New Testament Greek," *NovT* 27 [1985]: 201–26). This does not mean that the readers were not surprised; however, that this cannot be substantiated by the tense of the impv. alone.

Ἐν ὑμῖν is a locat. of place, "among you" (not "in you"), and is attrib. (modifying τῇ πυρώσει) not adv. (modifying γινομένῃ). Πύρωσις, -εως, ἡ (BDAG 900a; Turner, *Words* 445; LSJ 1559d) relates to the process of burning (as in Rev 18:9, 18), here used as a graphic metaphor of a painful ordeal ("fiery trial," NLT, ESV; "fiery ordeal," NRSV, NASB, HCSB, NIV; "scorching flame of persecution," Weymouth; LN 78.37). Πειρασμός, -οῦ, ὁ, "trial," "test" (BDAG 793c; Turner, *Words* 440–43).

The language is similar to 1:6–7 (πειρασμόν—πειρασμοῖς, πυρώσει—πυρός), where faith is pictured as passing through a refining process in order to test its genuineness (cf. Ps 66:10; Prov 17:3; 27:21; Zech 13:9; Wis 3:1–6; Sir 2:1–6; 1 Cor 3:13; cf. 1QS 1:17–18; 8:3–4; 1QM 17:8–9; 1QH 5:16; *Did.* 16:5). This refining process is picked up in v. 17 below. The similarity between 1:6–7 and the current passage argues against the contention that 4:12ff introduces a new situation of suffering or that it is an actual situation as opposed to a mere potential scenario discussed previously (*pace* Beare 188–96).

The second use of the dat. pron. ὑμῖν could be taken with the ptc. γινομένη, but this creates a redundancy given the first usage of the pron. More likely it belongs with πρὸς πειρασμόν, either as a dat. of ref. (Dubis 147), or more likely, given Peter's perspective on suffering, as a dat. of advantage. The ptc. γινομένη can be cstr. in two ways:

(1) attrib. with τῇ ἐν ὑμῖν πυρώσει, which would give "the fiery ordeal that is coming among you to test you." On the anar. ptc. functioning attrib., see R 1106. This is the position taken by virtually every commentator and EVV.

*(2) causal, modifying μὴ ξενίζεσθε, giving "do not be surprised at the fiery trial that is among you, because it is happening to test you" (Bigg 176).

Option (2) is to be preferred. The prep. phrase πρὸς πειρασμόν indicates purpose (BDAG 874c; Harris, 189–90), i.e., the fiery trial constitutes a test. So grammatically, the entire ptc. clause gives the reason why the readers are not to be surprised ("because it is happening to test you"), while the prep. phrase works at a secondary level, giving the purpose of the trial ("to test you").

ὡς ξένου ὑμῖν συμβαίνοντος

Ὡς functions here as a marker introducing the perspective from which an activity is viewed (BDAG 1104d), indicating a perspective that is untrue ("as though," NRSV, NIV). Ξένος, -η, -ον, "strange," "unfamiliar" (BDAG 684b; Spicq 2.555–60). In this gen. abs. cstr. it functions as the subj. of the ptc. It also forms a word play with μὴ ξενίζεσθε. The reason why Peter's readers should not be surprised about such testing circumstances will be elaborated on in the vv. that follow. Συμβαίνοντος gen. sg. neut. of. pres. act. ptc. of συμβαίνω, "happen" (BDAG 956b), is synonymous with γινομένη in the previous clause. Elliott's contention (774) that the pres. tenses of these ptcs. indicate a continuation of existing suffering rather than a new situation is a case of overinterpretation of vb. tense.

VERSE 13

ἀλλὰ καθὸ κοινωνεῖτε τοῖς τοῦ Χριστοῦ παθήμασιν χαίρετε

Ἀλλά correlates with μή in v. 12 to provide a positive-neg. contrast (Dubis 146). Believers are not to be surprised at their fiery ordeal but are to rejoice. Καθό (an abbreviated form of καθότι; see R 967) could express degree, i.e., "to the extent that" (Weymouth, NKJV, NASB; BDAG 493a; LN 78.53; Michaels 262; Dubis 148) or provide the rationale, i.e., "because/in view of the fact that" (Elliott 774; Goppelt 315 n. 8). The former option allows for various scenarios, while the latter focuses on the actuality of suffering. Contextual support could be claimed for either, and a final decision is difficult.

Κοινωνεῖτε 2 pl. pres. act. indic. of κοινωνέω, "share in" + dat. (BDAG 552b; J. Schattenmann, *NIDNTT* 1.639–44; Turner, *Words* 163–68). Apart from the cognate adj. in 5:1, this is the only use of the κοινων- word group in this epistle. With respect to the sufferings of Christ, we should probably understand this in the sense of following his example already discussed in 2:21–24, rather than any sense of mystical union as found in Paul (Michaels 262). The sufferings may include death, but what is primarily in view is the slander and abuse hurled by unbelievers.

Τοῦ Χριστοῦ is a subj. gen. (Dubis 148 [cf. LN 24.78], takes it as attrib., "messianic sufferings"). Πάθημα, -ατος, τό, "suffering" (BDAG 747d). The vb. χαίρετε recalls 1:6–8 where rejoicing is linked with suffering, but there ἀγαλλιάω is used. In contrast to this earlier passage (see on 1:6), here rejoicing is called for in the midst of suffering. The use of the pres. impv. with its unfolding aspect is consistent with a general exhortation (Fanning 325–88). In the following clause, the two verbs are juxtaposed. The relationship between the terms will be discussed below (see also on 1:6).

ἵνα καὶ ἐν τῇ ἀποκαλύψει τῆς δόξης αὐτοῦ χαρῆτε ἀγαλλιώμενοι

The purpose of rejoicing in the midst of trials is expressed by means of the ἵνα clause, with καί adv. "also." Ἀποκάλυψις, -εως, ἡ, "revelation" (Turner, *Words* 381–82). Ἐν τῇ ἀποκαλύψει τῆς δόξης αὐτοῦ is a locat. of time and is elsewhere referred to as the revelation of Jesus Christ (1:7, 13). The ref. is to the Parousia at the final day. Τῆς δόξης is an obj. gen. and clearly refers to Christ's glory (1:11, 21). In 1:7 this glory is shared by believers at his revelation.

The vb. χαιρῆτε is now supported and modified by the ptc. of manner ἀγαλλιώμενοι (nom. pl. masc. of pres. mid. ptc. of ἀγαλλιάω, "be full of joy"; BDAG 4c–d; Turner, *Words* 148–50; E. Beyreuther, *NIDNTT* 2.352–56), which serves to intensify χαρῆτε, resulting in the mng. "overjoyed" (NIV), "be glad and shout for joy" (NRSV), "even greater happiness" (CEV). The intensity of joy echoes the "inexpressible and glorious joy" of 1:8.

It should be stressed that the sense of the purpose clause is not that future rejoicing depends on the ability to rejoice in the midst of present distress per se. It is more that a proper perspective on suffering in the present enables one to endure and hence not succumb to external pressure (Achtemeier 306). Furthermore, it also indicates that undeserved suffering is the basis for eschatological vindication (Jobes 287). So, great joy awaits believers when Jesus Christ is revealed and their faith is vindicated. It is this "eschatological perspective on their problems" (Davids 166) that enables joy in the midst of present suffering. We also find that, in the end, two attitudes are called for under duress: joy and proper conduct. Both are based on the fact that believers follow in the footsteps of Jesus.

VERSE 14

εἰ ὀνειδίζεσθε ἐν ὀνόματι Χριστοῦ, μακάριοι

The cond. clause (first class cond. introduced by εἰ) parallels εἰ καὶ πάσχοιτε διὰ δικαιοσύνην, μακάριοι ("even if you suffer on account of righteousness, you are blessed") in 3:14, although here the indic. rather than the opt. mood is employed (see comments there for the sense of the opt.). To be insulted is to suffer, and to suffer for righteousness is to suffer in the name of Christ. This will be summed up shortly as suffering ὡς Χριστιανός, "as a Christian" (v. 16).

Ὀνειδίζεσθε 2 pl. pres. pass. indic. of ὀνειδίζω, "insult," "reproach" (BDAG 710c; Spicq 2.585–87). The vb. is one of several synonymous terms that Peter uses for abuse directed at followers of Jesus by unbelievers: λοιδορέω/λοιδορία (2:23; 3:9), ἐπηρεάζω (3:14), and καταλαλέω/καταλαλία (2:1, 12). Elliott (779) correctly notes that this conglomeration of terms reinforces the likelihood that the persecution directed at the recipients of this epistle was "verbal abuse and public humiliation rather than . . . official incrimination."

Ἐν ὀνόματι Χριστοῦ is instr. of cause (i.e., "because of the name of Christ," NIV; most EVV have the more ambiguous "for"). Ὀνειδίζω ἐν is a Heb. (Turner, *Style* 130). The adj. μακάριοι is pred. (with ἔστε implied) and forms the apod. of the cond. The language recalls the Beatitudes, particularly Matt 5:11//Luke 6:22 where the vb. ὀνειδίζω is also used.

ὅτι τὸ τῆς δόξης καὶ τὸ τοῦ θεοῦ πνεῦμα ἐφ᾽ ὑμᾶς ἀναπαύεται

The reason for the blessing is expressed by means of the ὅτι clause, with echoes of Isa 11:2 LXX (καὶ ἀναπαύσεται ἐπ᾽ αὐτὸν πνεῦμα τοῦ θεοῦ, "and the Spirit of God will rest upon him;" see Beale and Carson 1040–41). The repetition of the art. in τὸ τῆς δόξης καὶ τὸ τοῦ θεοῦ πνεῦμα is problematic:

1. τὸ τῆς δόξης is to be treated as a subst. ref. to the *Shekinah* (Selwyn 222–24). However, in cstrs. such as this (see Matt 21:21; 1 Cor 10:24, 33; Jas 4:14; 2 Pet 2:22; 1 John 4:3) the sense of the neut. art. is quite clear from the context, but that clarity is not present here;
2. τὸ τῆς δόξης is an anaphoric ref. to the glory just mentioned (Achtemeier 309 [possibly]);
*3 the expression is a hendiadys, expressing a single idea (ESV, NIV; R 767; BDF §442[16]; Elliott 782; R 785 believes that the two arts. serve to emphasise each of the gens.); or

*4   an epex. expression, "the Spirit of glory, that is, the Spirit of God" (Weymouth,
NRSV; T 187; Dubis 150). Here καί is explicative.

Options 3 and 4 are evenly weighted and are similar in mng.

The art. τῆς with δόξης could still be anaphoric (Michaels 264), referring back to the
glory mentioned in the previous verse (i.e., "the spirit of that glory"), or alternatively
is particularizing the quality.

It is unclear whether the presence of the Spirit and the consequential blessing is
meant to indicate:

1. the empowerment of the Spirit to endure persecution (Jobes 288; Goppelt
   325);
2. a foretaste of the coming eschatological glory (cf. 1:7; 4:13; Davids 168;
   Achtemeier 309); or
3. that the glory of God is seen in them (Davids 168).

In place of τὸ τῆς δόξης καὶ τὸ τοῦ θεοῦ πνεῦμα ("the Spirit of glory, even the Spirit of
God") read by 𝔓⁷² B Ψ and part of the majority text (K L), there are several alternative
rdgs. Parts of the Latin text omit the second τό, possibly an attempt to avoid the notion
of two separate Spirits. A number of mss. including ℵ* ℵ² (both with minor variations) A and parts of the majority text, together with some versions, read τὸ τῆς δόξης
καὶ δυνάμεως καὶ τὸ τοῦ θεοῦ πνεῦμα ("the Spirit of glory and power, even the Spirit
of God"), maybe linking the ideas of glory and power from the preceding doxology
(4:11). The shorter rdg., with the inclusion of both instances of τό should be retained.

There are also a number of alternative rdgs. for ἀναπαύεται (3 sg. pres. mid. indic.
of ἀναπαύω, "rest"; BDAG 69c). A and some other mss. read the double compounded
ἐπαναπαύεται, whereas several minuscules read the pf. mid. form ἀναπέπαυται. 𝔓⁷²
ℵ² read the pf. form ἐπαναπέπαυται. There is also an interesting longer reading that
follows ἀναπαύεται with κατὰ μὲν αὐτοὺς βλασφημεῖται, κατὰ δὲ ὑμᾶς δοξάζεται
("according to them is blasphemed, according to you is glorified"), which is supported by the majority text (K L P) and parts of the Latin, Syriac, and Coptic versions.
Although this longer reading does conform to Petrine style (e.g., 4:6; cf. 2:4; 3:18),
it has scant early support. The shorter ἀναπαύεται should be retained on the basis of
ℵ* B etc., as it best explains the rise of the other rdgs. See Michaels 265 for a defense
of the longer rdg.

VERSE 15

μὴ γάρ τις ὑμῶν πασχέτω ὡς φονεὺς ἢ κλέπτης ἢ κακοποιὸς ἢ ὡς
ἀλλοτριεπίσκοπος

Rather than γάρ introducing the basis for the previous v. (*pace* Achtemeier 309), it
introduces a caveat to it ("but," NKJV, NRSV, CEV, ESV; "however," NLT, HCSB; so
Davids 168). The sentiment of 2:20 and 3:17 is again presented. Suffering for doing
good, for the name of Christ, receives a blessing, but suffering for doing evil is no

credit whatsoever. The difference in the present passage is that four examples of evil-doing are mentioned.

The indef. pron. τις with the neg. μή is "no one," which functions as the subj. of the 3 sg. impv. πασχέτω. Ὡς is not comp. but introduces the perspective from which a person is viewed (BDAG 1104d).

Φονεύς, -έως, ὁ, "murderer" (BDAG 1063c) and κλέπτης, -ου, ὁ, "thief," "robber" (BDAG 547b) could be drawn from a stock list of vices, rather than expressing a genuine concern of the author that his readers may commit such crimes (so Goppelt 326; Michaels 266; Elliott 784; Davids 169 n. 12). Another possibility is that these terms involved some of the accusations leveled against believers by their antagonistic pagan neighbors (Jobes 289). Achtemeier (311), however, believes the terms should be taken at face value and are genuine warnings against committing such acts. Κακοποιός, -όν, here used subst., "evildoer," (BDAG 501a), is the most general of the terms (cf. 2:12, 14) and is probably intended as an umbrella term for all actions inappropriate for believers.

There is considerable uncertainty concerning the final term ἀλλοτριεπίσκοπος, -ου, ὁ, of which this is the first attested use in Gk. literature (possibly coined by the author). First of all, there are a variety of forms for ἀλλοτριεπίσκοπος in the ms. tradition. P 1739 and the majority text have ἀλλοτριοεπίσκοπος, A Ψ 69 and a couple of other mss. read ἀλλότριος ἐπίσκοπος, whereas 𝔓⁷² has ἀλλοτρίοις ἐπίσκοπος. The spelling in the text (ἀλλοτριεπίσκοπος) should be retained on the strength of ℵ B 33, 81, and a couple of other minuscules, together with the fact that this rare form best explains the rise of the variant rdgs. (on the spelling, see MH 92, 272; R 204).

The term elsewhere appears only in two later Christian writers, Epiphanius in the fourth century (*Anc.* 12.5 and *Pan.* 3.128.7) and Dionysius the Aereopagite in the fifth century (*Epistle* 8.1), both with the sense of meddling in another person's affairs. The two components of the noun are also used in close proximity by Epictetus (*Diss.* 3.22.97) in defending the charge that Cynic philosophers were busybodies. In etym. terms the noun derives from ἀλλότριος, "belonging to another," and ἐπίσκοπος, "overseer," which gives a sense of one who oversees the affairs of another. In a neg. sense this would be a "busybody" (NKJV, CEV), "meddler" (ASV, NASB, HCSB, ESV, NIV), or the like (Jobes 289; Elliott 786). Elsewhere in the NT, such a person is described using the terms περίεργος (1 Tim 5:13) and περιεργάζομαι (2 Thess 3:11).

Some commentators consider that such meddling hardly constitutes criminal activity along the lines of the first two terms in the list. Consequently, other meanings such as "spy," "informer," "concealer of stolen goods," "one who defrauds," have all been canvassed (Achtemeier 312–13; see his helpful excursus, "On the Meaning of ἀλλοτριεπίσκοπος"; also J. K. Brown, "Just a Busybody? A Look at the Greco-Roman Topos of Meddling for Defining *allotriepiskopos* in 1 Peter 4:15," *JBL* 125 [2006]: 549–68; Elliott 785–88; Turner, *Words* 332; BDAG 47b; ZG 714).

Nevertheless, most commentators (Michaels 267; Selwyn 225; Elliott 785; Davids 169; Jobes 289) and EVV (though note "informer," NJB; "mischief maker," NRSV) follow the basic etymology and render as "busybody" or something similar. Some

Christians may have considered themselves to be the "guardians of public morality" (Michaels 267; Davids 169) or have moved outside of appropriate cultural/social
boundaries. Either way, this would bring Christianity into disrepute in a society where
busybodies were not well liked (see Plutarch, *Mor. 515–17*). The use of ὡς highlights
this final term, not so much as something less criminal (as Michaels 268), but as an
activity more subtle and probable (Elliott 785). 𝔓⁷² and the majority text also insert ὡς
with the middle two nouns, more likely looking for consistency than having any claim
to originality.

VERSE 16

εἰ δὲ ὡς χριστιανός, μὴ αἰσχυνέσθω

The prot. of this cond. is elliptical. Although the first-class cond. parallels v. 14 to
some extent, the fact that ὡς continues the structure from the previous v. argues that
the 3 sg. πάσχει and the subj. τις should be understood (Dubis 152). Δέ correlates with
μή in v. 15 to provide a neg.-positive contrast. This is one of only three NT uses of the
subst. χριστιανός. In Acts 11:26 we are told that believers were first called "Christians"
in Antioch. Acts 26:28 supports the view, held by most today, that it was originally
a derogatory term coined by outsiders. Nevertheless, although the term was used to
deride followers of Christ, "suffering as a Christian" does not, in itself, indicate persecution by the state.

Ἀἰσχυνέσθω 3 sg. pres. mid. impv. of αἰσχύνω, "put to shame," "be ashamed" (BDAG
30b; H.-G. Link, *NIDNTT* 3.562–64). The 3 sg. impv. μὴ αἰσχυνέσθω constitutes the
beginning of the apod. EVV are divided in their treatment of the ellipsis and this impv.
Most retain 3 sg. throughout the cstr. ("If anyone [of you] suffers . . . let him not be
ashamed," ASV, RSV, NASB, HCSB, ESV), NIV has 2 sg. throughout ("If you suffer
. . . do not be ashamed"), whereas NRSV combines 2 and 3 sg. ("If any of you suffers,
do not consider it a disgrace"). The encouragement to feel no shame recalls 2:6. Thus
the readers are encouraged to maintain a subjective attitude that reflects the objective
reality of their vindication by God (Michaels 269).

δοξαζέτω δὲ τὸν θεὸν ἐν τῷ μέρει τούτῳ [μέρει reflects the text of the forthcoming
fifth edition of the UBS *Greek New Testament*. The fourth edition reads ὀνόματι.]

The apod. continues with δέ providing the shift from a neg. to positive impv. Rather
than feel ashamed for suffering as a Christian, believers are to glorify God.

The rdg. of UBS⁴ ὀνόματι ("in this name"), which is supported by the earliest and
most reliable mss. (𝔓⁷² ℵ A B Ψ etc.), has been amended in the forthcoming UBS⁵,
following the *Editio Critica Maior*, to μέρει ("in this part/matter"). The latter rdg. (P
049 and majority text) is clearly the more difficult of the two, as it is not at all apparent
why a scribe would change ὀνόματι to μέρει, whereas a change the other way is con-
ceivable on the basis of ὀνόματι in v. 14. Nevertheless, the ms. evidence to the contrary
is early and reliable and should probably be retained. If we do retain ὀνόματι, the dat.

ἐν τῷ ὀνόματι τούτῳ can be variously cstr. (bearing in mind the "name" is "Christian," not "Christ" from v. 14):

1. instr. of means, "by this name," i.e., by being identified as a follower of Christ (Davids 170; Goppelt 328; Elliott 796);
2. instr. of cause, "because of this name" (NRSV; sim. CEV, NIV, ZG 714; NLT: "praise God for the privilege of being called by his name!");
*3 locat. of sphere, "in/under this name" (ASV, RSV, NASB, ESV; Moule 78; Achtemeier 315; Dubis 153).

If the dat. is instr. (means or cause), then the likelihood is that glorifying God is an attitude of praise/thankfulness. If it is a locat. of sphere, then it more likely involves some activity or action. This could entail acknowledging one's faith in the midst of distress (3:15; Michaels 269; Achtemeier 314; Goppelt 328), maintaining a proper non-retaliatory response (2:23; 3:9), or even more widely of having a lifestyle that is consistent with this name (1:15; 2:12, etc.).

A final decision rests on logical priority. Do we begin with the sense of the dat. and find a corresponding sense for δοξαζέτω? Or do we first interpret δοξαζέτω and let that control the sense of the dat.? The latter approach is favored because not only is the dat. ambiguous, but this epistle has such a strong ethical focus that it is difficult to imagine the author thinking of glorifying God merely in subjective terms. Consequently, glorifying God should be understood as maintaining appropriate ethical conduct, including a non-retaliatory response to abuse. Consistent with this interpretation, the dat. is best taken as a locat. of sphere.

If we do accept μέρει as the correct rdg., then the dat. ἐν τῷ μέρει τούτῳ can be cstr. as either instr. of cause ("because of this matter," i.e., of suffering), or dat. of respect ("in this matter").

VERSE 17

ὅτι ὁ καιρὸς τοῦ ἄρξασθαι τὸ κρίμα ἀπὸ τοῦ οἴκου τοῦ θεοῦ

῞Οτι is clearly causal, but it is not at all apparent what it modifies. The options include:

1. εἰ δὲ ὡς χριστιανός (suffering as a Christian, v. 16a);
2. μὴ αἰσχυνέσθω (not being ashamed, v. 16b);
3. δοξαζέτω δὲ τὸν θεὸν ἐν τῷ ὀνόματι τούτῳ (glorifying God, v. 16c; Achtemeier 315);
*4 the entire thought of vv. 12–16, namely the fiery trial of suffering ridicule as a Christian and, rather than being surprised, maintaining a proper perspective and attitude (Goppelt 329; Elliott 797; Michaels 270, followed by Dubis 153, contend that it modifies only vv. 15–16).

Καιρός is an appropriate or critical point in time, here the beginning of eschatological judgment (cf. 4:7). The noun can either be taken as the subj. of an implied ἥκει ("for the time has come," NRSV, NKJV, NLT, HCSB), or pred. with an implied ἔστιν ("it is time," ESV, NIV; R 395).

The gen. art. τοῦ is attracted to the inf. ἄρξασθαι and is untranslated (BDF §400; R 512, 1066–68, 1076; M 216–18). The inf. ἄρξασθαι (aor. mid. inf. of ἄρχω, "begin") is epex. to καιρός ("it is time to begin"). τὸ κρίμα is the subj. (acc. of respect) of the inf. The noun κρίμα does not necessarily imply judgment in the sense of punishment. Although it can refer to legal action taken against someone (1 Cor 6:7), it can also denote the action or function of a judge (BDAG 567a; F. Büchsel, *TDNT* 3.942). Understood in light of 1:6–7, this judging function is clearly for refining purposes (Jobes 293). The referent is clearly the πυρώσει ("fiery trial") introduced in v. 12, which is explained in the ensuing vv. as suffering reproach for the name of Christ/as a Christian. Most commentators understand this to be a reference to the messianic woes, which in Jewish thought would precede the end time. The author has adapted this Jewish tradition and applied it to the persecution his readers are experiencing at the hands of their pagan neighbors. Seen from a larger perspective, this persecution actually constitutes the beginning of God's eschatological judgment.

The prep. ἀπό here indicates the point from which something begins (BDAG 105c). The idea is that judgment begins with the household of God and moves outward from there. Τοῦ οἴκου τοῦ θεοῦ recalls 2:4–6. Although there is disagreement as to whether the controlling metaphor is the temple as God's house (Michaels 271; Dubis 154) or the familial household (Elliott 799–800), given the ref. in 2:5 to believers as a οἶκος πνευματικός ("spiritual house"), the distinction is one of degree rather than kind.

εἰ δὲ πρῶτον ἀφ᾽ ἡμῶν

The prot. is again elliptical with an implied ἀρχέται ("it begins"). Πρῶτον is adv. with the implied vb. The switch to the 1 pl. pron. ἡμῶν paves the way for a more universal expression of the suffering of God's people in 5:9. See above on ἀπό.

τί τὸ τέλος τῶν ἀπειθούντων τῷ τοῦ θεοῦ εὐαγγελίῳ

The apod. is expressed as a rhetorical question introduced by τί, with ἔστιν again implied (ZG 714). By means of an *a fortiori* argument the implication is that the "outcome" (NASB, HCSB, ESV, NIV), "terrible fate" (NLT) (τὸ τέλος) of those who disobey the gospel is not pleasant. This obviously has pastoral intentions. To endure persecution in the present is far preferable to being on the neg. side of God's eschatological judgment in the future (Achtemeier 316).

Ἀπειθούντων gen. pl. masc. of pres. act. ptc. of ἀπειθέω, "disobey" (BDAG 99d). "The disobedient" have already been introduced in 2:8 as those who stumble on account of their rejection of Jesus Christ the cornerstone. Here, in what amounts to the same thing, they disobey the gospel. Ἀπειθέω takes the dat. of the person or thing disobeyed. Τοῦ θεοῦ is a gen. of source/origin, not obj. (*pace* Elliott 802; Dubis 155).

"The gospel of God" appears to be a standard designation in the early church for the Christian message (Mark 1:14; Rom 1:1; 15:16; 2 Cor 11:7; 1 Thess 2:2, 8, 9), of which Christ is its focus. Consequently, God should be understood as the originator of the message rather than the One being proclaimed. As noted by Dubis (155), this v. prepares for the following citation of Prov 11:31 LXX both structurally and conceptually.

VERSE 18

καὶ εἰ ὁ δίκαιος μόλις σῴζεται

Scriptural support for the statement regarding the fate of the wicked is employed from Prov 11:31 LXX (see Beale and Carson 1042), introduced by a simple καί. The structure mirrors that of v. 17b quite closely. The prot. is almost proverbial, making the pres. tense σῴζεται gnomic. The adv. μόλις can refer to what is not ordinarily the case, what is not ordinarily expected (Rom 5:7), and what is difficult to accomplish (BDAG 657b–c). Clearly the first two uses are not the intended sense here, and the point would appear to be that the cost of salvation is not cheap (cf. 1:19); further, perseverance in the midst of difficult circumstances is not easy (2:2; 5:8–9; so Davids 172; Goppelt 333; Jobes 294; Elliott 803). It is another way of saying that the road or gate (cf. Luke 13:23–24) that leads to salvation is narrow (Beale and Carson 1042). The implication of the citation is hardly that the salvation of sinners is more difficult than that of the righteous (*pace* Elliott 804). This overlooks the fact that the righteous were sinners previously (1:14, 18; 4:2–3) and that sinners can become believers (see on 2:12).

ὁ ἀσεβὴς καὶ ἁμαρτωλὸς ποῦ φανεῖται

Ἀσεβής, -ές, "ungodly," "irreverent" (BDAG 141c), here synonymous with ἁμαρτωλός. An example of the Granville Sharp Rule, whereby two substs. with a single art. joined by καί refer to the same person (see Wallace 270–90). Both terms are generic sg. (T 22; R 763) and equate to ἀπειθούντων τῷ τοῦ θεοῦ εὐαγγελίῳ ("those who disobey the gospel of God") from the previous verse. The apod. is again rhetorical and like the previous v. proceeds in an *a fortiori* manner. So rather than clarify the fate of the wicked, the scriptural citation reinforces the rhetorical point.

Ποῦ is an interr. adv. of place, equally as vague yet equally as ominous as τὸ τέλος of the previous v. The fut. indic. φανεῖται looks forward to the final judgment. The entire apod. is lit. "where will the ungodly and the sinner appear?" and is idiomatic for "what will become of the ungodly and the sinner?" (e.g., NRSV, NASB, HCSB, ESV, NIV; LN 13.118). The ref. appears to be to the world to come, with the implication that the sinner has no part thereof (Dubis 156–57).

VERSE 19

ὥστε καὶ οἱ πάσχοντες κατὰ τὸ θέλημα τοῦ θεοῦ πιστῷ κτίστῃ παρατιθέσθωσαν τὰς ψυχὰς αὐτῶν ἐν ἀγαθοποιΐᾳ

The function of καί is not entirely clear. It can be taken with:

1. the impv. παρατιθέσθωσαν, with the sense that those who suffer should also (as well as glorifying God [v. 16]) commit themselves to God (Bigg 181; Elliott 805);

2. the ptc. οἱ πάσχοντες, with the idea that those who suffer should also commit themselves to God along with others who do not suffer (Kelly 194; Goppelt 334 n. 59);

*3 the opening ὥστε, "and so," introducing a summation of the entire passage (Achtemeier 317; Michaels 272–73).

Option 2 has little to commend it as the entire section, indeed the entire epistle, focuses on those who do suffer. The word order would favor the latter option. Ὥστε with the impv. (BDAG 1107a; Moule 144) thus introduces an independent clause expressing consequence ("therefore," [NRSV, NASB, ESV]; "so then," [NIV]). This v. virtually encapsulates everything that the author has said so far concerning suffering.

First of all, suffering is linked with the will of God (κατὰ τὸ θέλημα τοῦ θεοῦ) as it is in 2:19–21; 3:17; and implicitly in 1:6. Nevertheless, there are two strands of thought associated with suffering in accordance with God's will. The first is ethical; suffering only receives divine endorsement and blessing when it is undeserved, and thereby follows the example set by Jesus (2:19–20; 3:9, 14, 17; 4:14–16). The second is eschatological; suffering is the evidence of God's judgment beginning with his own household (4:17; cf. 1:6). While the immediate context favors the latter, it is extremely difficult to rule out the former because of its consistent emphasis throughout the epistle. In fact, this emphasis is also seen in the climactic finale to this v. with ἐν ἀγαθοποιΐᾳ (Elliott 804–5; Davids 173).

Οἱ πάσχοντες κατὰ τὸ θέλημα τοῦ θεοῦ functions as the subj. of the impv. παρατιθέσθωσαν with τὰς ψυχὰς αὐτῶν the dir. obj. The vb. παρατίθημι has the sense of placing something in the care of one who is trusted with its safekeeping (C. Maurer, *TDNT* 8.162–64). The idea of committing one's life to God while suffering unjustly recalls 2:23 and its example of Jesus who committed his cause to him who judges justly (παρεδίδου δὲ τῷ κρίνοντι δικαίως).

Κτίστης, -ου, ὁ, "Creator" (BDAG 573c). Παρατιθέσθωσαν 3 pl. pres. mid. impv. of παρατίθημι, "set before," mid: "commit," "entrust" (BDAG 772a). On ψυχή, see on 1:9. Ἀγαθοποιΐα, -ας, ἡ, "doing good" (BDAG 3a; Spicq 1.1–4). God is here depicted as πιστῷ κτίστῃ ("faithful Creator"), which highlights God's character of faithfulness thereby providing the rationale for entrusting oneself to him. God as Creator affirms his sovereignty over all things including human suffering, and may also be intended to underline his authority to judge (cf. 4:17; Michaels 274).

Although the noun ἀγαθοποιΐᾳ is a NT *hapax* (the dat. pl. ἀγαθοποιΐαις is read by 𝔓⁷² A Ψ 33, 81, 323, 945, 1241, 1739 and others, which has the effect of focusing on good deeds themselves rather than on doing good as a lifestyle), the cognate vb. has already been used in 2:15, 20; 3:6, 17, and the noun ἀγαθοποιός ("one who does good") in 2:14. The emphasis throughout the epistle on doing good, together with the emphatic position ἐν ἀγαθοποιΐᾳ occupies, virtually turns the dat. into an impv. in its own right (as RSV, Barclay, CEV, NLT, NIV). Michaels (274) understands it in a temp. sense "while doing good" (ESV), but it is better cstr. as instr. "by/in doing good" (ASV, NKJV, NASB; Achtemeier 318), as it is in a nonretaliatory and proper response to suffering that people in fact demonstrate that they are not seeking to take matters into their own hands but are committing their cause to God.

FOR FURTHER STUDY

See For Further Study §§ 13, 14, 23, 38.

HOMILETICAL SUGGESTIONS

The Fiery Ordeal (4:12–19)

1. The fiery ordeal (v. 12)
   (a) constitutes a test (v. 12a)
   (b) is not something strange (v. 12b)
2. Sharing the sufferings of Christ (v. 13)
   (a) should occasion rejoicing (v. 13a)
   (b) results in even greater joy at the Parousia (v. 13b)
3. Suffering in the name of Christ/as a Christian
   (a) results in blessing (v. 14a)
   (b) evidence of the Spirit's presence (v. 14b)
   (c) must not be for unlawful behavior (v. 15)
   (d) should not bring shame (v. 16a)
   (e) should result in glorifying God (v. 16b)
   (f) is evidence that God's eschatological judgment has begun (v. 17)
      (i) for believers first (v. 17b)
      (ii) for unbelievers (v. 17c)
      (iii) salvation of believers is costly (v. 18a)
      (iv) the fate of unbelievers is dire (v. 18b)
4. Summary statement regarding suffering (v. 19)
   (a) must be according to God's will
   (b) commit oneself to God the faithful Creator
   (c) continue to do good

B. THE RESPONSIBILITY OF ELDERS (5:1–5a)

STRUCTURE

The opening vb. παρακαλῶ ("I exhort") is given its content with the impv. ποιμάνατε ("shepherd") in v. 2. The dir. obj. of the exhortation πρεσβυτέρους ("elders") appears first in the section as the topical frame. The remainder of v. 1 is an amplification of the subj. of the vb. παρακαλῶ, providing justification for the authority of the exhortation, with the def. art. ὁ governing three nouns: συμπρεσβύτερος ("fellow elder"), μάρτυς ("witness"), and κοινωνός ("sharer"). Verses 2–3 present three contrasting pairs (μή . . . ἀλλά) indicating both inappropriate and appropriate attitudes and motives for those who shepherd God's flock. V. 4 shifts the focus to eschatological reward, whereas v. 5a is a brief address to the younger men to accept the authority of the elders (see below).

1   πρεσβυτέρους τοὺς ἐν ὑμῖν
                          παρακαλῶ
      ὁ συμπρεσβύτερος
      καὶ μάρτυς τῶν τοῦ Χριστοῦ παθημάτων,
      ὁ καὶ τῆς μελλούσης ἀποκαλύπτεσθαι δόξης κοινωνός·

2   ποιμάνατε τὸ ἐν ὑμῖν ποίμνιον τοῦ θεοῦ
            ἐπισκοποῦντες
                  μὴ ἀναγκαστῶς
                  ἀλλὰ ἑκουσίως κατὰ θεόν,
                  μηδὲ αἰσχροκερδῶς
                  ἀλλὰ προθύμως,
3   μηδ᾽ ὡς κατακυριεύοντες τῶν κλήρων
                  ἀλλὰ τύποι γινόμενοι τοῦ ποιμνίου·

4   καὶ φανερωθέντος τοῦ ἀρχιποίμενος κομιεῖσθε τὸν ἀμαράντινον τῆς δόξης στέφανον.

5a   ὁμοίως, νεώτεροι, ὑποτάγητε πρεσβυτέροις·

VERSE 1

Πρεσβυτέρους τοὺς ἐν ὑμῖν παρακαλῶ [τούς reflects the text of the forthcoming fifth edition of the UBS *Greek New Testament*. The fourth edition reads οὖν.]

In place of the art. τούς (read by P, 33, 1739, and the majority text), the conj. οὖν is supported by 𝔓⁷² A B 614, 630, and a couple of other minuscules. Some other mss. (ℵ Ψ 623, 2464) have the conj. followed by the art. The inclusion of the art. alone is the preferred text of the forthcoming UBS⁵, following the *Editio Critica Maior*. Nevertheless, the conj. alone is probably the more difficult reading as the connection with the previous material is not that apparent. Furthermore, the article is probably an attempt to specify the elders more precisely.

At a literary level, the connection is provided by the term παθημάτων, "sufferings," but the logical connection may be that proper pastoral oversight of the Christian community is crucial if it is to survive external threat. Some commentators contend that the connection lies more in the elders being the first to be judged in God's household (4:17; Michaels 279; Jobes 300; Dubis 159).

The dir. obj. πρεσβυτέρους stands first in the clause to highlight those to whom the exhortation is directed. The term could simply refer to older members of the congregation, as opposed to the younger members (νεώτεροι) addressed in v. 5, or could signify some form of leadership. It is clear that the πρεσβυτέρους have the function of pastoral oversight (v. 2), and given that the author describes himself as a συμπρεσβύτερος, "fellow-elder," it is reasonably certain that those responsible for leading the community are being addressed (CEV: "church leaders"). The lack of the def. art. points to the term being used in a rather loose way and not as it would be in later Christian literature as part of a developed hierarchical leadership (see Achtemeier 322–23; Elliott 813–15; Jobes 302).

This is only one of three instances in the letter where the author speaks in the first person singular (2:12; 5:12 twice). It indicates not only a transition in thought (as it does in 2:12 and 5:12), but also signifies the authority with which he writes.

ὁ συμπρεσβύτερος καὶ μάρτυς τῶν τοῦ Χριστοῦ παθημάτων

This is a fairly lengthy parenthesis where the author gives his credentials. First, he is ὁ συμπρεσβύτερος, "the fellow-elder," a term not attested prior to this and probably coined by our author. He obviously understands himself to have a role of pastoral oversight, although not oversight of a local Christian community, but of the entire church. This role is eminently displayed in the penning of this epistle. It is possible he wants the elders in these local congregations to see their ministry as an extension of his own (Achtemeier 324). At a rhetorical level it expresses unity and collegiality.

Second, he is μάρτυς τῶν τοῦ Χριστοῦ παθημάτων, "witness of the sufferings of Christ." The single art. ὁ governs both συμπρεσβύτερος and μάρτυς, indicating the close linking of the roles in the same person (Granville Sharp Rule; see Wallace 270–90). Although some have taken this statement to be evidence that the author was an eyewitness of the crucifixion (e.g., Selwyn 228), this cannot be substantiated by the use of the Gk. term μάρτυς alone. A witness is one who testifies to something, not necessarily one who observes it (as in Rev 2:13; 11:3; 17:6; see Goppelt 342; A. A. Trites, *NIDNTT* 3.1038–50). The linking of συμπρεσβύτερος and μάρτυς in this manner may also be meant to indicate that the roles are necessarily linked, possibly suggesting that one only becomes an elder by taking on the role of witness to the sufferings of Christ (Goppelt 343; Achtemeier 324).

Τῶν παθημάτων is an obj. gen., whereas τοῦ Χριστοῦ is subj. The latter could be trans. "of Christ" (most EVV; Michaels 276; Achtemeier 320), or "of the Christ," i.e., of the Messiah (Weymouth; Elliott 820). Other passages that speak of the sufferings of Christ provide no real help, with Χριστός appearing without the art. in 2:21; 3:18, but with the art. in 4:13.

ὁ καὶ τῆς μελλούσης ἀποκαλύπτεσθαι δόξης κοινωνός

The art. belongs with κοινωνός, -οῦ, ὁ, "sharer" (BDAG 553d; Turner, Words 163–68), with the remainder of the clause written between the article and the noun for stylistic effect. Μελλούσης gen. sg. fem. of pres. act. ptc. of μέλλω. Ἀποκαλύπτεσθαι pres. pass. inf. of ἀποκαλύπτω, complimentary with μελλούσης. The gen. τῆς μελλούσης ἀποκαλύπτεσθαι δόξης is obj. ("sharer in the glory"). This refers not only to the revelation of Jesus Christ and his glory (4:13) but also to the participation that believers have in that glory (1:7). Μελλούσης implies the imminence of this revelation (cf. 4:7). Καί following the art. is more likely to be adv. "also," in which case the implication of this third credential would be that the author also shares in the sufferings of Christ along the lines of 4:13 (Michaels 282).

VERSE 2

ποιμάνατε τὸ ἐν ὑμῖν ποίμνιον τοῦ θεοῦ

Ποιμάνατε 2 pl. aor. act. impv. of ποιμαίνω, "shepherd," "tend" (BDAG 842d; Turner, Words 314–15). The aor. impv. gives the content of the exhortation begun in v. 1. The aor. is not the typical tense for general precepts and here may have an ingressive sense of taking up the role (Beare 199; Goppelt 343; Davids 178; see the discussion on "The Use of the Imperative in 1 Peter" in the Introduction).

Ποίμνιον, -ου, τό, "flock" (BDAG 843c). Τοῦ θεοῦ is a poss. gen., with the "flock of God" being a metaphor that has a long tradition in Jewish thought (Ezek 34; Jer 13:17; Zech 10:3; CD 13.7–9). Those who oversaw the flock were originally the leaders of the nation, then during times of apostasy there was the anticipation of a messianic Shepherd (Ezek 34:23). The metaphor became entrenched in early Christian tradition, with Jesus depicting himself as shepherd of the flock (Matt 15:24; Mark 6:34; John 10:1–18), then according to the Johannine tradition, delegating this role to Peter (John 21:15–19). The image of God's flock has already been implied in 2:25, where Jesus is the shepherd. The elders are thus to fulfill the same function in a delegated sense, a sense made clear in v. 4 where Christ is termed the ἀρχιποίμενος, "Chief Shepherd." Here ἐν ὑμῖν has a distributive sense; the flock present in each separate location ("in your charge" [NRSV; ZG 714], "under your care" [NIV]; Selwyn 230; Michaels 283; Goppelt 344; Elliott 824).

ἐπισκοποῦντες μὴ ἀναγκαστῶς ἀλλὰ ἑκουσίως κατὰ θεόν

The ms. tradition is quite confused. The text ἐπισκοποῦντες μὴ ἀναγκαστῶς ἀλλὰ ἑκουσίως κατὰ θεόν ("overseeing not under compulsion but willingly before God") is supported by 𝔓[72] ℵ² A P Ψ a number of minuscules and most versions. A few minuscules substitute a var. form of spelling ἐπισκοπεύοντες for ἐπισκοποῦντες (see MH 258). The majority text omits κατὰ θεόν, whereas both ℵ* and B omit ἐπισκοποῦντες ("overseeing"), with the latter also omitting κατὰ θεόν. Although a longer reading, κατὰ θεόν does conform to Petrine style (4:6) and should be retained. The inclusion of ἐπισκοποῦντες is more difficult to decide, but given early and widespread support it should probably be retained as well.

Ἐπισκοποῦντες nom. pl. masc. of pres. act. ptc. of ἐπισκοπέω, "take care of," "oversee" (BDAG 379a; Turner, *Words* 44–46; LN 53.70), expressing the manner in which the flock is to be shepherded. It also has derived impv. force by its dependence on the impv. ποιμάνατε (see the discussion on "Imperatival Participles in 1 Peter" in the Introduction). An aor. impv. followed by a pres. ptc. is characteristic of this epistle (2:18; 3:9; 4:8–11).

The μή (δε) . . . ἀλλά cstr. presents three contrasts, expressing first in a neg. and then in a positive sense, how this role of overseeing should be discharged. The first contrast utilizes the antonymous advs. ἀναγκαστῶς, "under compulsion" (NRSV, ESV; BDAG 60d; NJB: "not simply as a duty"), and ἑκουσίως, "willingly" (NRSV, ESV; BDAG 307b). Κατὰ θεόν (see also 4:6) refers to what God requires, but is somewhat ambiguous. It could mean that oversight is God's will, that it is to be done as God himself would do it, or that it is to be done in a manner approved by God, i.e., God's standard (Dubis 161; Jobes 304–5). The first option is rather obvious, while the difference in the latter two is slight. The focus is on oversight performed with a due sense of accountability to God.

μηδὲ αἰσχροκερδῶς ἀλλὰ προθύμως

The second contrast of three focuses on motive. Αἰσχροκερδῶς, the neg. element, refers to greed or a desire for financial gain ("sordid gain," NASB). The adv. is nowhere else attested in Gk. literature, although the cognate adj. αἰσχροκερδής, -ές, is reasonably common (BDAG 29c). This does not necessarily imply that elders were compensated for their duties, though such compensation was viewed favorably by both Jesus and Paul (Matt 10:10; 1 Cor 9:3–12). It may also indicate responsibility for money within the community (Acts 5:1–5; 2 Cor 8:20; Achtemeier 326–27; Goppelt 346; Elliott 829; NLT: "not for what you will get out of it"). The positive contrast προθύμως, "eagerly" (BDAG 870b), is not really its opposite but is virtually synonymous with ἑκουσίως above.

VERSE 3

μηδ' ὡς κατακυριεύοντες τῶν κλήρων

The third contrast concerns the attitude of elders toward those in their care and probably takes its cue from the saying of Jesus recorded in Mark 10:42. Ὡς does not introduce a metaphor, as this does not work with the contrasting element (Achtemeier 327, who correctly notes that the first ptc. would need to be subst.), but introduces the perspective from which a person is viewed (BDAG 1104d).

Κατακυριεύοντες nom. pl. masc. of pres. act. ptc. of κατακυριεύω (+ gen.), "be master of," "subdue" (BDAG 519b–c), here in a neg. sense of "domineering" (ESV; most EVV: "lord it over"). This and the following ptc. γινόμενοι could modify either the impv. ποιμάνατε or ἐπισκοποῦντες with virtually no difference in meaning. The structure of vv. 2–3 favors the latter option, although the use of the ptcs. themselves favor the former (Achtemeier 327). Either way they should be cstr. as modal, yet too have derived impv. force (Michaels 285; see the discussion on "Imperatival Participles in 1 Peter" in the Introduction).

Κλῆρος, -ου, ὁ, "lot," "share" (BDAG 548c). Originally, the noun referred to a lot that was cast, then that which was received by lot, then more generally of an allotted portion or share (J. Bichler, *NIDNTT* 2.295–303). Here it refers to what has been assigned, a sphere of responsibility (LN 35.49). The most obvious reference is to the flock, with the idea that the relationship between those giving and those receiving the oversight has been divinely ordained (Jobes 306). The pl. is best understood as referring to the respective communities and their various leaders (so Achtemeier 328; Davids 347; Michaels 286). The poss. pron. ὑμῶν is understood.

ἀλλὰ τύποι γινόμενοι τοῦ ποιμνίου

See above on γινόμενοι. Τύπος, -ου, ὁ, "model," "example" (BDAG 1020b; Turner, *Words* 170–73; Spicq 3.384–87; LN 58.59), here used of a moral example (cf. Phil 3:7; 2 Thess 3:9; 1 Tim 4:12; Titus 2:7) similar to ὑπογραμμόν in 2:21. Pred. nom. with γινόμενοι.

Τοῦ ποιμνίου is an obj. gen.; the flock receive the example of proper leadership from the elders (Dubis 162, takes it as a gen. of ref.). Thus, as Elliott (830) states, "the antithesis as a whole contrasts a hierarchical exercise of authority to a horizontal demonstration by example."

VERSE 4

καὶ φανερωθέντος τοῦ ἀρχιποίμενος

The use of καί and the fut. indic. κομιεῖσθε in the main clause, following the impv. focus of vv. 2–3, virtually makes vv. 2–4 a cond. sentence where vv. 2–3 form the prot. and v. 4 the apod. In other words, the reward spoken of here is dependent upon exercising oversight in the appropriate manner (Achtemeier 329).

The ptc. φανερωθέντος is temp. in this gen. abs. cstr. Ἀρχιποίμην, -ενος, ὁ, "chief shepherd" (BDAG 139c; BDF §118[2]; cf. *NewDocs* 2:18–19). Christ, previously depicted as ποιμένα καὶ ἐπίσκοπον ("shepherd and guardian") in 2:25, is now chief shepherd (cf. Heb 13:20 ποιμὴν μέγας, "great shepherd"). The appearance of the chief shepherd mirrors previous passages that have spoken of the revelation of Jesus Christ (1:7, 13; 4:13). The implication is not only that the role of oversight given to the elders is a delegated one but also they are accountable for their actions to the chief shepherd.

κομιεῖσθε τὸν ἀμαράντινον τῆς δόξης στέφανον

Κομιεῖσθε 2 pl. fut. mid. indic. of κομίζω, "receive," "obtain" (BDAG 557d), with the idea of recompense of some sort (LN 57.126). The mid. voice indicates special interest or involvement of the subj. in the activity or outcome (McKay 21). The vb. is also used in 1:9 of receiving salvation as the outcome of one's faith. Here salvation is again spoken of, but in metaphorical terms of receiving the victor's crown of glory. Ἀμαράντινος, -η, -ον, "unfading" (BDAG 49c), is lit. "made of amaranths," a dark red flower known for its resistance to fading ("the never withering wreath of glory," Weymouth). The word is very closely related to ἀμάραντον used in 1:4 of the unfading inheritance preserved in heaven.

Στέφανος, -ου, ὁ, "crown," "wreath" (BDAG 943d; NewDocs 7.240; 9.1–3). The crown is a common NT symbol of the reward for the righteous ("immortal crown" [1 Cor 9:25]; "crown of righteousness" [2 Tim 4:8]; "crown of life" [Jas 1:12; Rev 2:10]), but here is the only time it is linked with δόξα in the NT. The gen. τῆς δόξης could be quality, "the glorious crown" (T 212–13; Achtemeier 330), but in the sg., and obviously as a metaphor, it is more likely epex., i.e., the crown that is glory (R 498; Michaels 287; Elliott 835; Dubis 163). In this sense the crown is the eschatological glory in which all the faithful will share at the revelation of Jesus Christ (1:7).

VERSE 5a

ὁμοίως, νεώτεροι, ὑποτάγητε πρεσβυτέροις

Ὁμοίως, together with ὑποτάγητε, recalls the language of the Household Code (as to whether this v. was originally part of the Household Code, see the discussion and refutation in Achtemeier 330–32). Specifically, the aor. impv. ὑποτάγητε echoes 2:13 and the general admonition to be subject to every human creature. In both instances, the aor. is employed for a general admonition and should be seen to have programmatic force (see the discussion on "The Use of the Imperative in 1 Peter" in the introduction).

The address is directed specifically to the νεώτεροι (comp. of νέος, -α, -ον, "new," "young"). These have been variously understood as:

1. recent converts (Elliott 838–40);
*2   younger men (NLT, NASB, HCSB; Dubis 163–64);
3. younger members of the Christian community (most EVV; Davids 184); or
4. the remainder of the Christian community apart from the elders (Achtemeier 331; Jobes 307; Goppelt 351; Michaels 289).

Although we might expect ὁμοίως to introduce the reciprocal side of the equation (as it does in 3:7), νεώτεροι is a strange term to use for the entire church apart from the elders. Given usage in other early Christian literature (1 Clem. 1:3; 21:6), it is also unlikely to be inclusive of women. Consequently, 2 is the preferred option. Πρεσβυτέροις is more likely to have the same sense as it does in v. 1, rather than a more general reference to those who are older in age (pace Selwyn 233; Kelly 205).

FOR FURTHER STUDY

40. Church Government in the NT (5:1–5a)

Beckwith, Roger T. Elders in Every City: The Origin and Role of the Ordained Ministry. Carlisle, UK: Paternoster, 2003.

Bromiley, Geoffrey W. *ISBE* 1:696–98.

Burtchaell, James T. *From Synagogue to Church: Public Services and Officers in the Early Christian Communities.* Cambridge: Cambridge University Press, 1992.

Clarke, Andrew D. *A Pauline Theology of Church Leadership.* London: T&T Clark, 2008.

*Giles, Kevin N. *Patterns of Ministry among the First Christians.* Melbourne: Collins-Dove, 1989.

_____. *DLNT* 219–26.

Holmberg, Bengt. *Paul and Power: Authority in the Primitive Church as Reflected in the Pauline Epistles.* Lund: Gleerup, 1978.

Knight, George W. "Two Offices (Elders or Bishops and Deacons) and Two Orders of Elders (Preaching or Teaching Elders and Ruling Elders): A New Testament Study." *Presbyterion* 11 (1985): 1–12.

_____. "The Number and Functions of the Permanent Offices in the New Testament Church." *Presbyterion* 1 (1975): 111–16.

MacDonald, Margaret Y. *The Pauline Churches: A Sociohistorical Study of Institutionalization in the Pauline and the Deutero-Pauline Churches.* Cambridge: Cambridge University Press, 1988.

Maier, Harry O. *The Social Setting of the Ministry As Reflected in the Writings of Hermas, Clement and Ignatius.* Waterloo, ON: Wilfred Laurier University Press, 1991.

Merkle, Benjamin L. *The Elder and Overseer.* New York: Peter Lang, 2003.

Safrai, Shmuel, and Menahem Stern. *The Jewish People of the First Century: Historical Geography, Political History, Social, Cultural and Religious Life and Institutions.* 2 vols. Philadelphia: Fortress, 1974–76.

William, Ritva H. *Stewards, Prophets, Keepers of the Word: Leaders in the Early Church.* Peabody, MA: Hendrickson, 2006.

See also For Further Study § 14, 24.

HOMILETICAL SUGGESTIONS

The Responsibility of Elders (5:1–5a)

1. The fellow-elder (v. 1)
    (a) command to the elders (v. 1a)
    (b) witness of the sufferings of Christ (v. 1b)
    (c) sharer in the glory about to be revealed (v. 1c)
2. Tending the flock of God (vv. 2–4)
    (a) not grudgingly but willingly (v. 2b)
    (b) not for gain but eagerly (v. 2c)
    (c) not domineering but setting an example (v. 3)
    (d) the reward: the crown of glory (v. 4)
3. Submission of younger men to the elders (v. 5a)

Blessings Associated with the Final Revelation (Parousia) of Jesus in 1 Peter

1. Final Salvation (1:5)
2. Praise, glory, and honor (1:7)

3. Grace (1:13)
4. Inexpressible joy (1:8; 4:13)
5. Unfading crown of glory to elders who discharge their role appropriately
    (5:4)

C. HUMILITY AND RESOLUTENESS (5:5b–11)

STRUCTURE

In this section, vv. 5b, 6, 8, and 9 all open with an impv. The remainder of each v. then provides the reason (vv. 5c, 8b, 9c) or purpose (v. 6b) for the command and the manner/means by which it is to be performed (vv. 7, 9b).

5b πάντες δὲ ἀλλήλοις τὴν ταπεινοφροσύνην <u>ἐγκομβώσασθε</u>,
ὅτι
Ὁ θεὸς ὑπερηφάνοις ἀντιτάσσεται,
ταπεινοῖς δὲ δίδωσιν χάριν

6 <u>ταπεινώθητε</u> οὖν ὑπὸ τὴν κραταιὰν χεῖρα τοῦ <u>θεοῦ</u>,
ἵνα ὑμᾶς ὑψώσῃ ἐν καιρῷ,
7 πᾶσαν τὴν μέριμναν ὑμῶν ἐπιρίψαντες ἐπ' αὐτόν,
ὅτι αὐτῷ μέλει περὶ ὑμῶν.

8 <u>νήψατε</u>, <u>γρηγορήσατε</u>.
ὁ ἀντίδικος ὑμῶν διάβολος ὡς λέων ὠρυόμενος περιπατεῖ ζητῶν τινα καταπιεῖν·

9 <u>ᾧ ἀντίστητε</u>
στερεοὶ τῇ πίστει
εἰδότες τὰ αὐτὰ τῶν παθημάτων τῇ ἐν κόσμῳ ὑμῶν ἀδελφότητι ἐπιτελεῖσθαι.

Verse 10 then shifts attention to God's action, with the four fut. indics. stressing his vindication of those who suffer for a little while (ὀλίγον παθόντας). The section concludes with a doxology (v. 11).

10 ὁ δὲ θεὸς πάσης χάριτος,
ὁ καλέσας ὑμᾶς εἰς τὴν <u>αἰώνιον</u> αὐτοῦ δόξαν ἐν Χριστῷ ὀλίγον παθόντας
αὐτὸς καταρτίσει,
στηρίξει,
σθενώσει,
θεμελιώσει.

11 αὐτῷ τὸ κράτος εἰς τοὺς <u>αἰῶνας</u>. ἀμήν.

VERSE 5b

πάντες δὲ ἀλλήλοις τὴν ταπεινοφροσύνην ἐγκομβώσασθε

Πάντες δὲ ἀλλήλοις belongs with what follows rather than what precedes (i.e., πάντες is the subj. of ἐγκομβώσασθε, not ὑποτάγητε; NKJV incorrectly takes it with both). These exhortations are addressed to all in the Christian community and begin with a plea for humility. Ταπεινοφροσύνη, -ης, ἡ, "humility" (BDAG 989d; Turner, Words 216–18; W. Grundmann, TDNT 8.1–26; LN 88.53), a positive virtue in Christian literature as opposed to its use in secular Gk. to depict the mindset of the slave. It reinforces the general exhortation to mutual love (1:22; 2:17; 4:8) and the specific command to humility in 3:8.

Ἐγκομβώσασθε 2 pl. aor. mid. impv. of ἐγκομβόομαι, a NT *hapax* and rare word. Another clothing metaphor (cf. 1:13), relating to tying a garment around the body (BDAG 274a; G. Delling, *TDNT* 2.339; Spicq 1.404; LN 49.9). The point is that humility must be wrapped around oneself (a direct mid.; R 808) like a garment (TEV: "put on the apron of humility"). Like many other aor. impvs. in this epistle, this instance should be taken in a programmatic sense (see the discussion on "The Use of the Imperative in 1 Peter" in the Introduction).

The dat. ἀλλήλοις could possibly be cstr. as a dat. of advantage, "for the benefit of one another," but is better taken as a dat. of respect, "toward one-another" (NJB, CEV, NASB, HCSB, NIV; Elliott 847; Achtemeier 333 n. 174; NRSV: "in your dealings with one another").

ὅτι ὁ θεὸς ὑπερηφάνοις ἀντιτάσσεται

Ὅτι is causal and again "introduces the theological foundation for an ethical directive" (Goppelt 354; cf. 2:31; 3:18; 4:8). Ὑπερήφανος, -ον, "proud," "arrogant" (BDAG 1033d). Ἀντιτάσσεται 3 sg. pres. mid. indic. of ἀντιτάσσω, "resist," "oppose" (with dat. of person of thing opposed; BDAG 90d; LN 39.1).

The citation is from Prov 3:34 LXX and reflects the common biblical motif of a reversal of fortunes (the only alteration is a substitution of θεός for κύριος; the same citation occurs in Jas 4:6, where it is also followed by a plea to resist the Devil and a promise that God will exalt the humble; see Beale and Carson 1042–43).

On the neg. side, humility is necessary because the proud find themselves on the wrong side of God. Ἀντιτάσσεται could be a futuristic pres. referring to eschatological judgment (cf. 4:18) or gnomic indicating what is true of God's nature. The encouragement regarding eschatological vindication that follows (vv. 6, 10) favors the former cstr.

ταπεινοῖς δὲ δίδωσιν χάριν

Ταπεινός, -ή, -όν, "humble" (BDAG 989c; Turner, *Words* 216–18). See on ταπεινοφροσύνη above. On the positive side, the humble receive God's favor. Χάριν, "grace," is expounded in the vv. that follow.

VERSE 6

ταπεινώθητε οὖν ὑπὸ τὴν κραταιὰν χεῖρα τοῦ θεοῦ

Ταπεινώθητε 2 pl. aor. pass. impv. of ταπεινόω, "lower," "humble" (BDAG 990a; Turner, *Words* 216–18; see on v. 5). The inferential conj. οὖν together with a repetition of the stem ταπειν- clearly indicates a continuation of thought with v. 5b. The pass. ταπεινώθητε is literally "be humbled," and although some commentators (Goppelt 355; Michaels 295) and most EVV give it the force of the mid. voice (or the act. with reflexive pron.) "humble yourselves," the pass. impv. is quite rare (also found in Jas 4:10, a passage that also speaks of future exaltation by the Lord) and demands special attention. Achtemeier is no doubt correct in linking it to the readers' situation of persecution and social ostracism, which is again highlighted in the vv. that follow. The point is that they must accept the state of humiliation imposed on them (a permissive pass.; Wallace 441), in one sense by unbelievers but in another sense by God (4:17), not that they must humble themselves (Achtemeier 338; cf. Elliott 850). Thus, in all likelihood, the aor. impv. may be indicating a specific command rather than being another example of Peter's preference for the aor. impv. with general precepts (see the discussion on "The Use of the Imperative in 1 Peter" in the Introduction).

Κραταιός, -ά, -όν, "mighty," "powerful" (BDAG 564b; LN 76.9). "The mighty hand of God" has connotations of both judgment and deliverance (Exod 3:19; 6:1; 13:3, 9, 14, 16; Deut 3:24; 4:34; Ezek 20:34, etc.) and also discipline (Job 30:21; Ps 32:4). It appears to have this double-edged function here as well. On the one hand, it recalls 4:17 regarding judgment first upon the household of God. On the other, it prepares for the following v. regarding God's care and concern. The adj. κραταιάν echoes the cognate noun κράτος in the doxology of 4:11 and prepares for its further use in the concluding doxology of 5:11.

ἵνα ὑμᾶς ὑψώσῃ ἐν καιρῷ

Ὑψώσῃ 3 sg. aor. act. subjunc. of ὑψόω, "lift up," "exalt" (BDAG 1045d). The purpose of accepting humility is expressed by means of ἵνα with the subjunc. The idea is of divine reversal. Ἐν καιρῷ, "in due time" (NRSV, NIV) "at his own time" (ZG 715), is eschatological (cf. ἐν καιρῷ ἐσχάτῳ in 1:5) relating to the Parousia, or in the language of this epistle, the revelation of Jesus Christ and his glory (1:7, 13; 4:13). Being exalted by God is equivalent to receiving a share of this glory (1:7).

After καιρῷ, some mss. (A P Ψ several minuscules and some versions) add the gen. ἐπισκοπῆς ("time of visitation;" Ψ also adds ὑμῶν). The addition may have been prompted by 2:12 and appears to be an attempt to underscore the eschatological nature of the ref.

VERSE 7

πᾶσαν τὴν μέριμναν ὑμῶν ἐπιρίψαντες ἐπ᾽ αὐτόν

Μέριμνα, -ης, ἡ, "worry," "care" (BDAG 632b). Πᾶσαν τὴν μέριμναν is emphatic by position, with the adj. πᾶς stressing the total aspect of the noun. For repetition of the prep. (ἐπί) with the compound vb., see R 560; Moule 91. The ptc. ἐπιρίψαντες (nom. pl. masc. of aor. act. ptc. of ἐπιρίπτω, "throw," "cast upon"; BDAG 378a; W. Bieder, *TDNT* 6.991–93) is dependent on the impv. ταπεινώθητε in the previous v. and thus has some derived impv. force (see the discussion on "Imperatival Participles in 1 Peter" in the Introduction). EVV treat it either as attendant circumstance (ASV, NKJV, NASB, HCSB, ESV; also Dubis 167), or as a separate impv. (NRSV, CEV, NIV). Nevertheless, it could further be cstr. as instr., i.e., "be humbled by casting all your care upon him"

(Wallace 630), or a ptc. of result (i.e., "be humbled and so cast all your care upon him"). In either sense, the point is that an attitude of humility does not seek to take matters into one's own hands but trusts in God (cf. 4:19; LN 25.250; Achtemeier 339; Davids 187). The cares and anxieties addressed here no doubt refer to the feelings of shame and social ostracism received on account of being a Christian.

ὅτι αὐτῷ μέλει περὶ ὑμῶν

῞Οτι is causal and provides the rationale for entrusting one's cares to God. Μέλει 3 sg. pres. act. indic. of μέλω, an impersonal verb indicating concern (BDAG 626d; Moule 28; R 1217), and so αὐτῷ μέλει is lit. "it is of concern to him." The thought, though not the language, is paralleled in the Gospel tradition (Matt 6:25–25; Luke 12:24, 28).

VERSE 8

νήψατε, γρηγορήσατε

Νήψατε 2 pl. aor. act. impv. of νήφω, "be sober" (BDAG 672c), used in its common metaphorical sense of staying alert (cf. 1:13; 4:7; *NewDocs* 2.69; O. Bauernfeind, *TDNT* 7.1097–1104; P. J. Budd, *NIDNTT* 1.514–15). Γρηγορήσατε 2 pl. aor. act. impv. of γρηγορέω, "watch," "be alert" (BDAG 208a; LN 27.56), often used in eschatological contexts in the NT (Matt 24:42; 25:13; Mark 13:35; Rev 3:3; 16:15). The aor. impvs. are virtually synonymous (cf. 1 Thess 5:6) and indicate that casting one's care on God (v. 7) is not to be equated with lethargy. The aor. tenses could be seen as programmatic but also carrying a sense of forcefulness due to the urgency conveyed by the context (see the discussion on "The Use of the Imperative in 1 Peter" in the Introduction).

ὁ ἀντίδικος ὑμῶν διάβολος

$\mathfrak{P}^{72}$ אׁ² L Ψ 049ᶜ and a number of minuscules insert ὅτι after the impvs., thereby explicitly introducing their rationale. The shorter rdg. is the more difficult and should be retained also on the strength of א A B P 049* *Byz*.

Ἀντίδικος, -ου, ὁ, a legal term denoting an opponent at law (as in Matt 5:25; Luke 12:58; 18:3), although in the LXX it has a more general sense of an adversary or enemy (BDAG 88c; H. Bietenhard, *NIDNTT* 1.553–55; LN 39.9). Clearly the setting here is not the courtroom, but the world at large (Michaels 298). Elsewhere in 1 Peter, the opponents of believers are the pagans who revile them (2:12; 3:8–9, 13–17; 4:3–4, 12–16). Ὑμῶν is an obj. gen.

Διάβολος is in appos. to ἀντίδικος (T 206; BDF §268[2]). As an adj. it means "slanderous" (1 Tim 3:11; 2 Tim 3:3; Titus 2:3), but more often in the NT it functions as a subst. "the Devil," which is a Gk. trans. of the Heb. *śāṭān*, "Satan" ("adversary"), and refers to the archenemy of God and his people (see Elliott 854–56). As a monadic noun it is often anar. (R 794–95; cf. Wallace 249). Although the cstr. is grammatically independent of the previous two impvs., it clearly provides the rationale for them. The idea may well be that the Devil is the one ultimately responsible for instigating slander and abuse against Christians (Goppelt 361–62; Davids 189; Elliott 857–58; Achtemeier 341).

ὡς λέων ὠρυόμενος περιπατεῖ ζητῶν τινα καταπιεῖν

There is quite a degree of textual uncertainty at this point. Τινα καταπιεῖν ("someone to devour") is read by ℵ K L P and a number of minuscules. On the other hand, 𝔓⁷²
A 436, 945, 1067, 1409, 2298, the majority text and most versions read τίνα καταπίη ("whom he may devour"). The inf. καταπιεῖν alone is found in B Ψ 0206ᵛⁱᵈ 69 and a few others. The problem is exacerbated due to the earliest mss. being unaccented. It is possible that the inf. existed alone, and τινα was added later to provide a smoother rdg. Confusion then resulted as to whether it was to be read as an interr. (accented) or an indef. The existence of τινα in some form in the overwhelming majority of mss. argues for its inclusion. See Metzger 626–27.

Ὡς here introduces a comparison (BDAG 1103d), with the imagery echoing LXX Ps 21:14 (see Beale and Carson 1043–44; also *NewDocs* 3.50–51). Λέων, -οντος, ὁ, "lion." Ὠρυόμενος nom. sg. masc. of pres. mid. ptc. of ὠρύομαι, "roar" (BDAG 1103d). Καταπιεῖν aor. act. inf. of καταπίνω, "devour" (BDAG 524c). The ptc. ζητῶν ("seeking") is telic, which together with the epex. inf. καταπιεῖν indicates the intent of the Devil. In the thought of this epistle, being devoured by the Devil is equivalent to either giving in to fleshly desires (2:11; 4:2–4) or responding in an inappropriate way to suffering (2:18–21; 3:8, 13–17; 4:12–19).

VERSE 9

ᾧ ἀντίστητε στερεοὶ τῇ πίστει

Ἀντίστητε 2 pl. aor. act. impv. of ἀνθίστημι, "resist," "oppose" (BDAG 80a; LN 39.18; also in Jas 4:7 of resisting the Devil). Another aor. impv. for a general precept, although in this case it may be simply that -μι vbs. prefer the aor. tense in the impv. form (see the discussion on "The Use of the Imperative in 1 Peter" in the Introduction). This vb. takes the dat. (due to the compound; R 542), hence the rel. pron. ᾧ.

Στερεός, -ά, -όν, "firm," "solid," "steadfast" (BDAG 943b; G. Bertram, *TDNT* 7.609–14). Pred. with an implied ὄντες (Dubis 169). Στερεοὶ τῇ πίστει can be understood in three ways:

1. modifying the subj. of the impv., i.e., "resist him you who are firm in faith" (suggested by Achtemeier 342);
2. impv. as per the adjs. in 3:8, i.e., "be firm" (CEV, NLT; Michaels 300);
*3. instr., i.e., the Devil is resisted by means of steadfast faith (most EVV give this sense; Davids 191; Jobes 314; cf. Achtemeier 342).

The dat. τῇ πίστει can be cstr. either as a dat. of respect (Elliott 860; Dubis 169) or a locat. of sphere, with little difference in sense. The clear implication of this statement, as elsewhere in the NT (cf. Eph 6:10–17), is that faith can triumph over evil. *Pace* Michaels (300), who argues that this call for resistance indicates that the Devil is not attacking believers via the harassment by non-believers, the contrast between resistance (of the Devil) and nonresistance (of people) demonstrates how Peter understands the true nature of the hostility and problems facing the church. The Devil is the ultimate source, therefore resistance is to be directed at him.

εἰδότες τὰ αὐτὰ τῶν παθημάτων τῇ ἐν κόσμῳ ὑμῶν ἀδελφότητι ἐπιτελεῖσθαι
[This reflects the text of the forthcoming fifth edition of the UBS *Greek New Testament*. The fourth edition reads [τῳ] before κόσμῳ.]

Εἰδότες nom. pl. masc. of pf. act. ptc. of οἶδα. Εἰδότες with the inf. has the same sense as εἰδότες ὅτι (thus explaining the addition of ὅτι by 𝔓⁷² 614, 630, 1505, and a few others). The ptc. is causal ("because you know," NIV), yet it also has an impv. character; in essence the readers are being encouraged to reflect on this knowledge whether it be previously known or not (Michaels 301; cf. Turner, *Style* 128; see the discussion on "Imperatival Participles in 1 Peter" in the Introduction).

Ἐπιτελεῖσθαι pres. pass. inf. of ἐπιτελέω, "finish," "perform," "accomplish" (BDAG 383c; G. Delling, *TDNT* 8.61–62; LN 13.108; 68.22). The form should be taken as passive (*pace* T 55) as the will and purpose of God is implied (cf. 3:17; Michaels 302). EVV that render as "undergo" or the like (NRSV, NLT, ESV, NIV) miss the goal-orientated notion of completion inherent in the vb. (Dubis 170). Better ASV, NASB: "accomplished."

In place of the pres. inf. ἐπιτελεῖσθαι ("to be accomplished") supported by B² P Ψ 1739 and the majority text, a number of important mss. (א A B* K 0206, 33, 614, 630, 1505, and a number of others) read the pres. mid. indic. ἐπιτελεῖσθε ("you are accomplishing"). Although the ms. evidence leans toward the pres. indic., the inf. is undoubtedly the harder rdg. and should be retained. Note that several of the minuscules that support the pres. indic. also include ὅτι in an attempt to smooth the text.

The subj. of the inf. (acc. of respect) is τὰ αὐτὰ τῶν παθημάτων ("the same kinds of sufferings") with αὐτά an identical adj. used subst. This awkward cstr. may be intended to equate to τὰ αὐτὰ παθήματα ("the same sufferings;" so ASV, Weymouth, NKJV; Goppelt 363 n. 22), but more likely is a deliberate attempt to be not quite as precise, i.e., "the same kind of sufferings" (most EVV; R 505, 687; ZG 715; Michaels 301). In other words, the sufferings of fellow Christians throughout the world may not be exactly parallel, but they are suffering because of their faith nonetheless. The gen. τῶν παθημάτων is either partitive (R 502; Michaels 301; BDF §164[1]: the cstr. is "strictly speaking incorrect") or a gen. of material (see Wallace 91–92; a subset of epex. gen. proposed by Dubis 170).

With the pass. inf. ἐπιτελεῖσθαι, τῇ ἐν κόσμῳ ὑμῶν ἀδελφότητι is an instr. of agency, "by your brotherhood" (in agreement with Achtemeier 343; Elliott 862; Dubis 170; not a dat. of disadvantage *pace* T 238; Goppelt 363 n. 22; Davids 193 n. 23). Previously, ἀδελφότητα was used of the local Christian community (2:17); here it has a universal focus with κόσμος used in a geographical sense (i.e. not the theological sense of the world under the domain of evil; see Achtemeier 343; Michaels 301). The prep. ἐν is distributive, "throughout" (HCSB, ESV, NIV; Elliott 163). Thus all believers are bound together by the bond of kinship with God as Father (1:17). They are to recognize that harassment and social ostracism for their faith is not unique to them, and a sense of solidarity should provide extra determination to resist their archenemy.

VERSE 10

Ὁ δὲ θεὸς πάσης χάριτος

Δέ is adversative, contrasting suffering and the struggle against the Devil with God's support and salvation (Elliott 864). "The God of all grace" could mean:

1. that all grace originates from God, i.e., a gen. of origin or a gen. of product (Dubis 171); or
2. God himself is all grace, i.e., a gen. of quality (Achtemeier 344 n. 119).

The two ideas are closely related. Grace is expressed in various ways in this epistle: ministry gifts (4:10–11), as a result of suffering for doing good (2:19–20), and that which will be further manifested at the revelation of Jesus Christ (1:13).

ὁ καλέσας ὑμᾶς εἰς τὴν αἰώνιον αὐτοῦ δόξαν ἐν Χριστῷ [This reflects the text of the forthcoming fifth edition of the UBS *Greek New Testament*. The fourth edition reads [Ἰησοῦ] after Χριστῷ.]

Ὁ καλέσας ὑμᾶς is yet another manifestation of grace, now expressed in election (cf. 1:2; 2:9). Εἰς τὴν αἰώνιον αὐτοῦ δόξαν is the glory that believers will share when Christ's glory is revealed (4:13; 1:7), with the adj. αἰώνιον providing a stark contrast to the short period (ὀλίγον) of suffering mentioned below (Michaels 302).

Ἐν Χριστῷ most likely relates to the calling, not the glory. The latter sense would normally require the prep. phrase to be written *inclusio* (although, as Dubis 171 notes, the overcrowding created by αἰώνιον αὐτοῦ may explain the position), or to be preceded with a repetition of the art. τήν (so Michaels 302; Achtemeier 345). It reinforces the idea of 1:3, 18–21 that Jesus Christ is the basis for human relationship with God (instr. of means "by Christ," NKJV, NLT; Achtemeier 345), and also that believers are united with Christ (instr. of association; TEV; Dubis 171; cf. 5:14).

Ἰησοῦ is included after Χριστῷ by 𝔓[72] A Ψ 33, 1739, numerous other minuscules together with the majority text, but omitted by ℵ B (B has the art. τῷ with Χριστῷ) 630, 1292, 1505, 1611, 2138 and others. The only time the two names appear together in 1 Peter they appear as Ἰησοῦ Χριστοῦ (1:1, 2, 3, 7, 13; 2:5; 3:21; 4:11) rather than the reverse as here. Thus despite the strong ms. evidence for its inclusion, this is probably a case of the scribal expansion of sacred names (see Metzger 627).

ὀλίγον παθόντας αὐτὸς καταρτίσει, στηρίξει, σθενώσει, θεμελιώσει

Ὀλίγον, "a little while," is an adj. functioning adv. and recalls ὀλίγον ἄρτι in 1:6. The temp. ptc. παθόντας is acc. relating to ὑμᾶς from the previous clause. Αὐτός here functions as a verbal intensifier ("he himself") for the following four fut. indics. and is meant to instill confidence in the readers by indicating that their restoration is God's task not their own (Achtemeier 345). Ὑμᾶς (see earlier in the verse above) not only functions as the antecedent to the ptc., but also as the implied dir. obj. of the four vbs. (Michaels 303, who believes that the pron. is omitted in order to universalize the promise; the pron. is included by some mss. including the majority text).

Some mss. have aor. opt. endings instead of the fut. indic. A number of mss. also omit one or more of the four vbs. The text is supported by א 33^vid 436, 945, 1241, 1739*, 1852, 1881, 2464 and others and should be retained. The omissions can be explained by homoioteleuton (similar endings), whereas the opt. is only found in later texts and is a stylistic modification, common in entreaties at the close of letters (cf. 1 Thess 5:23; Heb 13:20).

Καταρτίσει 3 sg. fut. act. indic. of καταρτίζω, originally a medical term for the setting of a bone, came to mean to repair or restore something in general (BDAG 526b; G. Delling, *TDNT* 1.475–76). In the NT it has a sense of "repair" (Mark 1:19), "restore" (Gal 6:1), or "equip/supply" (Eph 4:12; Heb 13:21). The sense in this passage is closer to "restore" in the sense of making complete (LN 75.5; Achtemeier 346).

Στηρίξει 3 sg. fut. act. indic of στηρίζω, used in the NT of establishing or fixing something, but more commonly in the sense of "strengthen" (Luke 22:32; Rom 1:11; 16:25; 1 Thess 3:2, etc.; BDAG 945b; G. Harder, *TDNT* 7.653–57; Spicq 3.291–95; LN 74.19). Σθενώσει 3 sg. fut. act. indic. of σθενόω, "strengthen" (BDAG 922a; LN 74.14), occurs only here in the NT (and is rare in Gk. literature, although the form σθένω is more common, see LSJ 1595c). Θεμελιώσει 3 sg. fut. act. indic. of θεμελιόω, which comes from a root meaning to lay a foundation, and in its NT uses means "establish" or "set firmly" (BDAG 449b; J. Blunck, *NIDNTT* 1.660–62).

Building a "rhetorical crescendo" (Jobes 316), Peter uses these four semantically related vbs. to reiterate and clarify ἵνα ὑμᾶς ὑφώσῃ ἐν καιρῷ ("that he may exalt you in due time") in v. 6 (Michaels 302; Dubis 172 suggests the sense of the quadruplet is "God will make everything right beyond your wildest dreams"). The fact that the vbs. are in the fut. tense first of all highlights them as a promise rather than a wish (Davids 194), and second, together with the fact that they follow the short time of suffering, points to them being chiefly eschatological in focus (Michaels 302; *pace* Goppelt 365–66, who interprets them primarily in terms of a present strengthening to stand firm against the adversary). It is not that suffering in this life will soon end to be replaced by a different set of earthly circumstances without hostility, for suffering is part and parcel of what it means to be a Christian (4:12–19; Davids 194). Neither should we understand this in the sense of a short time of suffering being a prerequisite for God's strengthening so that further suffering can be endured.

So the tone is tempered slightly by Peter reminding the readers of their present situation of suffering (cf. Rom 8:18; 2 Cor 4:17). Thus Peter concludes where he begins: there is a time of suffering but that time is short, for the end is near and vindication awaits (4:7). It is part of the author's rhetorical strategy that this is not mentioned first (contrary to the word order in NRSV, NASB, ESV), but embedded within the v. among refs. to God's grace and restoration.

VERSE 11

αὐτῷ τὸ κράτος εἰς τοὺς αἰῶνας, ἀμήν

This is a shorter form of the doxology found in 4:11. The omission of ἔστιν could make the doxology a wish rather than a statement of fact: "to him be the power" (most EVV), but given the previous doxology we should probably supply it here: "to him is the power" (Achtemeier 346; Elliott 867; Dubis 172–73). Αὐτῷ is a dat. of possession. Κράτος, -ους, τό, "might," "power" (BDAG 565b). The majority of mss. add ἡ δόξα ("the glory") to τὸ κράτος, although the word order varies. The shorter rdg. with τὸ κράτος only has the support of 𝔓[72] A B Ψ 0206[vid] and a couple of others, yet should be retained. The longer rdg. has been influenced by the similar doxology in 4:11. Εἰς τοὺς αἰῶνας has also been expanded with the addition of τῶν αἰώνων by the majority of mss. including א A Ψ *Byz* (probably again under the influence of 4:11 if original there). Scribal expansion is typically found in doxologies, and the shorter rdg. supported by 𝔓[72] B is to be preferred.

Thus the body of the letter is concluded on a high note of praise. Τὸ κράτος standing alone emphasizes God's power to achieve what was stated in the previous v. (cf. τὴν κραταιὰν χείρα in 5:6), thereby further encouraging the recipients (Goppelt 366; Michaels 304; Achtemeier 347).

FOR FURTHER STUDY

41. Satan, Devil/Spiritual Warfare (5:8–9)

Arnold, Clinton E. *Spiritual Warfare: What Does the Bible Really Teach?* London: Marshall Pickering, 1997.
_____. *DLNT* 1077–82.
Bietenhard, Hans. *NIDNTT* 3.468–72.
Boyd, Gregory A. *Satan and the Problem of Evil: Constructing a Trinitarian Warfare Theodicy.* Downers Grove: InterVarsity, 2001.
Fuller, Daniel P. *ISBE* 4.340–44.
Garrett, Susan R. *The Demise of the Devil.* Minneapolis: Fortress Press, 1989.
Green, Michael. *I Believe in Satan's Downfall.* Grand Rapids: Eerdmans, 1981.
Hamilton, Victor P. *ABD* 5.985–89.
Murphy, Ed. *The Handbook for Spiritual Warfare.* Nashville: Thomas Nelson, 1992.
*Page, Sydney. *Powers of Evil: A Biblical Theology of Satan and His Forces.* Grand Rapids: Eerdmans, 1995.
Schreiber, Stefan. "The Great Opponent: The Devil in Early Jewish and Formative Christian Literature." Pages 437–57 in *Angels: The Concept of Celestial Beings–Origins, Development and Reception.* Edited by F. B. Reiterer et al. Berlin: Walter de Gruyter, 2007.
Sherman, Dean. *Spiritual Warfare for Every Christian.* Seattle, WA: YWAM, 1990.
Wagner, Peter C. *Confronting the Powers.* Ventura, CA: Regal Books, 1996.
Watson, Duane F. *ABD* 2.183–84.
White, Thomas B. *The Believer's Guide to Spiritual Warfare.* Ann Arbor, MI: Vine Books, 1990.

Wink, Walter A. *The Powers that Be: Theology for a New Millennium.* New York: Doubleday, 1998.

See also For Further Study §§ 13, 19, 23.

HOMILETICAL SUGGESTIONS

Humility and Resoluteness (5:5b–11)

1. Be humble toward one another (v. 5b)
   - (a) The reason: because God opposes the proud but gives grace to the humble (v. 5c)
2. Be humbled under God's mighty hand (v. 6a)
   - (a) The purpose: God will exalt you in due time (v. 6b)
   - (b) The means: by casting your anxieties on him (v. 7)
3. Be alert and vigilant (v. 8a)
   - (a) The reason: the Devil is looking for someone to devour (v. 8b)
4. Resist the Devil (v. 9a)
   - (a) The means: by being firm in faith (v. 9a)
   - (b) The reason: because suffering is the universal lot of Christians (v. 9b)
5. The God of all grace (v. 10–11)
   - (a) Called you to his eternal glory in Christ (v. 10a)
   - (b) Will restore, strengthen, confirm, and establish you (v. 10b)
   - (c) Is powerful (v. 11)

Resisting the Enemy (5:8–9)

1. Satan/The Devil: Terminology and background
2. His strategy is to destroy the faith of believers
3. He can be resisted by resolute faith (cf. Eph 6:10–17)

D. FINAL GREETINGS (5:12–14)

STRUCTURE

Verse 12 describes the purpose for the letter and the reliability of the letter bearer (see below). The concluding rel. clause εἰς ἣν στῆτε ("stand fast in it") picks up the immediately preceding ἀληθῆ χάριν τοῦ θεοῦ ("the true grace of God"). Verse 13 records greetings to the recipients, whereas v. 14 exhorts them to greet one another. The letter concludes with a blessing of peace.

12   Διὰ Σιλουανοῦ ὑμῖν
        τοῦ πιστοῦ ἀδελφοῦ,
            ὡς λογίζομαι,
        δι' ὀλίγων
<u>ἔγραψα</u>
        παρακαλῶν
καὶ ἐπιμαρτυρῶν
        ταύτην εἶναι ἀληθῆ χάριν τοῦ θεοῦ
            εἰς ἣν στῆτε.

13   <u>ἀσπάζεται</u> ὑμᾶς
    ἡ ἐν Βαβυλῶνι συνεκλεκτὴ
    καὶ Μᾶρκος ὁ υἱός μου.

14 <u>ἀσπάσασθε</u> ἀλλήλους
    ἐν φιλήματι ἀγάπης.

    εἰρήνη ὑμῖν πᾶσιν τοῖς ἐν Χριστῷ.

VERSE 12

διὰ Σιλουανοῦ ὑμῖν τοῦ πιστοῦ ἀδελφοῦ, ὡς λογίζομαι, δι' ὀλίγων ἔγραψα

As questions began to arise concerning the capacity of a Galilean fisherman to pen the quality of the Gk. in this epistle (see, however, the excursus in Jobes 325–38, who contends that the quality of the Gk. has been overstated), on the strength of διὰ Σιλουανοῦ ("through Silvanus") commentators began to emphasize Silvanus' role in the writing of the letter (Kelly 215; Selwyn 241; Davids 198). Weighty evidence has now been produced, however, that this use of διά refers to the letter carrier rather than the letter writer (see Acts 15:23 and further Michaels 306; Achtemeier 340–50; Elliott 872). Of course, this does not preclude the carrier having some role in the penning of the material, but that possibility cannot be substantiated.

Τοῦ πιστοῦ ἀδελφοῦ, "the faithful brother," is in appos. to Σιλουανοῦ (BDF §125[2]). This is the only use of ἀδελφός in this epistle, with ἀγαπητοί used of fellow Christians generally (2:11; 4:12). This may indicate that ἀδελφός should be taken here in the sense of "co-worker" (Davids 199). Most equate this Silvanus with the Silvanus of the

Pauline epistles (2 Cor 1:19; 1 Thess 1:1; 2 Thess 1:1) and the Silas of Acts (e.g., Acts 15:22, 32), but though highly probable, this cannot be established with certainty (see Achtemeier 351; Elliott 873–74). Ὡς is here used to introduce the perspective from which a person is viewed (BDAG 1104d). Ὡς λογίζομαι, "as I consider," expresses the author's personal recommendation of the faithfulness of Silvanus. This does not weaken the commendation but strengthens it with apostolic authority (Achtemeier 352; Michaels 307). This commendation appears to be more suited to the role of an emissary than a letter writer.

Ὑμῖν is normally rendered by EVV and most commentators as the indir. obj. of ἔγραψα, which is an epistolary aor. (past time from the perspective of the recipients). However, the placement of the pron. prior to τοῦ πιστοῦ ἀδελφοῦ rather than with ἔγραψα suggests that it should be cstr. as a dat. of respect: "through Silvanus, a brother who is faithful with respect to you" (Dubis 174; sim. KJV). Δι' ὀλίγων is idiomatically "briefly," and rather than being a ref. to the actual length of the letter (cf. Heb 13:22), appears to be a customary politeness, for long letters were not well received (Goppelt 372). It may also be used to express the importance of the subject matter (i.e., more could have been written).

παρακαλῶν καὶ ἐπιμαρτυρῶν ταύτην εἶναι ἀληθῆ χάριν τοῦ θεοῦ εἰς ἣν στῆτε

Ἐπιμαρτυρῶν nom. sg. masc. of pres. act. ptc. of ἐπιμαρτυρέω, "testify" (BDAG 375c). Στῆτε 2 pl. aor. act. impv. of ἵστημι, "stand." The ptcs. παρακαλῶν and ἐπιμαρτυρῶν are telic, expressing the purpose of the epistle in terms of exhortation (2:11; 5:1) and testimony. The testimony (cf. μάρτυς, "witness" in 5:1) relates to what God has done, continues to do, and will do on behalf of believers in Jesus Christ, while the exhortation relates to appropriate Christian living in the midst of hostile surroundings (Goppelt 372). These two ptcs. thus refer to both the theology and the parenesis of the letter.

The clause ταύτην εἶναι ἀληθῆ χάριν τοῦ θεοῦ serves as the indir. discourse content for the ptcs. παρακαλῶν καὶ ἐπιμαρτυρῶν, or more likely the latter (NIV: "encouraging you and testifying that this is the true grace of God;" also Dubis 174–75). The antecedent of ταύτην is unclear. Although in grammatical agreement with χάριτος (v. 10), this is tautologous (Michaels 309). Some have suggested suffering/trials, but although suffering may be the will of God (4:19), this is not quite the same as labeling it the grace of God. The most likely antecedent is the letter as a whole (fem. in agreement with ἐπιστολή; Bigg 196; Michaels 309–10; Achtemeier 352; Jobes 324), with the acc. functioning as the subj. (acc. of respect) of the inf. εἶναι (R 1039).

Ἀληθῆ χάριν τοῦ θεοῦ is pred. (Wallace 192). Throughout the epistle χάρις refers to what God graciously gives, and the term is used in a consistent manner with this here. Consequently, τοῦ θεοῦ is best cstr. as a gen. of origin/source. The adj. ἀληθῆ is better rendered here as "reliable/dependable" (as in John 5:31–32; 21:24; Titus 1:13; 3 John 12; Elliott 878–79).

The rel. clause with the impv. εἰς ἣν στῆτε is quite awkward (rare but not unprecedented; see R 949), giving rise to some var. rdgs. In place of the aor. impv. στῆτε, "stand fast" (in it) read by 𝔓⁷² ℵ A B 33, 81, 323, 945, 1241, 1739, and others, P and the majority text read the pf. act. indic. ἑστήκατε, (in which) "you stand," whereas a couple of other minuscules read ἔστε, (in which) "you are." The impv. not only has superior ms. support, the rel. pron. followed by the impv. is clearly the most difficult rdg.

The prep. εἰς can be understood either as:

*1 having the force of ἐν, an increasing phenomenon in HGk. (BDF §205; T 255–56; Z §106, 111; Harris, 84–88; EVV; ZG 716; Achtemeier 352–53; Elliott 879); or

2. purpose (Michaels 310: "with this grace in view, stand," or "for this grace, stand").

Other NT uses of ἐν with ἵστημι (Rom 5:2; 1 Cor 15:1; Phil 4:1) support option 1 (Dubis 175–76).

The antecedent of the rel. ἥν is ἀληθῆ χάριν τοῦ θεοῦ. It is in this grace that the recipients are urged to "stand fast," noting the link to resisting the Devil in 5:9 with the compound form ἀντίστητε. Even though this final exhortation is obviously a general precept, the impv. forms of ἵστημι are solely aor. in the NT, a point typical of -μι vbs. in general (see the discussion on "The Use of the Imperative in 1 Peter" in the introduction).

VERSE 13

ἀσπάζεται ὑμᾶς ἡ ἐν Βαβυλῶνι συνεκλεκτή

Συνεκλεκτός, -ή, -όν, "fellow elect," "also chosen" (BDAG 968d). ἡ ἐν Βαβυλῶνι συνεκλεκτή is lit. "the fellow elect (feminine) in Babylon." This would be a rather oblique reference to Peter's wife (pace Bigg 197), and commentators are virtually unanimous that the fem. form is used in a collective sense of a Christian congregation (cf. the uncompounded form ἐκλεκτή in 2 John 1, 13). The prep. compound reinforces the idea of the worldwide Christian brotherhood mentioned in v. 9, and the fem. form of the adj. may be looking there to ἀδελφότητι as its antecedent (Elliott 882). Συνεκλεκτή also corresponds to ἐκλεκτοῖς in 1:1, thereby framing the entire work (Michaels 310). After Βαβυλῶνι, ℵ and a couple of other mss. and vgᵐˢˢ read ἐκκλησία ("church") by way of clarification. NRSV, NLT appropriately render as "your sister church in Babylon."

There were two actual places named Babylon in the ancient world (see *NewDocs* 3.147), one in Mesopotamia and the other in Egypt (old Cairo), but not only was the former almost desolate at this time, there is no tradition that attaches Peter to either. Consequently, most understand Βαβυλῶνι to be a metaphor for Rome (see Elliott 882–87). It is not used in the neg. sense as it is in the book of Revelation (Rev 14:8; 16:19; 17:5; 18:2, 10, 21) but functions as a metaphor for displacement and alienation, finding its roots in the Jewish exile of 587 BC and appearing consistently in Jewish and Christian literature after the fall of Jerusalem in AD 70. So just as Peter addresses those who are aliens and exiles, he, too, writes from a place which is not home (Michaels

311). The motif of displacement thus provides an additional frame (with election, see above) for the entire work (Achtemeier 354).

καὶ Μᾶρκος ὁ υἱός μου

Υἱός could be taken lit., but more likely should be understood in a fig. sense of "son in the faith" (cf. 1 Cor 4:17; 1 Tim 1:2; 2 Tim 1:2; Dubis 177; Michaels 312). Although Μᾶρκος was a common name, most equate him with John Mark the cousin of Barnabas (Col 4:10) and one-time resident of Jerusalem (Acts 12:12). He initially accompanied Paul on the first missionary journey, then deserted him (Acts 13:4–13; 15:37–39), but appears to have been reconciled at some later point (Col 4:10; Phlm 24; 2 Tim 4:11). Mark's association with Peter in Rome is confirmed by Papias (in Eusebius, *HE* 2.15.1; 3.39), and remains constant in the post-apostolic tradition (see Elliott 887–90).

VERSE 14

ἀσπάσασθε ἀλλήλους ἐν φιλήματι ἀγάπης

Φίλημα, -ατος, τό, "kiss." In this case, the aor. impv. ἀσπάσασθε may be governing a specific command, but the "kiss of love" is more likely to be intended as a habitual greeting (see the discussion on "The Use of the Imperative in 1 Peter" in the Introduction). Ἐν φιλήματι ἀγάπης is instr. of means—"with a kiss of love" (cf. Rom 16:16; 1 Cor 16:20; 2 Cor 13:12; 1 Thess 5:26). Ἀγάπης is a descriptive gen. signifying the type of kiss. The kiss of love underscores the insistence to love one another that occurs throughout the letter (1:22; 2:17; 3:8). Given that in the Greco-Roman world a kiss was a sign of affection between relatives and close friends (Elliott 890), this serves again to underline the familial relationship between believers as part of God's household (Michaels 313).

εἰρήνη ὑμῖν πᾶσιν τοῖς ἐν Χριστῷ

𝔓[72] omits this final clause. In line with typical scribal additions at the close of letters, A P 1739 and the majority text add Ἰησοῦ after Χριστῷ, while a P 1739[c] and the majority text conclude with ἀμήν ("amen"). While the final clause should be retained (𝔓[72] may have been following a damaged exemplar [Davids 205 n. 17]), the shorter reading in each case is preferred.

The omission of a vb. is typical in the final greeting or prayer wish (cf. 1 Cor 16:24; 2 Cor 13:13; Gal 6:18; Eph 6:24; Phil 4:23). In place of the traditional Pauline blessing of grace, εἰρήνη, "peace," is most appropriate for these beleaguered communities (cf. 3:11) and echoes the prayer wish in the opening salutation (1:2), forming yet another *inclusio* (Achtemeier 356; Davids 205).

Τοῖς ἐν Χριστῷ is instr. of association (Dubis 177) and should not be taken in the sense that some of the readers are in Christ and some are not. Rather, the expression is one and the same with being a Christian (4:16). Consequently, the letter concludes with a definitive statement of solidarity with Jesus Christ, both in terms of present suffering and the promise of future vindication and unsurpassed glory.

FOR FURTHER STUDY

42. The Use of "Babylon" as a Metaphor in the NT

Bauckham, Richard J. *The Climax of Prophecy: Studies in the Book of Revelation.*
Edinburgh: T&T Clark, 1993.

Beagley, Alan J. *The 'Sitz im Leben' of the Apocalypse with Particular Reference to the
Role of the Church's Enemies.* New York: Walter de Gruyter, 1987.

_____. *DLNT* 112–12.

Court, John M. *Myth and History in the Book of Revelation.* London: SPCK, 1979.

Fortune, A. W. *ISBE* 1.391.

Gregory, P. F. "Its End Is Destruction: Babylon the Great in the Book of Revelation."
Concordia Theological Quarterly 73 (2009): 137–53.

Koester, Craig R. "Roman Slave Trade and the Critique of Babylon in Revelation 18."
CBQ 70 (2008): 776–86.

Kuhn, Karl G. *TDNT* 1.514–17.

Malina, Bruce J. *On the Genre and Message of Revelation: Star Visions and Sky Journeys.*
Peabody: Hendrickson, 1995.

Thompson, Leonard L. *The Book of Revelation: Apocalypse and Empire.* New York:
Oxford University Press, 1990.

Walton, Duane. *ABD* 1.563–66.

HOMILETICAL SUGGESTIONS

Final Greetings (5:12–14)

1. The epistle (v. 12)
   (a) written briefly
   (b) sent via Silvanus, who is faithful
   (c) for the purpose of:
      (1) encouragement
      (2) testimony to the dependable grace of God
2. Greetings from (v. 13):
   (a) the sister church in "Babylon"
   (b) Peter's "son" Mark
3. Greet one another (v. 14a)
4. Final blessing of peace (v. 14b)

Grace in 1 Peter

1. Is Peter's prayer wish for his recipients (1:2)
2. Was prophesied by the OT prophets (1:10)
3. Is part of the benefits coming to believers at the future revelation of
   Jesus (1:13)
4. Suffering for doing right finds grace (favor) with God (2:19–20)
5. Husbands and wives are joint heirs of God's grace (3:7)
6. The diverse spiritual gifts are manifestations of God's grace (4:9–10)

7. God gives grace to the humble (5:5)
8. God is the origin of all grace (5:10)
9. His grace is dependable (5:12)

Exegetical Outline

I. Salutation (1:1–2)
  A. The author: Peter (v. 1a)
  B. The recipients: Christians in northern Asia Minor (v. 1b)
  C. Statement of election (v. 2a)
    1. Its basis/origin (κατά): the foreknowledge of God
    2. Its effecting (ἐν): the sanctifying work of the Spirit
    3. Its purpose (εἰς): obedience
  D. The greeting: grace and peace (v. 2b)
II. The Christian Hope (1:3–12)
  A. The living hope (1:3–5)
    1. Basis of the living hope (v. 3)
      a. The mercy of God
      b. The resurrection of Jesus Christ
    2. Content of the hope (1:4–5)
      a. An inheritance of great quality (v. 4–5a)
        (1) Kept in heaven
        (2) Guarded by God through faith
      b. Salvation (v. 5)
  B. Joy in the midst of trials (1:6–9)
    1. The nature of trials (v. 6)
    2. The refining of faith (v. 7)
    3. Love for and faith in Jesus in the midst of trial (v. 8)
    4. Salvation as the outcome of faith (v. 9)
  C. The prophetic witness to the Christian hope (1:10–12)
    1. With respect to the grace destined for believers (v. 10)
    2. With respect to their inspiration by the preexistent Christ (v. 11)
    3. With respect to the sufferings and the subsequent glory of the Messiah (v. 11b)
    4. With respect to serving believers as recipients of the gospel (v. 12)
III. A Call to Holy Living (1:13–2:3)
  A. Emulating the holiness of God (1:13–16)
    1. Be mentally prepared (v. 13a)

      2. Hope must be centered on Jesus (v. 13b)

      3. Leave behind past lifestyle (v. 14)

      4. Mirror the holiness of God (1:15–16)

  B. Precious redemption through Christ (1:17–21)

      1. Revere God (v. 17)

         a. He is Father

         b. He is the impartial judge

         c. Conduct one's life appropriately

      2. The gift of redemption (v. 18–20)

         a. The price was not mere gold or silver (v. 18)

         b. Christ the perfect lamb (v. 19)

         c. God's pre-ordained plan (v. 20)

      3. The privilege of believers (vv. 20–21)

         a. Christ revealed at the end of the ages (v. 20)

         b. Faith in Christ is the avenue to God (v. 21a)

         c. The resurrection of Christ and his subsequent glory provide the basis for faith (v. 21b)

  C. The new birth (1:22–25)

      1. New birth has its outworking in Christian community ethics (v. 22)

      2. New birth is effected through God's word (v. 23)

      3. God's Word is eternal in contrast to the ephemeral nature of humanity (v. 24–25a)

      4. God's Word is the gospel proclaimed (v. 25b)

  D. Mature Christian living (2:1–3)

      1. Leaving the past behind (v. 1)

      2. Longing for what is compatible with the Christian life (v. 2a)

      3. Salvation as a process (v. 2b)

      4. Experiencing the character of Jesus/God (v. 3)

IV. The People of God (2:4–10)

  A. Christ the living stone (vv. 4–8)

      1. Christ the living stone (v. 4)

         a. Rejected by humanity (v. 4a)

         b. Chosen by God and precious (v. 4b)

      2. Believers as living stones (v. 5)

         a. The house is still under construction (v. 5a)

         b. Believers as a holy priesthood offering spiritual sacrifices (v. 5b)

      3. Christ the cornerstone as the foundation for life (vv. 6–8)

         a. Belief in him brings honor (vv. 6–7a)

         b. Unbelief and disobedience result in stumbling (vv. 7b–8)

  B. Believers as the people of God (vv. 9–10)

      1. Election (v. 9a)

      2. Royal priesthood (v. 9a)

      3. Holy (v. 9a)

      4. God's possession (v. 9a)

      5. Moved from darkness to light (v. 9b)
      6. Proclaiming the mighty deeds of God (v. 9b)
      7. Recipients of God's mercy (v. 10)
V. Obligations of the People of God (2:11–3:12)
  A. Living as aliens and strangers (2:11–12)
      1. Christians as an estranged people (v. 11a)
      2. Appropriate conduct for an estranged people (vv. 11b–12)
        a. Avoid sinful desires (v. 11b)
        b. The internal war (v. 11b)
        c. Maintain good conduct in the midst of ridicule (v. 12a)
        d. Good conduct may win non-Christians to faith (v. 12b)
  B. Duty to the governing authorities (2:13–17)
      1. Christians are to submit to the governing authorities (vv. 13–14a)
      2. The role of government: punishment and commendation (v. 14b)
      3. Christians must engage in appropriate behavior (vv. 15–17)
        a. It is the will of God (v. 15)
        b. It exposes pagan ignorance (v. 15)
        c. Christian freedom must be used appropriately (v. 16a)
        d. Christians are slaves of God (v. 16b)
        e. Summarizing maxims (v. 17)
          (1) Honor everyone
          (2) Love the family of believers
          (3) Fear God
          (4) Honor the emperor
  C. Duty of slaves: the example of Christ's suffering (2:18–25)
      1. The submission of slaves to masters (vv. 18–21)
        a. Unjust treatment does not abrogate the need for submission (v. 18)
        b. Unjust suffering finds favor with God (vv. 19–20)
        c. Unjust suffering is part of the Christian calling (v. 21a)
        d. The suffering of Christ as an example (v. 21b)
      2. The example of Christ (vv. 22–24)
        a. He was blameless in character (v. 22)
        b. He did not return abuse (v. 23a)
        c. He committed himself to God (v. 23b)
      3. The achievement of the cross (vv. 24–25)
        a. Christ bore our sins (v. 24a)
        b. We now live for righteousness not sin (v. 24b)
        c. Sin has been dealt with (v. 24c)
        d. We are no longer wandering (v. 25)
  D. Duty of wives and husbands (3:1–7)
      1. Submission of wives to husbands (vv. 1–6)
        a. To win unbelieving husbands to the faith (vv. 1b–2)
        b. Proper adornment (vv. 3–4)
          (1) Not in externals (v. 3)

(2)   In a gentle and humble spirit (v. 4)
   c.   The example of the Jewish matriarchs (vv. 5–6)
  2.   Husbands must be considerate to their wives (v. 7)
   a.   They are physically inferior
   b.   They are joint heirs of grace that leads to life
   c.   So that prayers may not be hindered
 E.   Unity and love (3:8–12)
  1.   Five desirable qualities (v. 8)
  2.   Do not retaliate but bless (v. 9)
   a.   Part of the Christian calling
   b.   Will result in inheriting a blessing
  3.   Suporting citation (Ps 34:13–17 LXX) (vv. 10–12)
   a.   Turn from evil and do good (vv. 10–11)
   b.   The favor and disfavor of God (v. 12)
VI.   Suffering for the Cause of Righteousness (3:13–22)
 A.   Suffering unjustly (3:13–17)
  1.   Suffering for doing what is right (vv. 13–14)
   a.   Is less likely (v. 13)
   b.   Brings a blessing (v. 14a)
   c.   Do not fear those who instigate it (v. 14b)
  2.   Giving an accounting of the Christian hope (vv. 15–16)
   a.   Revere Christ as Lord (v. 15a)
   b.   Explaining the Christian hope (vv. 15b–16)
    (1)   to all who ask
    (2)   with the appropriate attitude
    (3)   shaming those who insult
  3.   Appropriate suffering (v. 17)
   a.   Suffering for doing good may be the will of God
   b.   Suffering for doing wrong is inappropriate
 B.   The suffering and vindication of Christ (3:18–22)
  1.   Christ suffered (v. 18)
   a.   for sins
   b.   once for all
   c.   as a righteous man
   d.   to lead us to God
  2.   Christ's proclamation to the spirits in prison (vv. 19–20)
   a.   in the spiritual realm (v. 19)
   b.   who disobeyed in the time of Noah (v. 20)
  3.   Christian baptism (v. 21)
   a.   corresponds to the flood
   b.   is not a magical rite
   c.   is effective through the resurrection of Jesus
  4.   The vindication of Christ (v. 22)
   a.   He has entered heaven

   b. He is at God's right hand
   c. He has authority over the spiritual powers
VII. Living Appropriate Christian Lives (4:1–11)
   A. Amongst unbelievers (4:1–6)
      1. Emulating the resolve of Christ (v. 1a)
      2. Leaving behind a life of sin (v. 1b–3)
         a. Preparedness to suffer as evidence (v. 1b)
         b. Not following human desires but the will of God (v. 2)
         c. The time is long past to follow past pagan practices (v. 3)
      3. The pagan response (vv. 4–5)
         a. Surprise (v. 4a)
         b. Blasphemy (v. 4b)
         c. Their accountability to God the judge (v. 5)
      4. Believers who have died (v. 6)
         a. Evaluated negatively by unbelievers
         b. Evaluated positively by God
   B. Amongst Believers (4:7–11)
      1. The end is near (v. 7a), the consequences of which (οὖν) are:
         a. Be focused on prayer (v. 7b)
         b. Show constant love for those in the Christian community (v. 8)
         c. Show hospitality (v. 9)
         d. Use spiritual gifts:
            (1) to serve one another (v. 10)
               (a) speaking gifts (v. 11a)
               (b) serving gifts (v. 11b)
            (2) to glorify God (v. 11c)
      2. To God belong all glory and power (v. 11d)
VIII. Final Instructions for a Suffering People (4:12–5:14)
   A. The fiery ordeal (4:12–19)
      1. The fiery ordeal (v. 12)
         a. constitutes a test (v. 12a)
         b. is not something strange (v.12b)
      2. Sharing the sufferings of Christ (v. 13)
         a. should occasion rejoicing (v. 13a)
         b. results in even greater joy at the parousia (v. 13b)
      3. Suffering in the name of Christ/as a Christian
         a. results in blessing (v. 14a)
         b. is evidence of the Spirit's presence (v. 14b)
         c. must not be for unlawful behavior (v. 15)
         d. should not bring shame (v. 16a)
         e. should result in glorifying God (v. 16b)
         f. is evidence that God's eschatological judgment has begun (v. 17)
            (1) for believers first (v. 17b)
            (2) for unbelievers (v. 17c)

          (3)   Salvation of believers is costly (v. 18a)

          (4)   The fate of unbelievers is dire (v. 18b)

    4. Summary statement regarding suffering (v. 19)

       a. must be according to God's will

       b. Commit oneself to God the faithful creator

       c. Continue to do good

B. The responsibility of elders (5:1–5a)

    1. The fellow-elder (v. 1)

       a. Command to the elders (v. 1a)

       b. Witness of the sufferings of Christ (v. 1b)

       c. Sharer in the glory about to be revealed (v. 1c)

    2. Tending the flock of God (vv. 2–4)

       a. Not grudgingly but willingly (v. 2b)

       b. Not for gain but eagerly (v. 2c)

       c. Not domineering but setting an example (v. 3)

       d. The reward: the crown of glory (v. 4)

    3. Submission of younger men to the elders (v. 5a)

C. Humility and resoluteness (5:5b–11)

    1. Be humble toward one another (v. 5b)

       a. The reason: because God opposes the proud but gives grace to the humble (v. 5c)

    2. Be humbled under God's mighty hand (v. 6a)

       a. The purpose: God will exalt you in due time (v. 6b)

       b. The means: by casting your anxieties on him (v. 7)

    3. Be alert and vigilant (v. 8a)

       a. The reason: the Devil is looking for someone to devour (v. 8b)

    4. Resist the Devil (v. 9a)

       a. The means: by being firm in faith (v. 9a)

       b. The reason: because suffering is the universal lot of Christians (v. 9b)

    5. The God of all grace (vv. 10–11)

       a. called you to his eternal glory in Christ (v. 10a)

       b. will restore, strengthen, confirm and establish you (v. 10b)

       c. Power belongs to him (v. 11)

D. Final greetings (5:12–14)

    1. The epistle (v. 12)

       a. Written briefly

       b. Sent via Silvanus who is faithful

       c. For the purpose of:

          (1) encouragement

          (2) testimony to the dependable grace of God

    2. Greetings from (v. 13):

       a. the sister church in "Babylon"

       b. Peter's "son" Mark

    3. Greet one another (v. 14a)

    4. Final blessing of peace (v. 14b)

Grammar Index

Scripture Index

"Greg Forbes has produced a thick reading of the Greek text of 1 Peter that is an exegetical goldmine. Forbes leads readers through the text and enables them to navigate their way safely around the various textual, semantic, syntactical, and lexical chasms. It is well informed by Greek scholarship, it models competent exegesis, and is user-friendly for students who are still developing their Greek competencies. The high standard of the EGGNT has been set even higher."

Michael F. Bird, *Ridley Melbourne College of Mission and Ministry*

"It is wonderful to see the Exegetical Guide to the Greek New Testament coming back into print and moving toward completion. In this volume on 1 Peter, Dr. Greg Forbes provides, in succinct form, the wealth of exegetical detail that pastors and students want and need but often do not have time to amass for themselves. This book simultaneously helps readers to keep their tools sharp, while reserving more time for theological reflection and homiletical preparation. It does not replace commentaries, but for readers with the requisite skills it should be read before reading commentaries."

D. A. Carson, *Trinity Evangelical Divinity School*

"Here is an exegetical treasure chest filled with the riches of structural layouts of the text, lexical studies, grammatical and syntactical analyses, interpretative difficulties, textual variations, and homiletical insights. It is presented in a concisely readable format that reflects interaction with the critical resources on 1 Peter. This valuable work will aid the interpreter to determine the meaning of the text with the goal of proclaiming it. The bibliographies for further study alone are a gold mine. No serious student of the Greek text of 1 Peter will want to ignore this superb volume."

Paul W. Felix, *The Master's Seminary*